JAMES J. WILHELM is an Associate Professor of Comparative Literature teaching in Livingston College, a branch of Rutgers University. He is a specialist in medieval studies, receiving his Ph.D. from Yale University after doing earlier work in Italian and Latin at the University of Bologna in Italy. He studied classics and creative writing in preparation for his B.A. from Yale in 1954, which was followed by an M.A. from Columbia in 1958. The subject of his master's thesis was an examination of Ezra Pound's treatment of Guido Cavalcanti. His doctoral thesis was published in an enlarged form by Yale University Press as *The Cruelest Month: Spring, Nature, and Love in Classical and Medieval Lyrics* (1965). His second book was *Seven Troubadours: The Creators of Modern Verse* (1970). His articles have appeared in *The Chaucer Review*, *Italica*, and other journals, and his translations, from several languages, are also widely disseminated. He is currently exploring new ways of discussing Italian and English medieval literature in comparison with art.

MEDIEVAL SONG

MEDIEVAL SONG

An Anthology of Hymns and Lyrics

Translated and Edited by

JAMES J. WILHELM

London

GEORGE ALLEN & UNWIN LTD

RUSKIN HOUSE   MUSEUM STREET

First published in Great Britain in 1972

© 1971 by James J. Wilhelm

ISBN 0 04 840002 5 *hardback*
0 04 840003 3 *paper*

This book is a photographic reprint of the American edition, and American spelling and usage have been retained.

Printed in Great Britain by
Lowe & Brydone (Printers) Ltd., London

For

PAUL SOREL

in return for Chopin

Grateful acknowledgment is made to the following for permission to quote from copyright material:

The Pennsylvania State University Press, University Park: Permission to reprint from my *Seven Troubadours: The Creators of Modern Verse* translations of the following poems included in the present volume: Nos. 52, 53, 59, 60, 61, 63, 64, 66, 67, 68, 69, 72, 73, 75, 79, 80, 83, 90, 91, and 92. Copyright © 1970 by The Pennsylvania State University.

Yale University Press, New Haven: Permission to reprint from my *The Cruelest Month: Spring, Nature, and Love in Classical and Medieval Lyrics* translations of the following poems included in the present volume: Nos. 1 and 65. Copyright © 1965 by Yale University.

Dell Publishing Co., Inc., New York, and Angel Flores: Permission to reprint from *Medieval Age*, ed. Angel Flores, translations of the following poems included in the present volume Nos. 76 and 96. Copyright © 1963 by Angel Flores.

Carl Winter Universitätsverlag, Heidelberg: Permission to reprint from *Carmina Burana: I. Band: Text. 2. Die Liebeslieder*, eds. A. Hilka and O. Schumann, 1941, the texts of the following poems included in the present volume: Nos. 44, 48, and 50.

Éditions Édouard Privat, Toulouse: Permission to reprint from *Poésies complètes du troubadour Marcabru*, ed. J. M. L. Dejeanne, Bibliothèque Méridionale, 1st Series, *12*, 1909, the text of the following poem included in the present volume: No. 62.

Max Niemeyer Verlag, Tübingen: Permission to reprint from *Bernart von Ventadorn: Seine Lieder*, ed. Carl Appel, 1915, the text of the following poem included in the present volume: No. 65.

Leo S. Olschki Casa Editrice, Firenze: Permission to reprint from *Le Rime della scuola siciliana*, ed. Bruno Panvini, *1*, 1962, the text of the following poem included in the present volume: No. 95.

Riccardo Ricciardi, Milano–Napoli: Permission to reprint from *Petrarca: Rime, Trionfi e Poesie latine*, ed. F. Neri, G. Martellotti, E. Bianchi, and N. Sapegno, 1951, the text of No. 134; and from *Poeti del Duecento*, 2 vols., ed. G. Contini, 1960, the texts of Nos. 105 and 108, all included in the present volume.

C. H. Beck'sche Verlagsbuchhandlung, München: Permission to reprint from *Die deutsche Literatur: Mittelalter*, 2 vols., ed. H. de Boor, the texts of the following poems included in the present volume: Nos. 188 and 190. Copyright © 1965 by C. H. Beck'sche Verlagsbuchhandlung (Oscar Beck).

Clarendon Press, Oxford: Permission to reprint from *Dante's Lyric Poetry*, eds. K. Foster and P. Boyde, 1967, the text for the following poem included in the present volume: No. 116. Copyright © 1967 by Oxford University Press.

Librairie Honoré Champion, Paris: Permission to reprint from *Chansons de Jaufré Rudel*, ed. A. Jeanroy, 2nd ed., 1924, the text for No. 63; to reprint from *Chansons de Guillaume IX*, ed. A. Jeanroy, 2nd ed., 1927, the text for No. 55; to reprint from *Œuvres de François Villon*, ed. A. Longnon and L. Foulet, 4th ed., 1958, the text for No. 171D; and to reprint from *Poésies de Charles d'Orléans*, ed. P. Champion, *2*, 1927, the text for No. 163, all included in the present volume.

Random House, Inc., New York, and Angel Flores: Permission to reprint from *An Anthology of Medieval Lyrics*, ed. Angel Flores, translations of the following poems included in the present volume: Nos. 77, 78, 81, and 107. Copyright © 1962 by Angel Flores.

CONTENTS

[I] THE END OF THE CLASSICAL LYRIC

[II] GREAT CHRISTIAN HYMNS

[III] LATIN LYRICS FROM 600 TO 1050

* Original texts for asterisked items appear in section X.

8 CONTENTS

CONTENTS

[VII] NORTH FRENCH SONGS

[VIII] GERMAN SONGS

[IX] SONGS OF GREAT BRITAIN

A. OLD ENGLISH LYRICS

B. MIDDLE ENGLISH LYRICS

C. SCOTTISH-ENGLISH BALLADS

[X] SELECTED ORIGINAL TEXTS

[XI] INDICES

PREFACE

In undertaking the task of presenting European medieval lyrics in translation I have been only too aware of the difficulties. Not the least of these is linguistic, which has limited my range somewhat. I have omitted Old Norse skaids, Welsh lyrics, and Arabic poems simply because I do not have the competence to deal with them. I have left out Spanish and Portuguese songs for another reason: although no one would contest the beauty of Juan Ruiz' *Libro de Buen Amor,* much of the rest of the work in Iberia falls below that level into simple dance songs or love poems imitative of the Provençal *canso.* Despite the belief of some medievalists that Arabic poetry had a profound effect on the shaping of the European lyric, I do not feel that it will be greatly missed. The Arabic poems can, in any case, be found elsewhere. Instead, I have stressed the interaction of sacred and profane literature, for I feel that the religious ethos of the Middle Ages created the rhetorical patterns and attitudes that caused the rise of the secular romantic lyric.

It is my hope that this anthology will demonstrate the great diversity of the medieval lyric, rather than its sameness. Despite the still fashionable phrase "courtly love," which has been used as a tab to label much of this work, one can find distinct differences among the various nations and even among the poets. The men of Provence have a delicate metaphysical wit that the others never quite caught; the Italians strive for supernatural solemnity; the Germans stress realistic elements; and the English have a rich folklore tradition that runs deep in their creations. There is a world of difference between the rough-hewn Marcabrun and the smooth, facile Charles d'Orléans, between the cynical Cecco and the brooding Cavalcanti, between the good-humored Chaucer and the spleen-filled Villon. If this collection stresses that diversity, it will have fulfilled its labor.

About my translations, I can say that I have tried to be faithful to the literal sense of the text, although I have never permitted myself to be unnecessarily hampered. Where I have taken liberties, I have often expressed them in the notes.

The poems presented here were composed over a period from 1954, when I won a Fulbright Award to study at the University of Bologna (where I worked on Cavalcanti), to the present day, when I have concentrated on the German and Anglo-Saxon works. Despite the variation in time, I believe that the renditions will show the continuity that comes from having been produced by a single hand.

A few selected texts are placed at the end solely as reference points to show what I consider the representative works of some given periods. Since this book is aimed for the reader who is not equipped with linguistic skills, I have not tried to be complete. I stress Latin literature simply because it has been omitted from so many other collections, and I feel that it is essential for understanding the period.

Over the years I have had cause to consult with numerous people who have given me assistance or advice, including Smith Palmer Bovie, Frederick Goldin, Gerald Bertin, Philip B. Miller, Robert P. Miller, Stephen G. Nichols, Jr., Thomas G. Bergin, Henry Grant, and William K. Wimsatt. I must thank Edward Stringham and Max Hofmann for their constant encouragement, as well as Paul Sorel, to whom the work is dedicated.

JAMES J. WILHELM

[I]
THE END OF THE
CLASSICAL LYRIC

As T. S. Eliot has suggested, cultures tend to end with whimpers, rather than with bangs, and the Roman Empire was not an exception. Although only a few poems of the decadence are included here, they show the same features: an obsession with sensual imagery, an elaborate treatment of nature, and an almost morbid preoccupation with time and death. These poems reveal the same languid qualities that the statues of the Late Empire betray (one thinks immediately of the *Dying Gaul*). They also express the celebrated "failure of nerve" that characterized late pagan culture. Only Number 5, by Paulinus of Nola, shows a different spirit, and this Christian poem is provided for contrast.

The most extravagant poem of the period, the authorless *Vigil of Venus*, has never been authoritatively dated. It is clearly a poem between two worlds, being both the most sensual hymn written to Venus in the Latin language, and at the same time expressing a romantic vision of the world that is more often associated with later medieval literature. There is, for example, a court of love here, and Venus herself behaves like the medieval god Amor, directing her worshipers to perform highly ceremonious acts with given sets of laws. Ultimately, though, the *Vigil* stands by itself as a brilliantly tragic expression of a man's desire to create a vision of earthly harmony, disrupted by the harsh world around him. The poem shows the inability of the aesthetic sense to function in a religious way, and more than the other poems in the section communicates the melancholy of a world view without a doctrine of salvation.

By contrast, the song of Paulinus of Nola on St. Felix' Day is filled with enthusiasm and joy. The fact that the festival day is January 14, but is treated as if it were a spring day, shows the working of Christian metaphysics. The new religion offered a way of solving the problems raised in the other poems presented here. Although Paulinus' hymn is artistically inferior, it voices a spirit that freed people trapped in the dark forests of romantic despair.

ANONYMOUS[1]

[1]

Vigil of Venus (*Pervigilium Veneris*)

Cras amet qui numquam amavit, quique amavit cras amet

1. Tomorrow he will love who has never loved;
   tomorrow he who has loved will love again.
   Spring is new, the spring of birdsong; in the spring our earth was
       born.
   In the spring hearts come together; in the spring the birds all mate.
   And the trees undo their tresses to the husband rain.
   Tomorrow the coupler of lovers in the forest shade   5
   Will weave green mansions from the myrtle boughs.
   Tomorrow Dione lays down laws, terrible from her high throne.
   Tomorrow he will love who has never loved;
       tomorrow he who has loved will love again.

2. Tomorrow's the day when Father Heaven held his marriage:
   He made the whole year out of his springtime showers,   10
   Falling as husband Rain to the lap of his lovely wife,
   Mixing seeds to nourish all in her broad body.
   Then the Sea from its foamy ball, from Saturn's floating blood,
   In the middle of sky-blue legions and squads of two-legged horses
   Made Venus shivering wet from the shower-sprayed foam.   15
   She herself rules mind and matter with inward-stealing spirit.

[1] Dated from second to fourth centuries. Attributed to Florus, Tiberianus, others. Strong alliteration, internal rhyme, with a tendency to end-rhyme. Can be read in both quantitative and accentual meters. Tendency toward syntax of Romance languages. The texts, of which only three survived, are all corrupt. Edition followed here (with new line numbers) that of Cecil Clementi (3d ed.; Oxford: Blackwell, 1936). I include the opening refrain and omit it after line 87. The "wife of Tereus" (line 85) is Procne, the swallow. Amyclae (line 91) is a town in Laconia (Greece) or Italy associated with the "cry wolf" legend.

The creatress governs all with her secret strength.
Over the land, the heavens, over the deep-dug sea
She sows her seed-path in a straight and uncut course,
Ordering the world to know the ways of birth.   20
Tomorrow he will love who has never loved;
    tomorrow he who has loved will love again.

3. She herself with jeweled flowers paints the purpling year;
   With the breath of the Western Wind, swells trembling bosoms
   Into blossoming buds; she sprinkles the sparkling dewdrops,
   Those glistening waters left by the winds of night.   25
   Look! those tears are trembling in their downward-falling force:
   Each little drop's a world trying to check its fated fall.
   Look! those dark-red flowers are confessing their inner shame:
   The tears that the stars let fall on tranquil nights
   Will strip those virgin breasts from their red, wet cloaks.   30
   Venus in the morning will tell the dewy roses to wed:
   Roses made from the blood of the Paphian, made from Cupid's
      kisses,
   Made from jewels and flames and the sun's red rays.
   Tomorrow they'll cast off the shame that lurks in their
      fiery cloaks
   As one by one they take their marriage vows.   35
   Tomorrow he will love who has never loved;
      tomorrow he who has loved will love again.

4. The goddess tells the nymphs: go to the myrtle groves;
   My son will be your friend. Yet nobody can believe
   That Love will take a holiday (if he carries arrows).
   Go, nymphs! He's thrown away his weapons. Love's taking a
      holiday.   40
   Venus told him: go unarmed. Venus told him: naked, go!
   Leave that quiver, leave those arrows, leave that torch aflame.
   But listen, nymphs, be careful. Cupid's a handsome boy.
   Even naked he has weapons that can thoroughly destroy.
   Tomorrow he will love who has never loved;
      tomorrow he who has loved will love again.   45

5. Diana, with your blushes, Venus sends you all her girls,
   Asking a single favor: leave us, virgin born at Delos,
   Leave our forest free from bloody hunts of beasts.
   Let the trees with green shadows cover the freshening flowers.
   Venus would gladly invite you if she could bend your modesty;   50
   Venus would ask you to come if you weren't the Virgin Queen.
   Soon for three nights you'll see us wandering with happy songs
   Hand in hand throughout your holy thickets,
   Wearing crowns of flowers in your myrtle mansions.
   Ceres will be there; so will Bacchus; and the god of poetry.   55
   We must hold the whole night back, keeping vigil with our songs.
   Venus, rule our forests! You, Diana, go away!
   Tomorrow he will love who has never loved;
      tomorrow he who has loved will love again.

6. Venus wants her court covered with Hybla's flowers;
   She, our judge, will hand out laws with the Graces at her side.   60
   Hybla, give her flowers; give whatever the year gave you.
   Hybla, wear a coat of flowers, wide as the fields of Etna wear.
   Girls from the countryside are coming; girls from mountains too;
   Girls from groves, girls from forests, girls who live in brooks.
   The mother of the winged boy tells them all to have a seat.   65
   She warns them: never trust in naked Love.
   Tomorrow he will love who has never loved;
      tomorrow he who has loved will love again.

7. She herself took her Trojan offspring to the land of Latium;
   She gave the girl Lavinia in marriage to her son,
   Took the blushing Vestal, gave her to the god of war;   70
   She herself arranged the wedding of Sabines with men of Rome,
   To make the Ramnes, make Quirites, and for the race of Romulus
   Make the future father Caesar and the nephew Caesar too.
   Tomorrow he will love who has never loved;
      tomorrow he who has loved will love again.

8. Desire makes our country fertile; it feels the spell of love.   75
   Love, the son of Venus, is himself a country boy.

Yes, Cupid was born in a meadow, then suckled at her breast.
She brought him up on the fragile kiss of flowers.
Tomorrow he will love who has never loved;
   tomorrow he who has loved will love again.

9. Look! the bulls and cows are stretching beneath the broom plants,   80
Each one safely held in the marriage bond.
Look! the bleating sheep in shadows are meeting their mates,
And the goddess is ordering the birds: don't be silent.
Noisy swan songs are echoing stridently through the swamps.
The wife of Tereus is singing in the shade of a poplar tree.   85
You'd think she sang love's measures with her melodious voice;
You'd never think she mourned a sister wronged by her husband's
   rape.
She is singing. I am silent. When will *my* spring ever come?
When will *I* be like the swallow, with my days of silence done?
I have lost my Muse by silence. Apollo never looks my way.   90
So Amyclae in its silence lost in death its silence too.
Tomorrow he will love who has never loved;
   tomorrow he who has loved will love again.

FLORUS[2]

[2]

Venerunt aliquando rosae

One day some roses came—
   Genius of the gentle spring!
Day one, and we saw
   The points of those flowers;

[2] Florus. Unknown poet of the *Latin Anthology,* a collection of poems made for the Vandal kings of Africa. Sometimes identified as Publius Annius Florus, a friend of Hadrian, or the historian Lucius Annaeus (Julius) Florus.

Day two, and those pyramids   5
  Swelled to a greater bud;
Day three came the baskets;
The fourth day marked the end of that toil.
  They die today
Unless they're plucked in the morning.   10

TIBERIANUS[3]

[3]

Amnis ibat inter arva valle fusus frigida

The river was flowing through chilly fields, wide in the valley,
With pebbly laughter, with the tint of flower-filled grass.
Overhead a breeze with gentle caressing was lightly swaying
The deep green laurels, the myrtles with olive sheen.
Below the tender grain was swelling with bursts of blossoms.   5
The earth lay golden with crocus glow, splendid in lilies,
And the grove was perfumed with the breathing of violets.
Among these gifts of the spring, these jewel-decked graces
Loomed the queen of all odor, the star of colors too,
The flame of the goddess Dione, the golden-hued rose.   10
The dew-covered grove was abundant with moistened grain;
From a welling stream rivulets murmured here and there.
Mosses and myrtles were covering over the caverns
Where meandering streams ran with a sparkling spray.
In all of these shadows every bird was a mastersinger,   15
Warbling chants to the spring with sighs that were sweet.
Here the murmurs of the talkative river rang in the greenboughs,

---

[3] Tiberianus (*fl.* 330). Attribution of poem questioned. Written in "popular verse," with fifteen syllables, a form considered crude by classical standards but much used in Middle Ages. Dione (line 10) is another name for Venus.

And the West-Wind Muse raised a song from the singing breeze.
So through the verdure perfume and music, birds and breezes,
River, flower, grove, and the shade delighted all who came.　　　20

AUSONIUS[4]

[4]

Ver erat et blando mordentia frigora sensu

It was spring, and the day wheeled back as the saffron morn
　　Breathed a brisk chill with a soft, caressing touch.
A harsher breeze preceded the yokes of the Dawn,
　　Offering the promise of a summery day.
I was wandering on the square-cut paths of my watered gardens　　5
　　Hoping to refresh myself before the day was ripe.
On the bent grasses I saw some formations of frost
　　Hanging or standing upon the tops of my greens. . . .
I saw my rosebushes rejoicing in their cultivation,
　　Stained by the dew from the risen morning star.　　10
A rare jewel of frost clung to the hoary hedges
　　About to perish in the rays of the primal day.
Consider: did Aurora steal her blush from the roses,
　　Or did the risen day stain the flowers red?
One dew, one color, one morning favored them both:　　15
　　The star and the rose, and Lady Venus too.
Perhaps there's one odor between them: though one in the skies
　　Is wafted, while the other clings to the buds.

[4] Decimus Magnus Ausonius (*ca.* 310–*ca.* 395). Attribution of poem questioned. Subtitled *De rosis nascentibus,* "On the Birth of Roses." Ausonius was a nominal and lukewarm Christian who tutored Gratian before that man became Emperor; he was rewarded by being named prefect of Gaul and imperial consul. A native of Bordeaux, he was a close friend of the next poet, Paulinus of Nola. Retired to France, where he wrote a long poem on the course of the Moselle River, as well as some delicate lyrics to his wife. A few lines omitted from this poem.

The goddess of Paphos is common to both the flower and the star,
   And the Tyrian dye is a property of both.   20
A moment goes by: the burgeoning seeds of the flowers
   Open, dividing into space after space.
This one is green, wearing her tight helmet of leafage;
   This one shows a crimson slash on her delicate stalk;
This one opens the high top of her budding obelisk,   25
   Loosing the sheath that covers her crimson head.
Now she shakes the coverings off her summit,
   Seeking to number herself within her leaves.
No delay: she reveals the glory of the smiling calyx
   As she brings forth the close-packed seeds from her golden heart.   30
And this one which now was all red in the fire of her foliage
   Lies pale and withered, with all of her petals forlorn.
I was marveling at the swift rape of fugitive time
   And how the roses even at their birth consent.
Look how that crimson head's bending downward;   35
   Even as I talk, earth is aglow with her red.
One day gives so much beauty, a profusion of newness,
   And that very same day snatches it all away.
I complain, Nature! The grace of the flower's too brief.
   The things you offer, too soon you grab away.   40
As long as a day is, this is the life of a rose:
   Its old age presses hard on its adolescence.
The child that the sun has spied in the morning
   It sees coming back a ruined woman in the dusk.
But although she will perish in a mere matter of days,   45
   The rose will live on in the ages of her seed.
Gather your roses, my girl, while the flower and youth are new;
   And remember—your time is also hurrying by.

PAULINUS OF NOLA[5]

[5]

Ver avibus voces aperit, mea lingua suum ver

Spring opens the voices of birds—
  My tongue calls St. Felix' Day its spring,
For in this light even the winter is flowering
  For joying people. Let there be black chill
Around wintry frost, the year hardened in whiteness;   5
But still the light within kindles happy joy
  Which creates this spring inside me.
Sadness is gone, exiled from the heart;
  The winter of the soul is over.
Clouds of sorrow scud from a heart serene.   10
Just as the gentle swallow acknowledges friendly days
  And the white bird darts on black wings
And the turtledove, kin to the kindly pigeon,
  With finches makes bushes resound with spring song—
Each darting mute now among the rasping hedges,   15
  But soon with spring come back, they will all be glad,
With songs as varied as the color of their wings—
So too I know my day, the holy festival
  That's renewed every year in honor of my great Felix.
Now happy spring is reborn for me with the earth rejoicing; 20
Now I must loosen my mouth in song, intoning my prayers,
Blossoming in fresh new strains. O God, fill my heart!
My Christ, satisfy this thirst for a heavenly spring!

[5] Paulinus of Nola (*ca.* 353–431). Student and friend of Ausonius. He became
Bishop of Nola in Italy, and wrote letters to Ambrose and Augustine. He honored
Felix, his patron saint and that of Nola, with many poems. This poem continues for
several lines.

[II]
GREAT CHRISTIAN HYMNS

Christian hymnology in western Europe was relatively late in flowering, for the earliest Christians either did not feel the necessity for artistic song or else they relied upon Eastern hymnology. When Christians did first try their hands at literary creativity, they tried to embellish the simple prose of the Latin Vulgate Bible or St. Jerome's translation by writing narratives based on biblical themes, but expressed in a Latin imitative of Vergil and other great classical writers.

At last in St. Ambrose, the Roman Church found its first great hymnologist. In his *Confessions*, Book VIII, Chapter 7, St. Augustine tells us how these hymns came into being. The congregation in Milan, where Ambrose was bishop, was besieged in its church by Justina, the mother of Emperor Valentinian, who was being led astray by the Arian heresy. Ambrose composed his songs in order to bolster the spirits of his anxious, beleaguered followers. Writing in easy, unrhymed octosyllabics—the so-called iambic dimeter that was used as the underlying beat for the marching songs of the Roman legions—the saint instilled his works with vigor and assurance. The meter is insistent, and the form is popular. The Christian poet concentrates upon the humble rooster, whom most classical poets would have ignored in a serious context, thereby showing the end of the aristocratic pretensions of Classical Latin poetry. The Christian poet uses simple objects to convey a message in an unadorned fashion.

Ambrose's treatment of Christ is usually abstract. He equates his God with figures of light and discusses him in terms of philosophical abstractions rather than by portraying him as a narrative character, the humble Nazarene. This treatment, in keeping with the Neoplatonic trend of the theology of the day, continues for several centuries in Catholic hymnology. Christ in Numbers 9 and 10, for example, is portrayed almost entirely through the symbolism of the lamb. In the celebrated hymns of Venantius Fortunatus (Nos. 10 and 11) the imagery stresses almost grotesquely the immolation of the god-man: Venantius seems to insist upon the horror of the Messiah hanging like a piece of butchered meat in order to make the physical repellent and to force the listener into acceptance of the miracle which rises over it. In Number 11, he transforms a simple tree into an awesome symbol, constantly changing its form to adapt it to his needs.

Only the brief excerpt from the poem of Prudentius (No. 8) relates to a historical event in direct, dramatic terms.

With the writing of hymns to Mary, the course of hymnology begins to change. The first sample, Number 12, which is taken from the 600s or 700s, is one of the earliest and best. It is simple and dignified, but when compared with the famous *Stabat mater dolorosa* (No. 19), it sounds spare and ascetic. Still, one can sense in the earlier specimen the stirring of a new cultus-worship that would have an extraordinary effect not only upon the later rhetoric of the Church, but also upon the secular language of love. Imagery begins to cluster around the Virgin (the rose, the lily, the star) and she is attended with a whole vocabulary of praise; these images and this diction have an unquestionable correlation with that of the later troubadours and writers of the *Carmina Burana,* for if the hymnologist sings to Our Lady (Madonna), the secular songster addresses his own (*mia donna*). The shift is gradual but inevitable.

In the 800s another art form begins to emerge: the drama from the Mass. Selection No. 14 contains the famous *Quem quaeritis* trope from the Easter Mass. A trope is a dramatic episode inserted into a Mass for a special effect; the music that accompanied it was usually quite elaborate. According to a popular theory of the evolution of drama (but one that is not unchallenged), these tropes grew more and more complex until they finally emerged as plays. It is interesting to note that the word *tropus* is related to the Provençal word *trobaire* (troubadour) through the Provençal verb *trobar,* which means "to find," "to invent." Both the secular poet and the embellisher of the Masses were thought of as creators, inventors, and the gulf between the two is not so great as many scholars have imagined. For example, Number 28, a Latin love song contained in the lyric section, was sung to the tune of a pilgrim song written in praise of Rome. Music, aside from diction, was one of the features allying secular and hieratic composition.

With the writing of Numbers 18 to 20 in the thirteenth century, Latin hymnology reached its high point. Many hymns were written later, but the greatest were composed in German, French, or English. Even within the limits of the Middle Ages, the finest hymns of the later period were composed by men like Petrarch, Villon, and Dante. The religious song had itself become secular.

ST. AMBROSE[1]

[6*]

Aeterne rerum conditor

1. Eternal Founder of all things
   Who rules the night and rules the day,
   And gives the limits unto time
   To take our worldly cares away:

2. The herald's sounding now the day;   5
   He's kept his vigil to the light,
   A beacon for each wanderer,
   Separating night from night.

3. Roused by him the morning star
   Has loosed the darkness from the pole,   10
   And all the bands of evil sprites
   Have left the pathways of the night.

4. He calls, and sailors gather strength;
   The seas and waters all grow calm;
   His cockcrow washed the sins away   15
   From that great Rock of our belief.

5. So let's all rise up earnestly;
   The rooster's rousing those who lie

---

[1] St. Ambrose (*ca.* 340–397). Father of Catholic hymnology and Bishop of Milan. His much-imitated "Ambrosian stanza" is four-lined and unrhymed, although it does contain much random assonance, which is imitated in the translations. Number 6 is a Dawn Hymn; the Rock in line 16 is St. Peter. Number 7 was meant to be sung on Christmas Eve.

* Original text appears in Section X, p. 375.

B

And castigates the ones who sleep,
Denouncing those who will deny.   20

6. The sound of crowing brings hope back;
   Health's poured again for all the sick;
   The robber's sword is put to sheath
   And to the lapsed returns belief.

7. O Jesus, watch us as we sway;   25
   O see us, teach us to obey;
   For at your look our lapses fail
   And guilt is washed with tears away.

8. You shining light upon our sense,
   Dispel the slumber from our sight;   30
   First let our voices sound your praise,
   Then issue prayers to your might.

[7]

Veni, redemptor gentium

1. Come, Redeemer of the world:
   Show that the Virgin gave you birth;
   Let every age stare on with awe,
   For such an issue fits our God.

2. Not from the seed that's spawned by man,   5
   But from a mystic breathing-on
   The Word of God was turned to flesh
   And fruit did flower in the womb.

3. The cleft in the Virgin's body swelled,
   But the portal of shame stood untouched;   10

The banners of her virtues gleamed,
For she was temple now for God.

4. Rise now out of that wedding chamber,
   From that royal hall of modesty,
   You giant of a double nature   15
   And run your course rejoicingly.

5. Away from his Father once he parted;
   Now to his Father he returns;
   He made a journey into Hell-depths;
   Now to the seat of God he turns.   20

6. O equal to the eternal Father,
   Gird your loins with trophy of flesh;
   Make the infirmities of bodies
   Strong with your eternal power.

7. Your cradle now is gleaming brightly;   25
   The night's afire with new light;
   May no darkness break these measures,
   But gleam forever with true might.

PRUDENTIUS[2]

[8]

Salvete, flores martyrum

1. Hail, my martyr flowers!
     Swept from the threshold of life
     By the persecutor of Christ
   As the whirlwind swirls the new rose.

---

[2] Aurelius Prudentius Clemens (348–*ca.* 405). Born in Spain, but active in the imperial court at Rome. His writings include poems for special days. His style, which

2. You, first victims for Christ,   5
    Tender flock of the immolated,
    Play now before his altar
  With your childlike palms and your crowns.

ANONYMOUS³

[9]

Ad cenam agni providi

1. Looking to the supper of the Lamb
    In our stoles of spotless white,
    After the crossing of the Sea of Red,
    Let us call Christ our potentate.

2. His holy body felt the heat   5
    Upon the altar of the Cross,
    And from a draught of his rosy blood,
    We find our life within our God.

3. Protected on this Passover Eve
    From the baleful angel of woe,   10
    We'll be snatched out of the grasp
    Of Pharaoh, that unholy lord.

---

is often prolix, was consciously literary; it was created for private friends rather than
for the people, in contrast to St. Ambrose's style. This famous selection is excerpted
from a much longer Hymn on the Epiphany and deals with the deaths of child martyrs
at the hands of the "persecutor" King Herod (line 3).

³ Hymn for Easter Eve, when the worshipers wore white robes ("stoles") for
Communion. The Jewish origin of the rites is preserved in references to the Passover.
Strong rhymes throughout, but not ordered.

4. Now our Passover is our Christ,
   Who was immolated like a lamb,
   Unleavened bread of sincerity;   15
   For our sake he gave up his flesh.

5. O true and worthy hostage for man
   For whom the walls of Hell were broken;
   Your captive people cries redeemed:
   The prize of life has been retaken.   20

6. Christ has surged up from the grave;
   He comes in triumph from the depths.
   He shoved the despot into chains,
   Unlocking the gates of Paradise.

7. We ask you, author of us all,   25
   In this your Easter joy:
   From every onslaught of cruel death,
   Keep your loyal people safe.

VENANTIUS FORTUNATUS[4]

[10*]

Vexilla regis prodeunt

1. They bring the standards of the King;
   There shines the mystery of the Cross
   On which in flesh the Founder of Flesh
   Was tortured on the forkéd yoke.

---

[4] Venantius Fortunatus (*ca.* 530–*ca.* 605). A North Italian who settled in Poitiers, France, as chaplain to the nunnery founded by St. Radegunde, who had earlier been the wife of King Clotaire (Chlotar) I of the Franks. He addresses Number 22 to her, as well as other poems. Numbers 10 and 11 celebrate the arrival in Poitiers of a piece of the True Cross sent from the East to Radegunde. The quotation in Number

2. His innards were transfixed with nails,   5
   His hands and feet they stretched out tight;
   To buy us back our share of grace
   He hanged there as our sacrifice.

3. They pierced him in an upper place
   With baleful blade upon the sword;   10
   And thus he purged us of our crimes
   With laving of his lymph and blood.

4. Fulfilled is all that David sang
   A time ago in loyal song
   When he said this to all the tribes: 15
   "God ruled upon the simple rood."

5. Ah, tree that's shining and is fair,
   Atint with royal crimson hue!
   Ah, tree trunk deeméd right to bear
   The limbs of such a holy one.   20

6. How blesséd are those boughs on which
   The ransom of the world was draped;
   A scale was made to weigh the flesh
   And snatch the prey from deepest Hell.

7. You pour an odor from your bark;   25
   The scent of nectar you overwhelm;
   Delighting in your rich new fruit,
   You applaud this victory great.

8. Hail, O altar! hail, O victim!
   Out of the glory of the Passion   30
   Life has suffered through its death
   And, dying, brought us back to life.

10, line 16, was based on Psalms 96:10 in the Old Latin Vulgate. The flowing rhythm of Number 11 is trochaic tetrameter catalectic.

* Original text appears in Section X, p. 376.

[11]

Pange, lingua, gloriosi proelium certaminis

1. Tell, O tongue, the grandest glory won from the middle of the
    strife;
    Speak of the triumph wholly noble grasped on the trophy of the
    Cross
    Where the Worldly Redeemer suffered sacrifice, then knew victory.

2. The Maker, melancholy over the fraud of the first-formed of men
    Who bit into the deadly apple and then toppled straightway into
    death,   5
    Seeing a tree had wrought the evil, took its bark to buy man back.

3. Order demanded this lowly labor for restoration of human health:
    The art of the devious Destroyer demanded the use of other art
    So that God could pierce to the middle where the Fiend had
    worked his wound.

4. When the fullness of the timing at last had reached the perfect
    round,   10
    The Son was sent from the fort of the Father; he was founder of
    the world,
    And wearing skin he then proceeded out of the womb of the
    untouched Maid.

5. He wailed his woe inside a manger, a baby hidden in its bowels;
    The Virgin-Mother wrapped him with a swath of swaddling
    clothes;
    His hands, his feet, his legs she bound with bands that held him
    tight.   15

6. When he had reached the age of thirty, filling out the limit of life,
    With free will, born for this very purpose, dedicated to Passion's
    way,
    He dangled lamblike from the boughs, immolated on the Cross.

7. See gall and vinegar! whips and nails! the spears and the spit!
Gentle corpse now perforated, setting blood and lymph aflow;   20
Now see the river laving the soil, cleansing sea and sky and stars.

8. O faithful Cross, sole noble stem that rises in the groves of green,
No stele bore a flower like yours, nor such foliage, nor such seed:
Sweet rod bearing a sweeter burden fastened tightly with sweet
nails.

9. Bend your branches, lofty arbor; loosen fibers now clenched tight.   25
Let the stiffness pass to softening, stiffness gotten at your birth.
Stretch the members of the Sky-King gently on your giant stalk.

10. You alone were deemed most worthy to uphold the Prize of Time.
You are ship for all the shipwrecked, a refuge he himself prepared,
Anointed with the blesséd blood that flows unending from the
Lamb.   30

ANONYMOUS[5]

[12*]

Ave, maris stella

1. Hail, star of the sea,
The blesséd Mother of God,
Virgin eternally,
Gateway to heavenly laud.

2. Taking the AVE—hail,   5
From the mouth of Gabriel,

[5] Hymn on the Annunciation to Mary, possibly written as early as the 600s. Some
stanzas rhyme *aabb*. Contains Ave-Eva anagram (stanza 2).

* Original text appears in Section X, p. 377.

In peace, we pray, O leave us,
Changing the name of EVA!

3. Sinners from shackles unbind;
Proffer thy light to the blind;   10
Let our evils all be gone,
Every blessing then be won!

4. Demonstrate that thou art Mother;
Let him through thee gather
Prayers, to whom thou gavest birth   15
That he should suffer life on earth.

5. Virgin, one from out the masses,
Ever gentle among the crass ones,
Make us mild and chastened too,
Free of the sinful acts we do.   20

6. Give to us the holy life;
Make that highway free of strife;
Let us see thy Jesus Son
With joy eternal for everyone!

7. Praise to God, who is our Father;   25
Honor to Christ, who is the Son,
And to the Holy Spirit honor,
Three in person, God in one!

[13⁶]

Veni, creator spiritus

1. Come, creator of the soul,
Visit the temples thou madest whole.

Inspire with thy heavenly grace
The breast of man thou didst create!

2. Consoler is the name we call   5
   Thee, gift of the highest Lord of all,
   Thou living fount, thou charity,
   Thou fire, thou balm for agony,

3. Thou finger on the Lord's right hand
   Which sendest seven-formed gifts to man.   10
   The Father to thee gave the oath
   To let the speech pour out of throats.

4. Kindle light in all our parts;
   Pour thy love into our hearts;
   Make our bodies full of strength,   15
   Working virtue for life's length!

5. Drive the enemy far away;
   Let peace reign for many a day.
   With thee as our future guide,
   We'll keep evil from our side.   20

6. Transmit the Father to everyone;
   Give knowledge also of his Son;
   And thou, third sharer of the power,
   Let us feel thee every hour!

6 Hymn to the Holy Ghost, probably written in the 800s. Often attributed un-
convincingly to Hrabanus Maurus. Much of the rhetoric is indebted to Ambrose's
Number 7. No fixed rhyme, but much assonance. A seventh stanza sometimes included.

[14[7]]

Quem quaeritis in sepulchro

ANGEL:
Whom are you seeking in the tomb, O Christ-worshipers?

THREE WOMEN:
Jesus the Nazarene crucified, O dweller in heaven.

ANGEL:
He is not here; he has risen, just as he foretold.
Go now, announce that he has arisen, and say—

THREE WOMEN:
Alleluia, he has risen, our God, today,   5
A lion strong, Christ Son of God;
Give thanks to God, exclaiming *eia!*

ANGEL:
Come and see the place where your Lord was put.
Alleluia, alleluia. Go quick and tell the disciples
Your Master has arisen. Alleluia, alleluia.   10

THREE WOMEN:
Our Lord has risen from the tomb
Who hanged for us upon the Cross.
           Alleluia.

[7] Trope from the Easter Mass (800s). For music, consult RCA Victor LM 6015
(2). See Karl Young, *The Drama of the Medieval Church* (Oxford, 1933), *1*, 201 ff.

WIPO[8]

[15]

Victimae paschali laudes

1. Let the Christians sacrifice
   Praises to the Easter prey.

2. For the lamb redeemed the sheep;
   Christ the holy innocent
   Reconciled all sinners   5
   To his Father's side.

3. Life and death have dueled
   In conflict wondrous to behold;
   The Lord of Life went into death
   And now he lives and now he reigns.   10

4. "Tell us, Mary, what did you see
   Coming to us here?"
   "The tomb of Christ the living,
   The glory of his rising,

5. "Angels as the witnesses,   15
   His clothes and then his shroud.
   Christ my hope has risen;
   He will pass his men into Galilee."

6. There is only one person to believe:
   Mary, who tells the truth;   20
   Never that lying crowd of Jews.

[8] Wipo (d. 1050). From Burgundy or Swabia, he held high positions in the courts of Holy Roman Emperors Conrad II and Henry III, composing lauds for both, as well as many moral verses and this Easter Sequence. A sequence occurs in the Mass between the gradual and the gospel, and is usually written in rhythmical prose. This one contains strophes rhyming *aabb,* with monorhyme in the last two stanzas.

7. For we know that our Christ has arisen;
   In truth he has left the dead.
   O victorious King, have mercy!

ABELARD[9]

[16]

O quanta qualia sunt illa Sabbata

1. How mighty, how manifold those holy Sabbaths
   Which forever are held in the curia on high!
   What rest for the weary, what prize for the valiant,
   When God will be everywhere scattered through all!

2. That heavenly city is the one true Jerusalem,   5
   Whose peace is forever, whose pleasure's supreme,
   Where desire aspires not over its objects
   Nor prize is despised as short of its goal.

3. Of that King and his kingdom, his marvelous palace,
   The peace and repose and the pleasure found there—   10
   O tell us, partakers of that heavenly glory,
   If tongue can transcribe what the senses felt there.

4. But meanwhile our duty is: lifting the spirit
   And seeking our homeland in all of our prayers:
   To go back to Jerusalem, leave Babylonia,   15
   Return from our exile with heavy despair.

---

[9] Peter Abelard (1079–1142). Famous French philosopher and teacher whose tragic love affair with Heloise is well known. This Hymn to the Eternal Sabbath, meant to be sung at Saturday Vespers, was written at her request for use in the Abbey of the Paraclete, which was built by Abelard but handed over to Heloise to direct as abbess. Composed in rhymed pairs of accentual dactyls grouped into quatrains.

5. There when all troubles have come to an ending
   Let us sing to our Zion secure in our song;
   Rendering thanks endless for the granting of graces
   This blesséd folk offers its praise to you, Lord.   20

6. There shall a Sabbath succeed every Sabbath,
   The joy of the day-resters last ever-long;
   Jubilation unceasing will be there ineffable
   Which we and the angels express in our songs.

7. To the Master Almighty be glory eternal,   25
   From whom, through whom, in whom all things flow;
   From him is the Father and through him is Jesus
   And in him the Spirit of Father and Son.

THE ROSY SEQUENCE[10]

[17]

Jesu dulcis memoria

1. Jesus sweet in memory
   Lends a true joy to our hearts:
   The sweetness of his presence mounts
   Over honey and all known things.

2. Nothing more gentle can be hymned;   5
   Nothing lovelier can be heard;
   Nothing more soothing known to mind
   Than Jesus, who is Son of God.

---

[10] Written in late 1100s. Long attributed to St. Bernard of Clairvaux, but now believed to be the work of an Englishman. The sequence consists of the first seven and last two stanzas of a forty-two-stanza work. It was inserted into the Mass for the Feast of the Name of Jesus as a sequence, although it does not have the proper sequence form. Monorhymed stanzas. For music, see the *English Hymnal*, Number 238.

3. Jesus, hope of the penitential,
   How merciful to those who seek,   10
   How kind to those who come to beg,
   How marvelous to those who find!

4. Jesus, sweetness of our hearts,
   Fount of truth and light of minds,
   Surpassing every other joy   15
   And every other known desire.

5. No tongue is able to express,
   No word can ever circumscribe
   The power gained from loving you:
   Only true knowers can reveal.   20

6. I'll call for Jesus on my bed
   From the locked chamber of my heart.
   In privacy and public place
   I'll shout for him with earnest cry.

7. With Mary when the dawn grows light,   25
   I'll call for Jesus at the tomb;
   With clamor of the heart I'll cry,
   I'll quest with soul and not with eye.

* * * * * * * * * * * * * * * * * * *

41. Jesus has gone back to his Father;
    He has gone into the kingdom of the sky.   30
    My heart has parted from my breast
    And after in his wake now flies.

42. O let us trace the steps of our Master
    With hymns and praises and with prayers,
    That he may grant us grace for enjoying   35
    The mansions of his heavenly realm.

THOMAS OF CELANO[11]

[18*]

Dies irae, dies illa

1. Day of vengeance, ah, that day!
   When the world shall burn away,
   As David and the Sibyl say.

2. Ah, the trembling! ah, the fearing
   As the Judge to us is nearing,   5
   Our world in pieces strict to lay.

3. Trumpets sprinkling awesome soundings
   In the graveyards and surroundings
   ᴡill drive us all before the throne.

4. Death stands gaping, as does Nature;   10
   While arises every creature
   Answering for his life alone.

5. Out will come the written books
   Where our actions yield to looks
   As the world is judged in fame.   15

6. As the Judge to judgment's veering
   All that's latent is appearing,
   Nothing hidden will remain.

---

[11] Thomas of Celano (*ca.* 1200–*ca.* 1255). Attribution of this Hymn for the
Funeral Mass sometimes questioned, but it is usually ascribed to this biographer of
St. Francis and staunch member of the Franciscan Order. The latter part of the
poem seems to have been added in the transition from personal hymn to sequence
for the Requiem Mass. Strong monorhymed tercets.

* Original text appears in Section X, p. 378.

7. Ah, poor me! what shall I mutter?
   To what patron shall I stutter? 20
   Since scarcely just men can be sure?

8. Monarch of mighty majesty,
   Who frees the men who should be free,
   Save me, fountain of the pure!

9. Ah, remember, loving Christ, 25
   I'm the causer of your life—
   Don't abandon me that day!

10. Seeking me, you sat all weary;
    Suffered Passion to come near me;
    This labor must not fade away. 30

11. O just judger of perdition,
    Give my soul gift of remission
    Before the issue of the Word!

12. I am groaning like one guilty;
    Redness now has overspilled me— 35
    Spare this kneeling man, O Lord!

13. You made Mary innocent,
    Heard the thief make his lament,
    Allowed me too some hope to earn.

14. All my prayers sound so lowly, 40
    But be kindly and be holy
    Lest in endless ash I burn!

15. Put me with your shriven sheep,
    No company with goats I'll keep,
    Standing ever at your right hand. 45

16. Let all evil be confounded
And with dire flames surrounded:
Summon me with the saved to stand.

17. I beg humbly, I beg bending,
Heart worn like an ember spending:
God, take care about my ending!

50

ANONYMOUS FRANCISCAN[12]

[19*]

Stabat mater dolorosa

1. There stood the Mother deeply sorrowing
At the Cross-side, tears outpouring,
As they hanged her Son, her Christ;
How her heart was gravely groaning,
Wracked with pain and full of moaning,
As the swords inside her sliced.

5

2. Ah, the grieving, great affliction
Heaped on this maid of benediction,
Mother of the Chosen One;
Full of suffering, filled with pining
She stood shuddering while divining
The penalties for her great Son.

10

3. Where's the man who is not weeping
As he sees Christ's Mother keeping

[12] The most famous Marian hymn (1200s), formerly attributed to Iacopone da Todi (see Numbers 100, 101), but now given to an anonymous Franciscan. Strong end and interior rhyme throughout, which the translation attempts to approximate. Set to music by Verdi, Rossini, Palestrina, and Pergolesi.

* Original text appears in Section X, p. 380.

    Watch upon such bitterness?   15
    Who's not filled with agitation
    In the Virgin's contemplation
      Of her Son's most dire duress?

4. She sees Jesus stretched on the yoke,
    Paying for the sins of other folk,   20
      Handed over to the whips;
    There she sees her Boy-Child mild
    In the death-grip, alone, defiled,
      As his man-soul from him slips.

5. Pious Mother, fount of loving,   25
    Let me bear with you the groveling,
      Let me suffer woe with you;
    Let my heart be filled with burning;
    For the Lord Christ set me yearning,
      Make your child love me too.   30

6. Holy Mother, please abide me—
    Let the nail-blows pound inside me,
      Let them strike within my heart;
    As I spy those sundering blows
    That your loved one undergoes   35
      Let me also share a part!

7. Let me with you stand there crying,
    Lending comfort at the crucifying
      For as long as I have breath;
    At the Cross-side let me stand   40
    Offering you a kindly hand
      As we keen the dirge of death.

8. Maiden, foremost among maidens,
    Let me not be overladen,
      Let me mourn along with you;   45
    Let the Christ-death be my ration,

Make me consort to his Passion,
Let me bear the beatings too!

9. Let me feel the flails aflying,
   Make me drunk in the crucifying   50
      In the blest love of your Son;
   Save me from the Hell-flames' kindling:
   Virgin! save this sinner spindling
      When the Judgment Day has come!

10. Let the Cross attend my breath,   55
    Stay with me until my death
       And the grace of princely prize;
    When this body knows it's dying,
    Let this soul go upward flying
       To the praise of Paradise.   60

ST. THOMAS AQUINAS[13]

[20]

Adoro devote, latens veritas

1. I adore you devoutly, O hidden truth,
   Lurking inside all these outward forms;
   To you my heart will gladly surrender,
   For in contemplation of you it fails.

[13] St. Thomas Aquinas (*ca.* 1225–1274). Foremost member of the Dominican Order, who reconciled Aristotelian philosophy with Catholic theology in his *Summas*. Attribution questioned, but the hymn shows the objective, intellectual spirit of Dominicanism as opposed to the more emotional spirit of Franciscanism. Widely known in a variant version as *Adoro Te devote, latens Deitas,* but see F. J. E. Raby, *Speculum, 20* (1945), 236–238; A. Wilmart, *Recherches de Théologie ancienne et médiévale, 1* (1929), 21–40, 149–176.

2. Taste, sight, and touch when near you falter;   5
   Only the hearing is wholly believed.
   I believe what the Son of God has uttered:
   There is nothing truer than the word of truth.

3. On the Cross Jesus' godhead was totally hidden;
   But here the humanity also hides;   10
   I believe in them both, I confess them:
   I cry what the thief penitential cried.

4. Unlike doubting Thomas, I do not see the woundings,
   But still I confess that you are my Lord.
   Make me believe in you always more strongly,   15
   Have stout hope in you and forever adore.

5. You, reminder of the death of our Master,
   Bread that offers true life to mankind,
   Offer my soul some life-stuff out of you,
   Allow it to savor your delicate taste.   20

6. Pity-filled pelican, Jesus, my Master,
   Purge my pollution with your holy blood.
   One single droplet can offer salvation
   And make the whole world free of its crime.

7. Jesus, I see you veiled and in darkness.   25
   When can I have what I strongly desire?
   When can I gaze on your face that's now hidden
   And bask in the glory that comes with this sight?

[III]
LATIN LYRICS
FROM 600 TO 1050

Although hymns were the greatest works produced in the central portion of the Middle Ages, the lyric never died. One can hardly say that the tradition flourished when divorced from theology, but there are nevertheless enough documents to assure us that a man like Venantius Fortunatus was aware of the beauty and the goodness of women, that a scholar like Alcuin could feel the lively dialectic between ascetic Winter and productive Spring, and that a writer like Sedulius Scottus was keenly aware of the lack of money for drink. Furthermore, in looking at the original texts, we can see a change from classical to biblical allusions, from quantitative to accentual meter, and from assonance to regular rhyme.

If there is any question as to why Boethius is included in this section, rather than among the hymnologists, the reply must be that his hymn, lifted from the *Consolation of Philosophy* (Book One, Poem 5), is executed in a thoroughly classical vein, against the tenor established by Ambrose. Its allusions are entirely Greco-Roman, and, like the large work from which it is extracted, the poem celebrates the apprehension of belief through reason. It is as much Neoplatonic as Christian.

Venantius Fortunatus has been included in both sections, for in him the connection between hymnologist and lyricist is even more obvious than it is in the other writers. Venantius does not write love poems to Lady Radegunde (who is also St. Radegunde), but rather poems of Christian or Platonic friendship. He composes in a flowing, elegiac line that would not sound harsh to Ovid. Venantius, more than the other writers of his period, prefigures the late medieval court poet who will address songs of love to his unsaintly lady. Venantius offers us the ambience if not the tone.

The most passionate poems of the Carolingian Revival are addressed to young men. Alcuin writes some very moving verses in his complaint about the defection of a boy nicknamed Cuckoo from his monastery in France (No. 24). Showing the ways in which the pagan could be blended with the Christian, Alcuin calls himself by the Vergilian shepherd name Menalcas (line 22); another of his friends is the familiar Daphnis (line 20); and many of the other youths in the monastery had bird-names. The poet's sensibility is warm and immediate, and the same feeling can be found in the tragic complaint of Gottschalk (No. 25), which is addressed to a nameless boy. It comes as no surprise that Number 28 is a love song written directly to a young man by an anonymous hand.

Throughout the poetry of this period there is a great devotion to nature. Alcuin's Conflict of Winter and Spring (No. 23) opens the gates for the return of the cuckoo, and with him, it seems, poems about nature and love. The lines which he gives to Palemon (who is himself in this poem) "come now, my cuckoo . . . my sweet love (lines 42, 43) are echoed in the opening line of Number 30, "Now, my sweet girl friend, come," with the woman replacing the bird. The fields that Sedulius Scottus lovingly describes in Number 26 are inhabited by birds in Number 29 or elaborated in the opening lines of Number 31. Scottus' "now-now-now" emphasis is felt in many later poems, especially the *Carmina Burana*.

The lyrics of the Carolingian period reveal two facets that are important for the lyrics of any age: an emphasis upon the self (rather than upon the Christian community) and a concern with dialogue and eventually dialectic. The Conflict of Alcuin establishes the form of the "debate poem" (*tenzone, tenso*) of later ages (although the real father of the genre is Vergil or perhaps a Greek pastoral poet). The dialogue poem Number 30 stems not only from classical pastorals but also from the Song of Songs; it establishes the form of the late medieval *pastourelle* (e.g., No. 62).

The self is apparent throughout this section in the emotions of the writers, but shows especially in the Apology of Sedulius Scottus (No. 27) and in the lovely Complaint to Spring (No. 31), where the closing line, adapted from the Song of Songs, voices that disparity between external nature and the ego that is bewailed in later generations. Like that influential book of the Bible, many of these poems could be allegorized, but they can also be read simply as expressions of the heart.

BOETHIUS[1]

[21]

O stelliferi conditor orbis

O founder of the starry dome,
    Seated ever on your throne,
Turning the heavens with rapid whirl,
    Forcing the stars to bear your laws—
Thus sometimes gleams with perfect orb,   5
    Basking in her brother's rays,
The Moon, who buries lesser lights;
    Yet sometimes pallid in her horns,
When near the Sun she loses force;
    And early in the hours of night   10
Hesperus drives the chilly stars,
    Changing his reins by morningtide
As Lucifer he palely glows.
    When leaves are chased by storms away,
You shorten the hours of our day,   15
    And when the fiery summer returns,
You make the night hours swiftly run.
    With might you govern the varying year:
The North Wind bears the leaves away
    Which West Wind carries back again;   20
Arcturus brings the corn to bloom
    That Sirius burns to blackened stalks.
Nothing free of your ancient laws
    Abandons the labor by which it stands;
You govern all with fixéd end,   25
    Disdaining only the deeds of man

---

[1] Anicius Manlius Severinus Boethius (*ca.* 480–524). Counselor and companion to Theodoric, King of the Ostrogoths, who executed him on a trumped-up charge of treason. Composed his *Consolation of Philosophy* to rationalize the injustice. This is Poem 5 of Book One.

To force, as ruler, in good measure.
    Why should Fortune with slippery hand
Direct the turns? The pure are vexed
    By punishment due those stained with crime;   30
Evil men are lording it on thrones
    And the bad now dare to tread upon
The necks of saints in a wicked turn.
    Goodness gleams faintly in the gloom
And the just man bears the unjust's guilt   35
    There is no perjury or fraud
To those who embellish all with lies;
    And when they want to flex their strength,
They love to cut down the highest kings
    Before whom the masses crouch in fear.   40
You, who bind the whole with law,
    Gaze down now on this wretched Earth!
We, not the vilest of your works,
    Are battered by the toss of luck.
Ruler, stop these rapid fluxes,   45
    And as you make the universe turn,
Make Earth stable with firm peace.

VENANTIUS FORTUNATUS[2]

[22]

O regina potens, aurum cui et purpura vile est

O mighty queen, who looks down on all purple and gold,
    With these little blossoms you are worshiped by one who loves you.
And even if color's not substance, still through these petals
    I send you purple in violets and gold in the crocus form.

[2] See note to Number 10. For line 16, I read *Isti vos cupiunt iam revidere foris.*

Rich in the love of God, you have shunned the wealth of the world.   5
  Despising the one, you will gather a store of the other.
Well, take this gift of a mixed bouquet that I send you,
  Even though you are summoned to a much more blesséd life.
For although you torment yourself here to be reborn in the future,
  Just look: these petals will show you the heavenly fields.   10
From these tender sprigs which I offer in all of their fragrance
  Gather in the scent of things that are yet to come,
And when you arrive there, I beg you: may that kind right hand
  That gathers these flowers gather me to its merited side.
But although the grace of those heavenly flowers awaits you,   15
  This earthly bunch would just like to see you outdoors.
And although those above will delight for their exquisite odor,
  These will charm even more when you come, adorning your hair.

ALCUIN[3]

[23]

Opto meus veniat cuculus, carissimus ales

SPRING:
I want my cuckoo to come, my most lovéd bird;
Before all others he was always a welcomed guest
Up on my rooftop, singing through reddish bill.

WINTER:
Let no cuckoo come! Let him sleep in his dark, dark caves.
For he's always bringing hunger wherever he goes.   5

---

[3] Alcuin (*ca.* 735–804). English scholar summoned by Charlemagne to the court at Aachen to perform literary and educational tasks. He later directed the Abbey of St. Martin at Tours, where he ascribed bird-names and epithets from classical pastorals to himself and his students. Both poems longer in the original.

SPRING:
I want my cuckoo to come with the happy blossoms;
Let him drive away cold, this long-time friend of the Sun;
Phoebus adores the cuckoo when the days are long and serene.

WINTER:
Let no cuckoo come! he creates all kinds of toil;
He promotes constant battles, he disrupts the blessèd peace;   10
He's a great troublemaker, stirring both land and sea.

SPRING:
Ah, slow old Winter, why are you hurling these charges?
You huddle in your shadowy den weighted down with torpor
After the banquets of Venus, after the cups of loose Bacchus.

WINTER:
These are my riches; these my happy carousings;   15
Ah, sleep is sweet with a warm fire in your hearth.
But this your cuckoo can't know; he just serves the corrupt.

SPRING:
Let the cuckoo come with flowers in his beak, ministering honey;
Let him build up his mansions and sail on a halcyon sea,
Engendering offspring and brightening happy fields.   20

WINTER:
Ah, how I hate all these things you so delight in!
I like to count up my hoard that I treasure in chests,
And have a big meal, and then slip away in slumber.

SPRING:
O heavy Winter, always ready to sleep, just tell me
Who would get you that hoard, would heap up that treasure   25
If Summer and I didn't work for you year after year?

WINTER:
You're right. And because you kowtow to all my details,
You're my slaves; you'll do anything that I bid.
Yes, servants to me, your lord, in all of your toils!

SPRING:

You our lord? Why, you're shabby, stingy, and proud!   30
You wouldn't be able to feed yourself one single day
If the cuckoo didn't come and bring you his sweet alms.

Then Palemon spoke rejoicing from his high throne
And Daphnis too, and the flock of pious shepherds:
That's enough, Winter. You talk too much; you're too harsh.   35
No, let the cuckoo come, sweet friend of the shepherds,
And let the gladdening seeds burst forth on our hills;
Let the cattle have pasture, let peace reign over the meadows
And branches green lift parasols for the weary;
Let the goats come to barnyard with udders swelling with milk,   40
And the birds salute the Sun with their varying songs.
For all of these reasons, come now, my cuckoo, come!
You are now my sweet love, a most welcome guest for all.
All things await you—the earth and the water and sky.
Hail, my sweet honor; yes, for all of the ages, hail!   45

[24]

Heu, cuculus nobis fuerat cantare suetus

Alas, my cuckoo who always used to sing for me,
    What cursèd hour has snatched you away?
O, o! my cuckoo, where, in what place, did I leave you?
    To me that was a most unfortunate day.
Every manner of man everywhere is lamenting you,   5
    For the cuckoo is lost; yes, that cuckoo—mine.
O don't let him be lost! Let him come in the springtime
    And coming let him sing for me happy songs.
Who knows if he'll come? I'm afraid he has drowned,
    Swirled in a whirlpool, dashed by the waves.   10
O God! if that Wine-God has drenched him in liquid
    Who gathers young men in his deadly whirls!

If he lives, let him come, let him run to our warm nest;
Let no crow grasp him with clutching claw.
O, my cuckoo, who grabbed you away from your father's home?   15
He stole you, he stole you; now will you ever come?
If you care for songs, cuckoo, then come quickly.
Come quickly, I beg! O yes, quick! come!
Don't delay, little cuckoo; I beg you: come running.
Your belovéd Daphnis wants to have you again.   20
The springtime has come; cuckoo, arise from your slumber.
Look! old father Menalcas wants you here.
The bulls are now grazing around in our pastures;
Only the cuckoo is absent; who pastures him?
O God! not that Bacchus, that impious Wine-God   25
Who's quick to turn every heart into ill.
Weep for the cuckoo. Yes, all men go on weeping.
He went rejoicing; I fear he'll come back in tears . . .
Alas, he has fled, he has fled; my lament is now bitter;
It's all I have left; my gentle cuckoo is gone.   30
Let me send my songs after him, songs of bereavement,
For singing might carry my fledgling home.
O I pray you: be happy wherever you wander;
Remember me, cuckoo, and forever—fare well!

GOTTSCHALK[4]

[25]

Ut quid jubes, pusiole

1. Why do you order, little boy-child,
   Why command me, little son,
      Telling me to sing a sweet song

[4] Gottschalk, Godescalc (*ca.* 805–869). German monk whose aristocratic Saxon father placed him in the Monastery of Fulda at a young age. He tried unsuccessfully to get out, but was refused. Later at Orbais he wrote an inflammatory treatise in

When I'm exiled far away
   Out at sea?   5
Why do you order me to sing?

2. Better for me, poor little young one,
  To do some weeping, little man;
    I'm for descant, not for chanting
    The kind of song that you demand,   10
      My sweet dear one.
  Why do you order me to sing?

3. You know I'd rather, little laddie,
  Have you join me, brother of mine,
    Weeping with an earnest heart,   15
    Sharing now my heavy mind
      In lamentations.
  Why do you order me to sing?

4. Well you know, divine novitiate,
  You know, heavenly protégé,   20
    I have been here long in exile
    Many nights and many days
      Always suffering.
  Why do you order me to sing? . . .

7. Yet since you desire it so strongly,   25
  Finest companion for a man,
    I shall sing to the Son and Father
    And of the Spirit that always ran
      Out of them both.
  This I'll sing voluntarily.   30

---

which he pronounced pre-Calvinistic views of man's predestination. Bitterly attacked by Hrabanus Maurus and John Scotus Erigena (who committed the opposite heresy of denying ultimate judgments). Apparently died after long imprisonment, when this Complaint was written to a young monk who had asked him for a song. Every one of the lines rhymes with -e. I have omitted the rather digressive fifth and sixth stanzas, which compare the captivity of the Jews with the poet's exile.

c

8. Blesséd art thou, holy Master,
   Father, Son, and Paraclete,
   God of might, of majesty,
   Just Divinity.
   This I *will* sing willingly.   35

SEDULIUS SCOTTUS[5]

[26]

Nunc viridant segetes, nunc florent germine campi

1. Now the grain is green, now field-grass is in flower;
   Now the vines are heavy; now's the best of the year;
   Now colored birds soothe the heavens with their songs;
   Now sea, now earth, now stars in the sky are laughing.

2. But not one drop disturbs me with sad-making swill,   5
   Since Mead and Beer and the gifts of Bacchus I lack.
   Alas! how I miss the multiple substance of flesh
   Which is born on the tender earth, in the dew-filled air.

3. I'm a writer (confession!), a musician, Orpheus Junior.
   I'm a treadmill ox. I wish you whatever you will.   10
   I'm your soldier of God armed with the weapons of Wisdom.
   For me, O Muse, beg the good Bishop for alms.

[5] Sedulius Scottus or Scotus (*fl.* 848–874). Irishman summoned to the continent by Emperor Charles the Bald in 848. He settled for a time with Bishop Hartgar of Liège, to whom his Begging Poem is directed.

[27⁶]

Aut lego vel scribo, doceo scrutorve sophiam

I read and write; I teach and I study wisdom.
  I obey the Heaven-throned One both night and day.
I glut, I swill, and rhyming invoke the Muses;
  Asleep I snore; awake to my God I pray.
My mind, conscious of evil, moans weak mortality: 5
  Have mercy, O Christ and Mary, on sinful me.

ANONYMOUS⁷

[28]

O admirabile Veneris idolum

O admirable image of Venus,
Of whose material
  Nothing is frivolous:
May the Great Ruler always look after thee
  Who set stars and poles   5
And fashioned the waters
  And made the earth whole;
May the cunning of thievery
  Never come near to thee
And Clotho who holds the life-cloth   10
  Look on thee tenderly.

---

⁶ Apology for His Life, a confession poem.
⁷ Dated in 900s or earlier. Contained in a manuscript from Verona, as well as in the *Cambridge Songs*. Love song sung to the tune of the pilgrim hymn *O Roma nobilis, orbis et domina*, which was also used for some troubadour songs. Consult RCA Victor LM 6015 (2). The allusions are entirely classical, including the "Great Ruler" (Greek *Archos*) in line 4. Two further stanzas omitted because of their pedantic quality.

CAMBRIDGE SONGS[8]

[29]

Vestiunt silve tenera ramorum

1. The woods are dressing their branches
   With tender spray, weighted with fruit buds.
   High overhead the pigeons are crooning
   Tunes for us all.

2. The turtledove's groaning; the thrush sings lushly;   5
   The age-old cry of the blackbird twangs again;
   The sparrow's not quiet, but high under the elm leaf
   Strikes with a chuckle.

3. Here now the nightingale's happy in green-leaf,
   While with syllables long on the night breeze   10
   The hawk in his ceremonious quaver
   Sets air aquiver.

4. The eagle soars to the stars, as through fields
   The lark looses many a trill of a song,
   Oft plunging down, striking a different key,   15
   Before touching earth.

5. Swift swallows force out raspings together;
   Jackdaw jaws; the quail's wail echoes;
   Thus all of the birds together are offering
   Everywhere summer songs.   20

[8] *Cambridge Songs.* Numbers 29–31. A collection made about 1050 of poems written earlier, some in the 900s. Contained in a manuscript in Cambridge, England, that was once housed in the Monastery of St. Augustine in Canterbury, possibly deriving from German sources. The collection contains selections from Horace and Vergil, laments for deceased monarchs, hymns, a *fabliau* (obscene narrative), and the text of Number 28. Edited by Walther Bulst (Heidelberg: Carl Winter Universitätsverlag, 1950).

6. But none of these creatures is like the bee,
   Who embodies the ideal of chastity—
   Only Mary, who carried Christ in her womb
   Untouched by man.

[30⁹]

Iam, dulcis amica, venito

MAN:
   1. Now, my sweet girl friend, come—
   I love you like my very own heart.
   Come inside my cubicle door,
   Where I have ornaments galore.

   2. There you'll find some couches spread,   5
   Tapestries hung up overhead,
   Flowers sprinkled everywhere
   With fragrant herbs to spice the air.

   3. A table laid out you will find,
   Weighted with food of every kind;   10
   There the sparkling wine will pour
   And whatever, dear, you adore.

   4. There you'll hear chamber music soft,
   And flutes will raise their shrills aloft.
   A learned girl, a little boy   15
   Will offer songs that you'll enjoy.

   5. He'll pluck a plectrum on his cithara;
   A lyre will strike a melody with her.

⁹ Dialogue Poem, often called "Invitation to the Beloved." Severely effaced by a monk who considered it sacrilegious. Restored by E. P. Vuolo, *Cultura Neolatina, 10* (1950), 5–25. Much indebted to the Song of Songs. The rhyme scheme is roughly *aabb,* but imperfect. A melody survives.

Serving men then will offer up
Winebowls brimming to painted cups.   20

GIRL(?)
   6. But all this carousing is not my care;
      It's the talking later I hold dear.
      It's not the richness of the material,
      Dear familiarity is all I will.

MAN:
   7. Come now, my chosen sister, the best   25
      Delight for me, before all the rest,
      Shining light to this pupil of mine,
      Greater part of this soul divine!

GIRL:
   8. I walked alone through forest spaces,
      Delighting in those hidden places;   30
      How often I fled the vulgar classes,
      Trying to avoid the common masses.

MAN:
   9. Snow and ice are no more to be seen.
      Flowers and grass are growing green.
      Philomela high takes her part: 35
      Love burns in the cavern of my heart.

  10. O dearest one, please don't delay!
      Be eager—yes, love me right away!
      Without you I just can't fend;
      We must carry our love to the end.   40

  11. Why keep deferring, my elect one,
      Things that later will have to be done?
      Do quickly everything you have to do.
      Me—I'm ready anytime for you!

[31[10]]

Levis exsurgit Zephirus

1. Now Zephyr's rising lightly
   While Sun comes on more brightly;
   Now Earth is opening up her lap
   And everything's aflow with sap.

2. Scarlet Spring comes walking out   5
   With gaudy clothes wrapped about,
   Sprinkling land with many flowers,
   Hanging fronds on woodland bowers.

3. Four-footed beasts prepare their lairs
   While nests are formed for those in air;   10
   On every branch among the wood
   The fowls are singing: joy is good.

4. But what my ears explain to me
   And what my eyes force me to see—
   Alas!—in the midst of this happiness   15
   Fill me instead with sorrowfulness.

5. For here I'm sitting all alone,
   Considering life, as white as stone,
   And the minute that I lift my head
   Every sound and sight is fled.   20

6. You at least, for the sake of the Spring,
   Go out and walk, considering
   The fronds and flowers and the grain—
   This soul of mine is sick with pain.

---

[10] Complaint to Spring. Escaped mutilation perhaps because of its melancholy tone
and allegorical possibilities. Written in Ambrosian stanzas with the regular rhyme
aabb.

[IV]
THE
CARMINA BURANA

The *Carmina Burana* are the stepchildren of European literature. They are a collection of poems written down in the latter half of the thirteenth century, although most of them were composed well before that time. The anthology was collected and stored at the Benediktbeuern Monastery in Bavaria, not far from Munich. The latter part of the monastery name supplies the Latin adjective *"Burana"* that describes these *carmina* or songs. For years this manuscript was left uncatalogued, known only to the monks who had access to it; but in the early 1800s when the Bavarian government was secularizing the Beuern complex, the anthology was brought to light.

Actually, many of the poems in the collection had long been known because they were included in other manuscripts found elsewhere. The authors of the *Burana* lyrics were by no means necessarily the monks who transcribed the words. They were clerics or laymen drawn from many parts of Europe. Some of the poems in the collection are written in a macaronic verse that blends Latin with French, Italian, or German, thus showing the varied sources of the writing. Furthermore, although it is romantic to imagine some of the authors as wandering scholars (*vagantes* or Goliards, based on the legendary author Golias), there is every reason to believe that the composers were often quite respectable men with roots who had a lively knowledge of music and rhetoric.

The collection itself is varied in genres. There are sequences and dramatic episodes within it, as well as a sizable section devoted to drinking songs, gambling songs, and love poems. Some of the most famous poems have been set to music by Carl Orff. Indeed, my translations of Numbers 32 to 39 follow his selection, and have been rendered into English with his music in mind as a possible background. Those who resent Orff's romantic approach can find a more authentic treatment in the Das Alte Werk series, Telefunken recording SAWT 9455-A, where twenty songs are performed from transcriptions of the original manuscript.

No matter how they are performed musically, the tone of the secular poems is clear. The Hymn to Fortune (No. 32), for example, could have been used as part of the celebration for a Black Mass, in which random Chance replaces the providential workings of God. As an entity, the *Burana* celebrate nature, love, and fortune, in a way that runs directly

counter to the supernatural doctrines of the Church. The Confession of
Golias (No. 33) purports to be a shriving of the soul, but is in actuality
an exaltation of the flesh. The speaker revels in his mortality, even
daring to mimic the last line of the *Dies irae* ("God, take care about my
ending!"), which is twisted in the *Burana* version to express the speaker's
"care . . . only for my skin."

Some of the poems, like the Dirge of the Roasted Swan (No. 34) and
the Gambling Song (No. 35), are almost grotesque parodies. The brutal
end of the cooked fowl must be viewed as a travesty of martyrdom, just
as the cry of the naked gambler ("Bitter Fate, O why hast thou forsaken
me?") mimics Christ's cry from the Cross. Sometimes, of course, the tone
is gentler, as in the Drinking Song (No. 36), where the whole world seems
to drown in liquid, or in Number 38, where the equation of men with
flowers seems more comic than sacrilegious.

However, lest we try to write off these poems as mere playful skits, we
must consider the haunting *Stetit puella* (No. 37), which parodies the
Stabat mater (No. 19). There is also the excerpt *Ave, formosissima* (No.
39), which masquerades as a tribute to Mary until it breaks forth into a
eulogy of the heroine Blancheflor, Helen of Troy, and Venus. If these poems
are comic, they are also diabolical, no matter how much like schoolbook
exercises they may seem. On the other hand, some of the most outrageous
pieces, like the Hymn to the Belly (No. 40), can obviously be read in a
moral way as the exposition of a glutton's weakness. Similarly, the portrayal
of the world buffeted in wild conflict (No. 41) can demand an acceptance
of order. As the *Burana* themselves remark in a pithy epigram (No. 42):
"in all that is/ It is good to have a mean."

The gradual working toward a mean is apparent in the love lyrics from
44 to 50. The earlier ones tend to view man's life in terms of the flowers,
as the late classical poets did, but they blend Christian assurance and even
assumption with their pagan acceptance of nature. The third stanza of
Number 44 is a marching song, with the vigor of a Christian hymn. The
first three stanzas of Number 45 are delicate and graceful; they play with
the words "virgin" and "love" in an ambiguous way, and only in the
fourth stanza are the material motives bluntly stated.

The *Carmina Burana* travesty classical rhetoric as well as Christian.
Number 46 is a violent reworking of Horace's famous *sententiae* "it's sweet
to be foolish in the right place" and "seize the day." Number 47 wreaks
havoc with Vergil's "Love conquers all." In the late medieval poems,

these statements are given their most extreme meanings, and the singsong quality of the verse helps to hammer the points home.

In poems 48 to 50, however, one is aware of a different sensibility. The sixth stanza of Number 48 plays with Ovid's famous remarks about the difficulty of maintaining one's balance in love; to this dilemma the poet adds the coloring of Christian suffering in stanzas 3 and 7. As a result, one gets more than a simple declaration of the necessity of sex; the natural world itself seems complicated, and perhaps not so far removed from the religious as the previous poems indicated. The beautiful Hymn to Sleep (No. 49), often attributed to Abelard (but without convincing proof), strikes a note of calm seriousness. This tone is sustained in Number 50, where the poet writes a love song to his lady employing standard Christian symbolism blended with classical allusions, all done with taste and assurance. At this point parody is left behind and one enters the brave new world of medieval secular composition, where passion has a new dignity (since it has The Passion as its backdrop). When the beloved is finally described like Mary as a star of the sky, we see the religious and the secular unite in a way that also occurs in the polished poetry of the troubadours.

In Numbers 32 to 39, where I have the Orff music in mind, I have used the third edition of J. A. Schmeller (Stuttgart, 1894). In other cases, I rely on the more authoritative edition of A. Hilka and O. Schumann, 2 vols. (Heidelberg: Carl Winter Universitätsverlag, 1930–1961).

ANONYMOUS[1]

[32]

O Fortuna

1. O Fortuna,
   Like the moon, you
Shift in everchanging state—
   Always waxing,
   Then collapsing,   5
Making man's life rife with hate;
   Hard perversely,
   Then with mercy
How you tease our reason's thrust!
   Poor one hour,   10
   Ah, comes power!
Which soon melts like ice's crust.

2. Luck is mighty
   Yet as flighty
As an ever-shifting wheel: 15
   High will stumble,
   Health will crumble
In a flow that will not heal.
   Wearing veils
   Along dark trails   20
Suddenly you gleam all stripped:
   Back all naked
   I'm paraded
Out to bear your sportive whips!

3. Slipping virtue,   25
   Health that hurts you—
All that's kind now cruelly chokes;

[1] Hymn to Fortune.

Fine condition
Feels perdition
Quickly lunging for its throat: 30
    Just one hour—
    O the power!—
Then the heart feels strokings deep.
    Luck starts crumbling—
    Knights go tumbling—   35
O my brothers, with me—weep!

[33²]

Estuans intrinsecus ira vehementi

1. As my inner self's on fire
       With a raging flame,
   In a blaze of bitter ire
       I address my brain:
   Manufactured out of matter,   5
       Air my element—
   I'm a bough the breezes batter
       With a playful bent.

2. Wise men who heed imprecations
       When their reason talks   10
   Carefully place their foundations
       On the mighty Rock.
   Idiot me! Shall you compare me
       To the river's run?
   A path pursued will never bear me   15
       Back where I've begun.

    ² Confession of Golias. Continues for about 14 stanzas as the speaker runs through
his sins in a rather exhaustive way. Attributed to a certain Archpoet (*ca.* 1130–1167),
an otherwise unknown German who was a friend of Rainald of Dassel, the Arch-
bishop of Cologne.

3. No, I'm swept on ocean foam
   Skipperless and drifting,
   A bird that flies skyways alone,
   Flitting, ever shifting.   20
   Chains will never fetter fast,
   Locks not last long whiles.
   I hunt friends of my own cast
   And bind me to—the vile!

4. Affairs high-serious belabor   25
   Hearts, too little funny.
   I love jokes; to me their savor's
   Sweeter far than honey.
   Labor bearing Venus' stamp
   Seems suavely empowered;   30
   She has never pitched her camp
   In the breasts of cowards.

5. Down life's open road meandering
   In the guise of youth,
   Ever given to philandering,   35
   Never shriven to truth,
   Greedy to try all lustful fare
   More than health to win—
   Dead in soul, O God! my care
   Is only for my skin! . . .   40

[34³]

Olim lacus colueram

1. Once I skimmed over inland seas;
   Once my white down was fine to see;
   I lived my swan-life peacefully—

───────────────

³ Dirge of the Roasted Swan. *Lacus* in title preferred to *latus*. The two omitted
stanzas say: "I would prefer to live in the water/ Always under the clear sky/ Than

Poor me! Poor me!
Now basted blackly   5
And roasted totally!

2. Turn me, turn me now the sculleries;
Burn me, burn me the rotisseries;
Here comes the serving boy to offer me—
Poor me! Poor me!   10
Now basted blackly
And roasted totally! . . .

5. Now on a serving-plate stretched out I lie,
Thinking in vain of flying through the skies;
Now gnashing molars start to catch my eye—   15
Poor me! Poor me!
Now basted blackly
And roasted totally!

[35⁴]

Ego sum Abbas Cucaniensis

I am the Abbot of Cuckoo-Ninny
And my counsel is always with drinkers like me,
And I follow the sect of Decius, Lord of the Dice,
And whoever runs after me mornings in taverns
At nightfall will issue naked   5
And stripped of his shirt will cry:
Wafna! Wafna!
Bitter Fate, O why hast thou forsaken me?
All the pleasures of this life
You have stolen away!   10

---

to lie here in hot pepper./ I was whiter than snow,/ prettier than any other bird./ Now I'm blacker than a crow." ˙

⁴ Gambling Song. *Cucaniensis* can be Cockaigne, a fictional land of luxurious life. *Wafna* is an emergency cry for help.

[36⁵]

In taberna quando sumus

1. In the tavern when we're toping
   No one sits with death-sighs moping—
   To the gambling we go rushing,
   Sweating from the heavy crushing;
   If you have a lust for mastering   5
   How we pass our time in casting
   (There where Penny summons schooners)
   Listen to these random rumors.

2. This one's slurping, that one's sporting,
   Someone's foolishly cavorting,   10
   But of those who stay for gambling
   Some will exit nudely scrambling,
   Some will put on fine apparel,
   Others sackcloth or a barrel;
   There where death is all forgotten   15
   Bacchus rules the lot of soddens.

3. First throw says who pays for wine,
   That liquid of the libertine.
   Next to prisoners toasts they're giving,
   Thrice saluting then the living;   20
   Four times for each Christian head,
   Five times for the faithful dead;
   Six for sisters who are bolting;
   Seven's a soldier who's not revolting.

4. Eight's for all the Brothers Perverse;   25
   Nine's for all those monks dispersed;
   Ten is for the sailor at sea;
   Eleven for brawlers constantly;

⁵ Drinking Song.

Twelve for the truly penitent;
Thirteen for men on missions sent.   30
Here's to the Pope. Here's to the King!
Everyone drink—no end to the thing!

5. Drinks the mistress, drinks the master;
   Drinks the soldier with the pastor;
   Drinks the Madame with Monsieur;   35
   Drinks the maid-girl with the steward;
   Drinks the slinker, drinks the slack one,
   Drinks the pinkie with the black one;
   Drinks the set man, drinks the bummer;
   Drinks the genius with his dumber.   40

6. Drinks the pauper and the weak one;
   Drinks Old Prelate with the Deacon;
   Drinks the exile, drinks the cipher;
   Drinks teen-ager with long-lifer;
   Drinks the sister, drinks the brother,   45
   Drinks old grandma with your mother;
   This girl's swilling; that churl's plundered—
   Thousands drinking—yes, and hundreds!

7. Six-hundred coins could not remotely
   Fill the bill, for there's no quota   50
   To this drink that knows no measure.
   And though nothing gives more pleasure,
   Still are some who pick and carp,
   Hoping to make our guilt pangs sharp.
   Let those carpers go depraved—   55
   Write their names not with the saved!

[37⁶]

Stetit puella

1. There stood the girl
    In the crimson dress—
    At the softest press,
    How that tunic rustled:
                Eia!   5

2. There stood the girl,
    Rosebud on a vine;
    Face ashine,
    Mouth a reddish bloom.
                Eia!   10

[38⁷]

Tempus est iocundum

1. Pleasant is the weather—you maidens!
    Now rejoice together—with young men!
        O! O! O!
        I flower from head to toe!
        I'm all on fire   5
        For the girl I desire;
        New's this love I cherish:
        New, new, new by which
                I perish. . . .

---

⁶ Parody of Number 19. A third stanza with mixed German and Latin has been
omitted. It equates "great charity" in Latin (*caritatem magnam*) with *hohe Minne*
("high love") in German.
    ⁷ Verses so arranged by Orff.

4. O the better solace—accepted!   10
   O the bitter malice—rejected!
   O! O! O! . . .

7. In cold Winter's fling—man's trusty!
   Comes the sudden breath of Spring—lusty!
   O! O! O! . . .   15

5. Virginity quite jestfully—speeds me;
   And yet simplicity—impedes me.
   O! O! O! . . .

8. Come with joy, my lady—abounding;
   Come, O come, my beauty—I'm floundering!   20
   O! O! O! . . .

[39⁸]

Ave, formosissima

Hail, most beautiful and good,
   Jewel held most dear by us;
Hail, honor of maidenhood,
   Virgin ever glorious—
Hail, thou light above all lights,   5
   Hail, rose of the world—
   Blancheflor
   And Helen,
              Venus,
              Venus,   10
              Venus noble-souled!

⁸ Parody of *Ave, Maria.* This stanza is the opening address of a man to a woman
in a longish *pastourelle: Si linguis angelicis,* ed. Hilka-Schumann, Number 77.

[40⁹]

Alte clamat Epicurus

1. Epicurus cries aloud:
   "A belly full is surer.
   Belly is my own true god—
   Throat is his procurer;
   Kitchen is their sacred shrine   5
   Where they sniff their goods divine.

2. "Behold! this god is awfully good;
   Fasts he does not cherish;
   And before the morning food,
   There's a burp of sherry;   10
   To him tables and big bowls
   Are the truly heavenly goals.

3. "Yes, his flesh is always bulging
   Like a bloated jug of sack:
   Ruby cheeks show his indulging;   15
   Lunch meets dinner back to back;
   When his desire stirs the veins
   It is stronger than a chain."

4. This religious cult expresses
   Devotion in its belched excesses;   20
   Belly folds in agony;
   Beer is battling burgundy;
   Yet life is blesséd with much leisure
   When its center's belly's pleasure.

5. Belly speaks now: "Not one damn   25
   Care I for anything but me;
   I just quietly want to jam

⁹ Hymn to the Belly. Epicurus is the Greek philosopher whom thinkers of the Middle Ages associated with hedonism and a denial of immortality.

Plenty of stuff inside of me,
And then above the chow and wine
To sleep, to rest in peace divine."   30

[41¹⁰]

Iste mundus

1. This old world
   In fury furled
   Sets false joys before our eyes—
   These all spill,
   Run downhill   5
   As the lily quickly lies.

2. Worldly schemes,
   Life's vain dreams
   Steal away the truer prize;
   They impel   10
   Man to Hell
   Where he fully buried lies.

3. Carnal matters,
   Law that shatters
   Truly full of frivolousness   15
   Falters, fades
   Like a shade
   That has lost its mesh of flesh.

4. All we spy,
   Hold close by   20
   In our fatherland today
   We'll dismiss,

---

¹⁰ Poem reflects the *contemptus mundi* or "contempt of the world" tradition.

Slowly miss
As the oak leaves drift away. . . .

6. Let us batter,   25
   Let us scatter
   All desires of the skin;
   Stand erect
   Among the elect
   And the justest of all men.   30

7. Heavenly pleasure
   We shall treasure
   Through the ages that never end!
                                        Amen.

[42]

Semper ad omne quod est

Always in all that is
   It is good to have a mean;
For without some measure
   The court of the king careens.

[43]

Non est crimen amor

Love is not wrong because
   If it were a crime,
God would never have used love
   To bind even the divine.

[44*]

Iamiam rident prata[11]

1. Now, yes now the fields are smiling;
   Now, yes now the girls agree
   In gaiety, while all beguiling
   Earth laughs too in harmony.
   Summer has entered on the stage,   5
   And, decked in flowers,
        Is all the rage.

2. Grove again wears greenish sleeves,
   Bushes with their budlets snap;
   Cruel Winter has taken leave.   10
   Young men full of joy and sap,
   Go be happy in the tendrils!
   Love is now enticing you
        To the girls.

3. Our resolution: let's all fight   15
   Together for our Lady Venus;
   Let's keep sadness out of sight—
   To us real violence is heinous.
   The looks and ah! the ploys,
   Hope and Love will lead us   20
        To our joys.

* Original text appears in Section X, p. 382.

[11] I read "rident" instead of "virent" in the opening line.

[45¹²]

Veris dulcis in tempore

1. In the time of pleasant spring,
   Under a tree that's blossoming
   Juliana with sister standing—
       O sweet love!
   Whoever lacks you in this hour   5
       'S all the poorer.

2. Look! the trees burst into flower,
   Birdies singing with lusty power,
   Virgins warming hour by hour—
       O sweet love!   10
   Whoever lacks you in this hour
       'S all the poorer.

3. Look! the lily's taken to flowering,
   And ranks of virgins start to sing
   Songs to the highest godlike thing—   15
       O sweet love!
   Whoever lacks you in this hour
       'S all the poorer.

4. If I could catch what I most covet
   In a dark wood—kiss and love it,   20
   There'd be no other joy above it—
       O sweet love!
   Whoever lacks you in this hour
       'S all the poorer.

¹² Follows Hilka-Schumann, Number 85.

[46¹³]

Omittamus studia

1. Let's put aside our studying:
   Sweet it is to play the fool.
   Let's seize all the sweeter things
   Youth offers in its languid rule.
   There'll be time for pondering   5
   Weighty things when life grows cool.
     Time too swiftly rushes;
       Study crushes;
     Young blood strongly urges
       Us to purge us.   10

2. Summer of age away is slipping,
   Winter soon comes rushing on;
   Life feels loss against it chipping
   Until the flesh with care's all gone;
   Heart is hardened; blood just trickles;   15
   One by one goes all that pleases;
   Old Age hails us with his sickle:
   Fodder for his family of diseases.
     Time too swiftly rushes . . .

3. Let's imitate the gods above!   20
   That's a maxim well worth heeding.
   Toward us come those nets of love
   To ensnare fair men of breeding.
   Be obedient to our prayers!
   That's the code the gods maintain.   25
   Let's go down then to the square
   And watch the virgins entertain.
     Time too swiftly rushes . . .

¹³ Two lines from stanza 1 omitted from manuscript. The Horatian poems parodied
are *Odes* IV.12 and I.11.

4. Ah, there's plenty there for grabbing
   If it's only with the eyes.   30
   Shiny arms the air are stabbing,
   Slender slink those splendid thighs—
   While the girls are leaping, stalking
   With the beat that never dies,
   I stand gaping; in my gawking   35
   Feel my soul outside me rise!
       Time too swiftly rushes . . .
           Study crushes;
       Young blood gently urges
           Us to purge us.   40

[47¹⁴]

Ianus annum circinat

1. Janus circles round the year;
   Spring announces Summer's back;
   Gradually toward Taurus veers
   Phoebus with his hoofbeats near
   Outside Aries' racing-track.   5
       Love can anything defeat,
       Love can turn the harsh to sweet.

2. Let all sadness fast depart;
   Let sweet pleasures consecrate
   The schoolhouse of the Queen of Hearts!   10
   Now's the time for euphony,
   You soldiers who will dedicate
   Your lives to our Lord Dione.

---

[14] Lines compressed from text. Refrain mimics Vergil, *Eclogue* X.69. The phrase *Dioneo lari* in stanza 2, translated "Lord Dione," relates to the masculinizing of the woman and is comparable with Provençal *midons* ("Milord"), which is used by troubadours to describe a lady.

Love can anything defeat,
Love can turn the harsh to sweet.   15

3. When I entered Venus College,
   A graduate of Pallas,
   Among those devotees of knowledge
   There was not one girl as
   Beautiful as one I spied: 20
   O her face was Helen's!
   Venus only with her vied
   In affairs of elegance.
   She was tops in modest pride.
   Love can anything defeat,   25
   Love can turn the harsh to sweet.

4. Different from other men,
   I love all uniquely.
   Once this novel flame begins,
   It flares within   30
   And never shows a weakening.
   There's no other girl more noble,
   Ever able,
   Beautiful and lovable,
   Never proving mobile,   35
   Not unstable,
   Ready ever for bowing,
   Never false to her vowing.
   To be aware she lives in bliss
   Would bring me great delight;   40
   And I'd feel even doubly blessed
   If I could share that plight.
   Love conquers everything!
   Love governs everything!

5. Spare this boy, you boy-god, spare;   45
   Venus, look with loving care;
   Move that fire,
   Stir desire,

And what I want, don't let it die!
Don't let her deceive us   50
As Daphne did Phoebus!
Once a freshman in Wisdom School,
Venus, Venus, I yield to your rule!
    Love conquers everything!
    Love governs everything!   55

[48*]

Axe Phebus aureo

1. Phoebus in his golden car
       Lights the firmament,
    And with rosy glows imparts
       His shaftings down to men.
    Cybele in elegance arrayed   5
       With her flowering face
    To Bacchus gives a fresh bouquet,
       While Phoebus beams with grace.

2. With the help of winds that blend
       All throughout the grove,   10
    Little birds their beauties lend
       As they chant of love.
    Philomel now renews her blame
       Of Tereus for wrongs,
    Joining the blackbird in refrains   15
       Adapted for their songs.

3. Now Dione's
    Chorus joyously
    Zealously answers
    Their various chants.   20

* Original text appears in Section X, p. 383.

And now Dione
In jest and in agony
Lightens, then tightens
Her worshipers' hearts.

4. Me too she pulls   25
   Away from my sleep.
Me too she rules:
   "Now vigil keep!"
Cupid's golden shaft
   I'm forced to bear;   30
Ire-filled fires
   Through my body tear!

5. Whatever I'm plied
   I recant.
For what I'm denied   35
   I will pant
In a mind severely swayed.
When a thing is ceded me,
   I waver;
Yet whoever won't heed me   40
   J favor;
About me you can truly say:

6. I'm faithful; I'll go to my grave
For her, or else for her I'm saved.
If she wants me, I'm all through.   45
If she taunts me, I pursue.
The more I've rejected the lawful,
The more I deflect toward the awful.
The more the unspiced one's allowed me,
The more the unlicensed one cows me.   50

7. O Dione's
Baleful decrees!
Poison to flee
Working inwardly,

Fearsome lechery,   55
Full of treachery.
Mistress of might,
Whose torture's a fright,
Your serfs you requite
With bitterness' bite,   60
Full of all slights
And fiery spite!

8. And so in me
    A fear is swelling,
   And down my cheeks   65
    The tears come welling.
   And so my face
    Looks frayed and pale:
   It is: in love I've been
    Betrayed, I fail.   70

[49¹⁵]

Dum Diane vitrea

1. When Dian with lamp of glass
   Arises in the evening skies
   Soft and glowing pinkly as
   Her brother's fires around her die,
   Zephyr's gentle breezes often   5
   Force the clouds on high to soften,
   Then steal away;
   Music too can sway
   Human breasts from inner broil,
   Subtly changing   10
   Heart, which ranges
   Nodding toward love's heavy toil.

¹⁵ Hymn to Sleep. Follows Hilka-Schumann, Number 62. Poem continues for
four more stanzas, which the editors regard as spurious.

D

2. Vesper's slender ray of light
   Gives the pleasing
   Dew that eases   15
   Entrance into dreamland's portals
   For weary mortals.

3. O how blessed is sleep's potion,
   Curing cares and worldly commotion!
   Stealthily stealing through pores of eyes,   20
   Joyous rival to love's enterprise.

4. Morpheus through the mind
   Draws a wind as kind
   As that which wafts a field of ripened grain;
   Murmuring rivers glide through sandy plains;   25
   Mill wheels circle slowly round and round—
   While we in sleep lie robbed of light and sound.

[50*]

Dira vi amoris teror

1. By the dire force of love I'm worn,
   By the chariot of Venus borne,
   By a fervent fire I lie choked:
   Bless éd one, remove this forkéd yoke!

2. You're the ember of this lively burning;   5
   Heart's standards feel you inside turning,
   While I recline on this fire too real
   And end with you as my mind's seal.

3. This heart is sad that once was joyous
   On that day when it saw you, glorious,   10

* Original text appears in Section X, p. 385.

Modest, with charms that never end:
It took you instantly for its friend.

4. Sighs come pouring out of my breast,
   Racks of sorrow that give me no rest;
   The vigor of love without remission   15
   Presses me into this chained condition.

5. Virgin lily, O send, I pray
   Help to guide me on my way!
   I, an exile on parade,
   Humbly call on you for aid.   20

6. I don't know what to do; I fail
   For the love of you by which I sail;
   Venus' shaftings will soon destroy
   Unless you rush to help this boy.

7. Orphan from the reign of Venus,   25
   Blessed with chastity to clean us,
   Face neat, ornate for all to see,
   Garbed in the robe of Philosophy:

8. To you alone I hymn my praise;
   O don't despise my earthly ways;   30
   Let me, I pray you, hold you high,
   Shining as lodestar of my sky!

[V]
PROVENÇAL SONGS

The Provençal lyric bursts upon the late medieval world like a welcomed ray of spring sunlight or, in terms of the imagery perpetuated by the Latin lyric, like the missing cuckoo. The first known poet is Duke William IX of Aquitaine, grandfather of the famous Eleanor and lord of most of southwestern France. In his work we can detect a transformation from cruder poems (Nos. 52 and 53), where women are treated as mere objects for possession, to the more refined but still masculinely dominated love lyric or *canso* (Nos. 54 and 55). William establishes many of the rhetorical patterns which recur in later compositions. He calls his woman *midons* (which I translate "Milord," or sometimes "Milordess," to preserve the wit), treats her like a medieval duke writing the real duke into her charter, and in short establishes that socially oriented world that is often associated with the overused phrase "courtly love." On the other hand, William's tone is often brusque and frankly Ovidian. His imagery runs the gamut from the castle bedroom to the cathedral. He speaks about his lady's being "whiter than any ivory creation" (No. 54, stanza 3) and he constantly plays with sacred allusions (St. George, nunneries, monks) in a way that makes his poems sound every bit as "churchly" in their overtones as courtly.

William's tampering with Christian mysticism can best be seen in his famous Riddle Poem (No. 56), where religious mysteries are transferred to secular paradox. Still, lest we see him merely as a rude parodist, his Hymn on His Own Death (No. 57) shows the bowing of the earthly lord to the Celestial Lord in clear, certain terms. William's stanzas, rhyme schemes, and rhetoric can all be related to Latin rhetoric and Christian hymnology, especially in his pilfering of the touchstone word "joy."

Cercamon continues the tradition admirably, preserving the Duke's easy colloquial flavor (which I have exaggerated in my translation of No. 58), yet also insisting on the divine madness of love. His supposed pupil Marcabrun voices the reaction to the new love credo that one might have expected in an age of faith. Marcabrun speaks about Good Love and Refined Love, which the troubadours use in their descriptions of their personal affairs, but he identifies Good Love in Number 59 with Christian charity and Low Loving, its opposite, with lust; in this way he is in accord with St. Augustine, not Duke William. Yet Marcabrun is no bland con-

servative; his Crusade Song (No. 60) is also a scathing attack on the
society of his day. His sensitivity shows especially in his handling of the
pastourelle, a form that he left his imprint on: Number 61 is still rather
crude, like some of the *Carmina Burana,* but Number 62 is indeed refined.
Here a highborn woman voices her love for her man, who is away on
crusade, refusing the comfort of the narrator, who tries to interest her in
God, although he is actually concerned with seduction. As an entity, the
poem expresses through the characters the love of this world in poignant
terms, but it also gives voice to the demands of the world beyond.

With Jaufre Rudel we encounter the ethereal and the mystical in a
secular context. His famous Number 63, which speaks of his burning
desire for his "far-off love," has led some people to interpret his poems
as expressions of Manichean or Catharist doctrine: they see the far-off lady
as a dim ideal of the Good shining bleakly upon a poet lost in a world of
Evil. The poem is not, however, Catharist, for stanza 6 says clearly that
God, not Satan, is the creator of the world. One can find a sense of idealism
contending with tragic separation in the mystical works of St. Bernard of
Clairvaux, Richard of St. Victor, and elsewhere. The situation is, in fact,
basic to the lyric of any time. The mysterious godfather of stanzas 7 and 8
is probably Adam, whose sin intensified the gap between ideals and reality
that forms the basic tension in the poem. Jaufre's Riddle Poem (No. 64)
is a further extension of the treatment of human love in a mystical frame-
work. It sounds sacrilegious, but the *Burana* proved that one can be that
without being heretical.

Bernart de Ventadorn is now usually considered The Master Singer.
A mixture of tones and gestures is an integral part of Bernart's method,
for he developed the Provençal *canso* into a sophisticated form that was
capable of many sudden turns. In his works, his woman appears as a
divine agent like Mary (that other "good woman"), like a lordly duke
(continuing William's Milord), and often, quite suddenly, like Eve, the
dark destroyer of man's dreams. Yet no matter how she is portrayed, the
medium of the poem is always graceful, witty, and polished. He can toy
with mentions of Christmas and Easter in Number 69 or play with a
reversal of seasons in Number 66, but Bernart will never be accused of
heresy; he expresses that willful acceptance of madness that is the property
of poets, lovers, and saints.

Unfortunately, the history of the *canso* after Bernart is one of decadence.

Striving for originality, some poets moved into obscurantism, embracing the so-called *trobar clus* or "closed-invention" style. One of the strongest exponents is Raimbaut of Orange, who in Number 71 expresses his determination to be highly individual, yet in a language that is still apprehensible. More typical is Arnaut Daniel, who in Numbers 84 and 85 shows what can and cannot be done with this attitude toward composition. One can admire the original Provençal for the experiments with sound, as Pound did, but when one translates for sense, there is something lacking.

On the other hand, some poets tried to do the simple thing. In Number 88, Raimbaut de Vaqueiras attempts to capture the quiet lilt of a folk song, as does Peire Vidal in Number 82. Both are successful individual attempts, but they did not establish a new tradition. Possibly the best love poem of the latter half of the twelfth century is Bertran de Born's Number 80, where he frankly confesses that his Self-Conceived Lady is a supreme fiction.

As South French society began to crumble under the incursions of the English and the North French, compounded by the Papacy's calling of the Albigensian Crusade, the poetry turned from the sweet style of love to bitter satire, usually expressed in a form called the *sirventes*. Bertran de Born communicates the anguish of living in a land torn by internal and external dissension. Peire Cardenal in Number 90 attacks the Church for its sinful hypocrisy, which is shown by the Monk of Montaudon (No.' 86). Cardenal paints the general scene in Number 91, when he writes of a society that has gone mad. Yet lest we believe that the tradition ended in heresy, we have Cardenal's reasoned Complaint to God (No. 92) and the beautiful religious Dawn Song of Folquet of Marseille (No. 89).

In one sense, the change of the whole tradition is mirrored in the Dawn Song or *alba*. We have the fresh, anonymous, popular alba (No. 51), which seems to emanate from pagan spring rites and yet suggests the aristocratic world of the beautiful queen, her young lover, and her jealous husband. We have the balanced creation of Guiraut de Bornelh (No. 74), where the references to the supernatural order are beautifully locked with the human. We have the rather slick, but still effective, piece of Raimbaut of Vaqueiras (No. 87), where one can sense the dilution of the tradition. Finally, the work of Folquet shows a complete turning away from the human in preference for the religious. After the Church and the Albigensian Crusaders conquered in southern France, the poets followed the lead of

Folquet (persuaded to no slight degree by the Inquisition that he helped to institute). Southern France thus reversed the trend of other countries by returning to hymns at the close of its golden age. Still, its unique contribution to Western letters was not lost. We must simply look to other countries to find the traditions that were carried on.

ANONYMOUS[1]

[51]

En un vergier sotz folha d'albespi

1. In a garden under a hawthorn bower
   A lover to his lady's closely drawn
   Until a watchman shouts the morning hour.
   O God! O God! how swift it comes—the dawn!

2. "Dear God, if this night would never fail   5
   And my lover never far from me was gone,
   And the watchman never saw the morning pale—
   But, O my God! how swift it comes—the dawn!

3. "Come, pretty boy, give me a little kiss
   Down in the meadow where birds sing endless song.   10
   Forget my husband! Think—just think of this—
   For, O my God! how swift it comes—the dawn!

4. "Hurry, my boy. The new games·end at morn.
   Down to that garden—those birds—that song!
   Play, play till the crier blows his horn,   15
   For, O my God! how swift it comes—the dawn!

5. "Down in the sweet air over the meadow hovering
   I drank a sweet draught—long, so long—
   Out of the air of my handsome, noble lover."
   O God! O God! how swift it comes—the dawn!   20

6. The lady's pretty. She has many charms.
   Toward her beauty many men are drawn.
   But she lies happy in one pair of arms.
   O God! O God! how swift it comes—the dawn!

[1] Oldest Dawn Song in a modern European language.

DUKE WILLIAM IX OF AQUITAINE[2]

[52]

Farai un vers, pos mi sonelh

1. I'll write a poem, then take a nap,
   And then go stand in the sun.
   Some ladies are really misguided;
      I know which ones:
   Those who turn the love of a knight   5
      Into grief.

2. A lady commits a mortal sin
   If she doesn't love a faithful knight;
   And if she loves a monk or a priest,
      She's very wrong;   10
   It's right that we should burn her
      At the stake.

3. In Auvergne, that side of Limousin,
   I was cruising all alone on the sly;
   Then I found the wife of Lord Guari   15
      And Bernard's too.
   All they did was salute me simply
      By St. Leonard.

[2] Duke William IX of Aquitaine, seventh Count of Poitou (1071–1126 or 1127). First known secular love poet after the Dark Ages. Owner of more territory than the kings of France in his day. Increased his holdings by marrying Philippa of Toulouse, who later abandoned him for the monastic life. Usurped church lands, for which he was excommunicated. Took a major part in the disastrous Crusades of 1101, barely escaping death in Asia Minor. Led a brief, successful skirmish against the Moors in Spain. Notoriously fond of songs, parties, and women, as the chroniclers fondly point out. Succeeded by his son, William X, father of Eleanor of Aquitaine. Eleven poems survive. This one, a *fabliau*, is one of the few examples of the obscene-story poem in Provençal.

4. Then one of them said in her dialect,
   "God protect you, sir pilgrim;   20
   You're a man of excellent breeding,
      I do believe;
   We see far too many fools around
      In this world."

5. Now hear what I said in reply: 25
     I didn't say this and I didn't say that,
   Didn't mention a stick, not a tool;
      All I said was:
   "Babariol, Babariol,
      Babarian."   30

6. Then Lady Agnes said to Lady Emma:
   "He's just what we're looking for.
   For the love of God, let's put him up!
      He's a mute.
   He'll never be able to tattle about   35
      What we do."

7. The one covered me up with her mantle
   And led me in to her bedroom fire.
   Listen! It was all pretty nice:
      A fire nice and warm,   40
   And it made me feel good to get heated
      By her coals.

8. They gave me some capons to eat,
   And listen! I had more than a few,
   With no cook or scullion hanging around—   45
      Just us three.
   The bread was white, the wine was choice,
      And the pepper hot.

9. "Sister, I think he's a sly one;
   Dropped his speech just for our account;   50

Let's bring out that big red tomcat
  Right this minute.
That'll loosen his tongue in a hurry
  If he's fooling."

10. Lady Agnes went out for the beast;   55
  It was big and had long mustaches.
  The minute I saw him come in,
    I was scared;
  I almost lost all of my courage,
    My nerve.   60

11. After we ate and we had some drinks,
  I shucked off my clothes as they asked.
  And they brought up that cat behind me—
    That evil thing!
  And the one dragged him along my flank   65
    Down to the heels.

12. Then all at once she pulls that cat
  By his tail, and does he scratch!
  They gave me more than a hundred strokes
    In just that time;   70
  But I wouldn't have moved an inch—
    Till brink of death.

13. "Sister," said Agnes to Emma,
  "He's mute, and that's for sure!
  Let's get him ready for his bath   75
    And a nice, long stay."
  I stayed there a good eight days or more
    In their oven.

14. And I screwed them this many times:
  One hundred and eighty-eight.   80
  And I almost fractured my straps
    And my gear.

And I'll never be able to tell you
  My later pain.

15. No, I'll never be able to tell you   85
   About that pain!

[53]

Companho, farai un vers covinen

1. Friends, I'll write a poem that will do:
   But it'll be full of fun
     And not much sense.
   A grab bag all about love
   And joy and youth.   5

2. A man's a fool if he doesn't get it
   Or deep down inside won't try
     To learn.
   It's very hard to escape from love
   Once you find you like it.   10

3. I've got two pretty good fillies in my corral:
   They're ready for any combat—
     They're tough.
   But I can't keep 'em both together:
   Don't get along.   5

4. If I could tame 'em the way I want,
   I wouldn't have to change
     This setup,
   For I'd be the best-mounted man
   In all this world.   20

5. One's the fastest filly up in the hills,
And she's been fierce and wild
   A long, long time.
In fact, she's been so fierce and wild,
Can't stick her in my pen.   25

6. The other was born here—Confolens way—
And I never saw a better mare,
   I swear!
But she won't change her wild, wild ways
For silver or gold.   30

7. I gave her to her master a feeding colt;
But I kept myself a share
   In the bargain too:
If he'll keep her one whole year,
I will a hundred or more.   35

8. Knights, your advice in this affair!
I was never so troubled by
   Any business before.
Which of these nags should I keep:
Miss Agnes? Miss Arsen?   40

9. I've got the castle at Gimel under thumb,
And over at Nieul I strut
   For all the folks to see.
Both castles are sworn and pledged by oath:
They belong to *me!*   45

[54]

Farai chansoneta nueva

1. I shall compose a new refrain
Before the ice and wind and rain;

My lady always tests and tries
To see if I am truly fond;
There is no blow to strike my side   5
That will make me break loose from her bond.

2. I render myself to her, I accede
   And let her write me into her deed,
   And don't think I'm completely drunk
   If I love my good lady this much,   10
   For without her, I'd lose all my spunk:
   I have such great hunger for her touch.

3. She's whiter than any ivory creation:
   No other will win my adoration.
   But if I don't get aid by and by   15
   To help me win my beautiful lady—
   By the head of St. George, I'll die—
   With no kiss in boudoir or bower shady.

4. What good will it do, my lady gay,
   If you move that love of yours away?   20
   It seems you will run to a nunnery.
   Ah, listen! love gives me such unrest
   That sadness soon will be stinging me
   If you don't make right these wrongs I protest.

5. What good for me, those cloister walls,   25
   If I'm not offering you my all?
   Every joy of the world we can share,
   Lady, if we'll just love each other.
   To Daurostre I send, my friend over there,
   This song that he sing with no special bother.   30

6. For her I shake, for her I tremble;
   For with good love I love this madam;
   No lady born remotely resembles
   Her bearing in the dynasty of Adam.

[55*]

Ab la dolchor del temps novel[3]

1. In the sweetness of the budding spring
   When woods are leafing, wingéd things
   Cast their songs in native speech
   By the verse of their own spring chant;
   Ah, then for men it's right that each   5
   Should have the easing that he wants.

2. From where all's goodness, all is beauty,
   Comes no seal, no runner on duty,
   And so my heart can't laugh or rest;
   And I dare not draw on for a task   10
   Till I know if my entire behest
   Will be fulfilled as I have asked.

3. Our love affair will be reborn
   Like a branch upon a hawthorn
   Which, trembling over the trunk, will sway   15
   At nighttime in the hail and rain,
   But come the dawn, the sun's bright rays
   Make leaf and branch all green again.

4. O I still remember that day
   When we signed a truce to our fray,   20
   And she gave me that gift I adore:
   Her loving, with ring in troth.
   God, let me live some more
   To put my hand beneath her cloak!

5. No strange Latin do I need   25
   To part my Good Neighbor from me:

---

* Original text appears in Section X, p. 386.

[3] Simile in stanza 3 adapted by Dante in *Inferno* II.127 ff. The *senhal* (secret name) Good Neighbor in stanza 5 deliberately seems to mimic Christian charity.

For I know how the gossiping spreads
In some quick talk that runs rife.
We don't need to brag how our love's bred:
No, we have the meat and the knife!   30

[56⁴]

Farai un vers de dreit nien

1. I'll write a verse about sheer nil—
   Not about me or any other guy.
   Of youth and love I've had my fill,
       As of other hack.
   I wrote this ditty with one half-open eye   5
       On my horse's back.

2. I don't know the hour I first saw the light.
   I'm not way up high, yet I'm not in a ditch,
   I'm not all involved, yet I'm not up-tight.
       (That's the way it's willed);   10
   With a fairy's wand I was bewitched
       Atop a high hill.

3. I don't know when I wallow in sleep
   Or when I wake—unless I'm told.
   My heart from my body would like to sneak   15
       To escape heart's care.
   All this for a single laugh could be sold—
       By Saint Martial I swear!

4. I'm sick. Lord, I'm afraid of dying.
   And I only understand what I hear.   20

---

⁴ Riddle Poem. The cause of the confusion is undoubtedly love; other elements
in the poem are not easily explicable.

I need a doctor for my fantasizing,
   But don't know who.
He'll be a good healer if he sets me clear—
   If not, I'm through.

5. I have a girl friend—don't know who—   25
   For I've never seen her (in faith I swear!).
She never solaced me, never abused—
   But what the hell!
A Norman or Frank never once dared
   Enter my *grand hôtel!*   30

6. I never saw her, but love her strong;
   She never did me good or bad;
When I don't see her, there's nothing wrong,
   It's an even score,
For a prettier, better one makes me glad,   35
   Who's worth a lot more.

7. I've made the *vers* about something or other
   And I'm sending it to a man I've pressed
To pass it onward through another
   Toward Anjou for me;   40
And let that one take from his secret chest
   The counterkey.

[57[5]]

Pos de chantar m'es pres talenz

1. Now that I've singing's bent
   I'll strike a tune for a lament
   Never to be love's obedient
   In Limoges or in Poitou.

[5] Hymn on His Own Death. Safest date of composition between 1112 and 1117, before the actual death, when William's son succeeded him under very peaceful

2. Now into exile I will go.   5
   In peril, in frightful woe,
   I leave my son to face war's throe
   And the wrongs my neighbors do.

3. O leaving the lordship of Poitou
   Is such a bitter thing to do!   10
   Watch my lands, Foulques d'Anjou—
   And your little cousin too.

4. If Foulques refuses to lift a hand,
   Like the King, grace of my land,
   Evils will come from those bands   15
   Of Gascons and men of Anjou.

5. Unless my son is wise, shows worth,
   Once I've left this native earth
   Tossing him over will bring them mirth
   Because he's weak and new.   20

6. Mercy I beg of you, dear friend.
   If ever I wronged you, make amends.
   To Jesus enthroned, I pray: defend!—
   In Provençal, in Latin too.

7. O I was a man of prowess and wit,   25
   But now I renounce each single bit;
   I'll go to him who sin remits
   Where men can end renewed.

8. Yes, I was a jaunty lord, and gay,
   But another Lord points another way.   30

---

circumstances. William conducted a long, adulterous love affair in his later years with the wife of Foulques IV (the Rough) of Anjou. "Vair" and "gris" in the last line are expensive furs. This poem was apparently not sung at William's funeral.

Now these shoulders, burdened, sway
As my end looms in view.

9. Now I abandon chivalry, pride,
Everything I was never denied.
What pleases him I'll abide: 35
May he hold me ages through!

10. At my funeral, friends, I pray:
Gather around, shout your praise,
For I've known many happy days
Far and near, and in Poitou.   40

11. But now I surrender my joy, my pleasure:
My vair and gris, my sable treasure.

CERCAMON[6]

[58]

Quan l'aura doussa s'amarzis

1. When the gentle breeze turns bitter
And the leaf snaps off the bough
And the birds reverse their twitter,
Then I have to weep and sigh,
For Love's got me in his clutches,   5
And power over him I've not had much.

[6] Cercamon (*fl.* 1130–1152). Gascon singer and composer who traveled widely (his name means Search-the-World); the supposed teacher of Marcabrun. His Lament on the Death of William X (1137) is datable. The translation attempts to suggest a certain primitiveness in the verse, which has an *ABABCD* rhyme scheme. (Note: capital letters for rhyme schemes indicate that the very same rhymes are used in every single stanza of the poem.)

2. Hell no! from Love I get zero,
   Except for some trouble and pain.
   It would take some hard-working hero
   To get what I've got on my brain,   10
   For nothing stirred up my envy so
   Like the thing from which there's always "No!"

3. A jewel has set me bounding with joy;
   To a finer one I never aspired;
   But when I'm with her I feel so low   15
   I can't even tell her of my desire,
   And when I'm away (it seems to me)
   Sense goes, with sensibility.

4. The prettiest one you ever glimpsed
   Next to her isn't worth a damn;   20
   When the world goes into full eclipse,
   She'll be a beacon in the gloom.
   O God! I pray: let me cling to her,
   Or watch her undressing in her room.

5. I hassle and I fret; I'm all up-tight   25
   For her love, asleep or awake.
   The thought of failing causes such fright
   It makes me afraid to make my demand.
   Okay, I'll serve her two years or three—
   This way she'll get the word from me.   30

6. I'm not alive or dead or well;
   I don't feel pain, but I've got a lot;
   Her love's a thing I just can't tell:
   Whether I'll get it or how or when.
   But the power of grace is in her all   35
   And that can lift me or make me fall.

7. I like it when she makes me crazy:
   I walk and gape or I stand and stare;

It's all right if she yaps at me
And bitches me constantly everywhere.   40
For after the evil comes the good—
Or at least it will if she thinks it should.

8. If she doesn't want me, I wish I'd died
   The day I put her high up above.
   O God! she killed deliciously   45
   When she gave me one fond look of love.
   She's cornered me in such a pen
   I can't see another woman again!

9. And so I go all hung up in this joy
   For if I respect and follow her,   50
   She'll make me false or make me fine,
   A conniver or a loyal courtier,
   A common peasant or a noble guy,
   All up-tight or flying high.

10. You can agree or feel affronts—   55
    She can retain me if she wants.

11. Cercamon says: to be debonair,
    Man, about Love you must never despair!

MARCABRUN[7]

[59]

L'iverns vai e·l temps s'aizina

1. Winter goes, and the time is pleasant,
   And the woods again are growing green,
   And flowers peep along the hawthorn,

[7] Marcabrun, Marcabru (*fl.* 1130–1150). According to the questionable *vidas* (biographies) in the songbooks, a Gascon orphan tended by Aldrics of Vilar and

As birds go bounding with their joy—
   Ay!   5
Now all men are gay with love;
Each one's drawn to his mate—
   Yeah!
According to his heart's desire.

2. Cold is quaking, drizzle rustles   10
   Against the gentle season's coming;
   Through the groves and thickets
   I hear the contests of those songs—
   Ay!
   And put myself to the trobar task,   15
   For I'll tell you how Love wanders,
      Yeah!
   And, maybe, how he rolls back too.

3. Low Loving spreads, confounding
   Control with gluttonous appetite,   20
   Searching for that sweet dish of meat,
   Ever warmed by those nasty fires—
      Ay!
   Once a man slips in there—
   For real or just for a try—   25
      Yeah!
   Got to leave his skin behind in the pot!

4. Good Love packs a panacea
   To heal his loyal followers;
   But Low Loving spanks his disciples   30

---

taught by Cercamon. First had the name Pamperdut (Lost Bread or Lost Britches),
but later acquired his current name, which means Dark Spot. Perfected the *sirventes*,
a nonamatory poem that is often satiric: example here. Supposedly murdered by
some lords of Guyenne because of his wicked tongue. Some forty-five poems
survive. Here, sense obscure in stanzas 5 and 8. The lord in stanza 9 is probably
Ebles II (the Singer) of Ventadorn. "Refined Love" in line 47 is *amor fina;* its
opposite in line 19 is *Amars.*

And sends 'em straight to Hell—
   Ay!
As long as the geld lasts here,
The poor fool thinks he's loved,
   Yeah!   35
But once the geld's gone, botch-up!

5. Low Loving lays a marvelous trap,
   Luring the dupe into his lime
From the top down to his toes:
All messed up! Shall I? No?   40
   Ay!
Want a blonde, brunette, or black?
And will I do it? Or won't I?
   Yeah!
This way a fool gets a skinny rump.   45

6. A lady who loves her farmhand
   Just doesn't know Refined Love.
No, she's got the bitch's instinct
Like the greyhound for the cur.
   Ay!   50
Out come those savage, mongrel rich
Who won't give you parties or pay—
   Yeah!
So swears Marcabrun!

7. The farmhand sneaks into the kitchen   55
   To warm up some fire among the twigs
And lap up some of the fresh bouquet
From the cask of Milady Goodfount—
   Ay!
I know how he stays and loafs there,   60
Separating the grain from the chaff—
   Yeah!
Impeasantizing his master.

8. Who has Good Love as neighbor
   And lives within his bondage   65
   Sees Honor and Worth inclining
   And Value—not any danger—
       Ay!
   Does so much with honest words,
   He need never fear the wrath—   70
       Yeah!
   Of that lecher-livin' Sir Aigline.

9. I'll never pledge my troth
   With Lord Eblés' pack of poets,
   For too often there good sense   75
   Falters, contrary to reason—
       Ay!
   I said, I say, and always will:
   High and Low Love have different cries—
       Yeah!   80
   And whoever blames Good Love's an ass.

[60⁸]

Pax in nomine Domini!

1. *Pax in nomine Domini!*
   Marcabrun made the words and the song:
       Hear what he says.
   The most gracious Lord of Heaven
   Out of his sweetness has fashioned   5
   For our use here a washing tub,
   Unlike any other (except the one

---

⁸ Crusade Song with strong *sirventes* flavor. Written for the Second Crusade, about 1147. The Count in line 70 is probably Duke William X, who died ten years earlier. Opening Latin line means: "Peace in the name of Our Lord!"

Overseas in the vale of Josephat).
But to this one I summon you.

2. And it's rightful that we should bathe   10
Our bodies from night till morn—
   I assure you.
Everyone has his chance to scrub.
And until he's healthy and hale,
He ought to go straight to the tub,   15
For there's our true therapy.
And if we pass first to death,
We'll fall to lowly lodging.

3. Small-Souledness and Lack-of-Faith
Part Youth from his good companion.   20
   Ach, what grief!
That most men prefer to go where
The winnings belong to Hell!
If we don't run quick to that big washtub
Before our mouths and eyes are closed,   25
Not a one's so puffed with pride
That he won't face death's stronger match.

4. For the Lord who knows all that is
And all that will be, and all that was
   Has promised us   30
Honor in the name of the Emperor.
And the beauty to come—do you know?—
For those who will go to the tub:
More than the star of morning joy,
If only they'll avenge the wrongs   35
To God, here and in Damascus.

5. In the line of Cain's descendants,
From that first villainous man,
   Come many heirs
Who won't bear their honor to God.   40
We'll see now who's his loyal friend.

For by virtue of the washing tub
We'll all own Jesus equally.
And let's throw back the loot
That accrues from luck and fortune.   45

6. And all those horny wineheads,
   Dinner-snatchers and brand-blowers,
      Highway-crouchers
   Can lurk behind in the lazy house:
   God wants the brave and the fair   50
   To step up to his washing tub;
   And those will keep his mansions safe
   And find the Adversary strong
   And, 'gainst their shame, I chase them out!

7. In Spain, over here, Marquis Ramon   55
   And those from the Temple of Solomon
      Suffer the weight
   And the pain of the Paynim pride.
   And so Youth gets a vile report.
   And the cry for this washing tub   60
   Rolls over the richest overlords
   Who're feeble, failing, bereft of nerve,
   For they don't value Joy nor Fun.

8. The Franks are all degenerates
   If they say no to the task of God   65
      That I commend.
   Ah, Antioch! Virtue and Valor
   Are mourned in Guyenne and Poitou!
   God our Lord, to your washing tub
   Bring the Count's soul in peace;   70
   And here guard Poitiers and Niort,
   O Lord who issued from the tomb!

[61⁹]

L'autrier jost'una sebissa

1. The other day along a hedgerow
   I found a lower-class shepherdess
   Who was rich with joy and sense,
   Seeming the daughter of a farmer,
   Wearing a hood and cape and gown,   5
   And a blouse of very rough stuff,
   With shoes and stockings of wool.

2. I approached her across the meadow:
   "Little girl," said I, "pretty thing,
   I'm worried the wind may sting you."   10
   —"Lord," said the little farm girl,
   "Thanks be to God and my nanny too,
   Little care I if the wind should blow
   Because I'm lighthearted and hale."

3. "Little girl," said I, "charming thing,   15
   I've torn myself away from the road
   To lend you some companionship,
   For a little farm girl like you
   Shouldn't go around pasturing beasts
   Without some equal fellowship   20
   In country like this, all by yourself."

4. "Sir," said she, "whatever I am,
   At least I know folly from sense.
   This equal fellowship of yours,
   Milord," said the little farm girl,   25
   "You can put where it rightly belongs,
   For whoever thinks she's got it
   In her grip's got only a pose."

⁹ Comic Pastourelle where courtly attitudes are misdirected toward a serious peasant girl. Strong rhyme: *aaabaab*.

5. "Little girl with noble manners,
   That man must have been a knight   30
   Who engendered you in your mother,
   And she was a courtly farm girl.
   The more I look, the prettier you are,
   And the joy of you makes me glitter.
   If only you'd be a bit humane!"   35

6. "Sir, my line and my heritage
   I see reverting directly back
   To the sickle and to the plow,
   Milord," said the little farm girl,
   "But some men pretend to be knights   40
   Who by right should be toiling away
   In fields for six days a week."

7. "Little girl," said I, "a kindly fairy
   Cast a spell when you were born,
   One of radiant enchantment   45
   Far beyond any other farm girl's;
   And this charm would even double now
   If I could see you just one time
   Below me, with me on top!"

8. "Sire, you've praised me so much   50
   You've made me completely annoyed.
   Since you've raised my value so,
   Milord," said the little farm girl.
   "Now you'll draw this reward
   As my good-bye: 'Gape, fool, gape!   55
   And stand there staring till mid of day!' "

9. "Little girl, a savage heart and fierce
   A man can tame with a little handling.
   I'm well aware, at this time,
   That with a little farm girl like you   60
   A man can have some fine company

In good, warmhearted friendship,
As long as one doesn't dupe the other!"

10. "Sir, a man screwed-up and mad
Will swear, pledge, put up stakes;   65
And so you'd bring me homage, eh?
Milord," said the little farm girl.
"But I, for a piddling entrance fee,
Don't want to change my name
From a virgin into a slut."   70

11. "Little girl, every creature
Reverts directly to his nature;
You and I, my little farm girl,
Ought to join our kindred spirits
In the bower down by the meadow;   75
There you'll feel much safer
When we do the sweet, sweet thing!"

12. "Sire, yes! but according to rightness:
A fool pursues his own folly,
A noble man a noble outcome,   80
And a farmhand with his farm girl;
Good sense is ruptured in that place
Where a man doesn't look for measure—
So say the ancient folk."

13. "Little girl, I never saw a figure   85
More mischievous than yours,
And I never met a heart more vile."

14. "Lord, the owl sends you this prophecy:
One man gapes at a painting
While the other prays for his manna.   90

15. "Never should he gape at the painting,
The man who expects his manna."

[62*]

A la fontana del vergier[10]

1. In the garden by a stream
   Along the sand where grass is green
   Under the shade of an orchard tree
   With flowers white for company
   And the usual spring refrains,   5
   I found alone, with no friend there,
   A girl who did not want my care.

2. She was a maiden with body sleek,
   Daughter of a lord of a doughty keep;
   And when I thought that birds and grass   10
   Were bringing joy to the precious lass,
   As well as the delicate new season,
   And that she'd listen to my talking,
   A sudden change arose to balk me.

3. Her eyes began weeping by that spring,   15
   And sighs from the heart came issuing:
   "Jesus!" she said, "King of this world,
   For *your* sake in this grief I'm whirled.
   It's *your* fault that I'm all confused.
   For the finest man on all the earth   20
   Goes serving you—ah, what great mirth!

4. "With you he goes, my gentle friend,
   The handsomest, noblest, richest of men!
   And here he leaves me in despair
   With constant grieving and constant care.   25
   Ach! curses on that King Louís!

* Original text appears in Section X, p. 387.

[10] Pastourelle in terms of dramatic action, but a Complaint on the Crusade in terms of the woman's lyric; tonally akin to Number 31. The King in line 26 is Louis VII of France, who embarked on the Second Crusade.

E

He issued the summons and sermons too
That let this pain come rushing through."

5. When I had heard her make lament
I walked to the brookside radiant: 30
"Beautiful," said I, "too much dejection
Spoils your features and complexion.
It doesn't pay to be so depressed.
To him who makes the woodland bloom
Open your heart and give joy room."   35

6. "Milord," said she, "I firmly trust
That God will grant me mercy just
In that other age forevermore
As he will to sinners by the score;
But *here* he's snatched away the thing   40
That brought me joy; I just can't pray
Because that man's too far away. . . ."

JAUFRE RUDEL[11]

[63*]

Lanquan li jorn son lonc en may

1. In May when the days are long
I like the sound of birds far away,
And when I depart from their songs

[11] Jaufrè Rudel (*fl.* 1140–1150). A noble from Blaye, on the Garonne River, believed to have taken part in the Second Crusade from a mention by Marcabrun. Hero of a romantic legend based on this poem, which states that he fell in love with the Princess of Tripoli from hearsay, crossed the sea to find her, and fell dead in her arms; out of sorrow she reputedly became a nun. Celebrated by Rostand's play, *The Far-Away Princess.* Only six poems usually attributed to him.

* Original text appears in Section X, p. 388.

I remember my love who's far away.
Head hanging I go, grief-torn.   5
No song, no flowering hawthorn
Do I admire more than winter ice.

2. And lord I'll rightly call the one
   Who'll help me see my love so far!
   But now instead of good I've won   10
   Two evils: he and I so far!
   Ah, I'd take to the pilgrim's way
   And stand with a staff, arrayed
   In a cloak, reflected by her eyes!

3. For the love of God, what bliss   15
   To seek out her hostel far away,
   Where, if she wants, I'll insist
   On lodging by her, now far away.
   Then talking will be truly dear
   When this far-off lover, near,   20
   Hears speech that brings me solace's prize.

4. Half joyed, half pained would I depart
   From sight of my love so far away;
   But now! when can I even start?
   Our lands are so very far away!   25
   O I'd just get lost in the maze
   Of those many lanes and highways. . . .
   But—in God the matter lies!

5. Never will I know happiness
   In love, without my love who's far.   30
   She's the most graceful, very best,
   In any place, either near or far.
   For her, so fine beyond comparison,
   Even in the realm of the Saracens
   I'd gladly suffer the captive's cries!   35

6. God who made all that comes and goes
   And created this far-off love:
   Over me strength and courage dispose
   So that I really see my far-off love
   Abiding in such a dwelling place   40
   That her room, that her garden space
   Will always assume palatial size!

7. You're right if you say I lust or
   Burn for my far-off love.
   All other joys lose their luster   45
   Compared to that from my far-off love.
   But what I want is now denied
   Just as my godfather prophesied:
   I'd love but not feel love's reprise.

8. So what I want is now denied.   50
   Curse that godfather who prophesied
   I'd love but not feel love's reprise!

[64¹²]

No sap chantar qui so non di

1. He can't sing who can't make tunes;
   He can't write verse who can't work words,
   And he doesn't fathom the ways of rhyme
   If he can't encompass the sense itself.
   But my song starts like this: 5
   The more you hear it, the more it'll mean.
   Ah, ah!

2. Nobody should wonder about me
   If I love a thing that will never see me,

¹² Riddle Poem.

For my heart never found any other joy 10
Except in that one I've never seen,
And for no joy does it laugh so much,
And I don't know what good will come—
Ah, ah!

3. Blows of joy strike me, they kill— 15
And the prick of love starts stripping off
My flesh, so my body's soon all bones;
Never was I so gravely stricken,
And for no other blow have I languished so,
For it's no comfort, nor fitting either— 20
Ah, ah!

4. Never did I sink sweetly to sleep
But that my spirit wasn't soon there;
Never did my heart feel such wrath here
But it soon found itself again back there; 25
And when I wake up in the morning,
All my good knowledge deserts me,
Ah, ah!

5. I know I never found joy in her
And never will she be rejoicing for me, 30
Nor ever consider me her friend;
Nor will she make me a pact to herself;
She never told me truth, nor lies,
And I don't know if she'll ever do it:
Ah, ah! 35

6. Good is the verse—I never once failed—
And everything here stands in its place,
And he who wants to learn from me
Should guard against jostling, breaking it,
For this way they'll get it in Quercy, 40
Sir Bertran and the Toulousain Count:
Ah, Ah!

7. Good is the verse—and there they'll do
   Something of which a man can sing,
   Ah, Ah!   45

BERNART DE VENTADORN[13]

[65*]

Can vei la lauzeta mover

1. When I see the lark moving
   His wings with joy toward the light,
   Then forget and let himself fall
   From the sweetness that enters his heart,
   O! what great envy I feel   5
   Toward whomever I see who's glad!
   I wonder why my heart
   Doesn't melt right away from desire.

2. Alas! how much I thought I knew
   About love, and how little I know!   10
   For I can't keep myself from loving
   Her who'll give me nothing in return.
   She's stolen my heart and all of me
   And all herself and all the world;
   And after she robbed me, left me nothing   15
   Except desire and a longing heart.

---

[13] Bernart de Ventadorn (*fl.* 1140–1180). Supposedly the son of a furnace-tender of Ebles (II or III) of Ventadorn (modern Ventadour, a ruined castle). After alleged misadventures with Ebles' wife, he was befriended by Henry II of England and Queen Eleanor in London; possibly joined Eleanor during her return to Poitiers. Later resided in Toulouse and Narbonne; believed to have died in the Monastery of Dalon. About forty-five works survive. Tristan in stanza 8 is either the secret name for the poet's lady (masculinized in keeping with the term Milord) or the name of a jongleur. Rhyme: *ABABCDCD*.

* Original text appears in Section X, p. 390.

3. Yes, I lost all power over myself,
   I wasn't mine from that moment on
   When she let me look into her eyes,
   Into a mirror I like so well.   20
   Mirror, since I first saw myself in you,
   Deep sighs have murdered me,
   And I lost myself the way
   Handsome Narcissus lost himself in the pool.

4. About women I feel great despair.   25
   Never again will I trust them.
   And although I used to protect them,
   From now on, I'm defecting,
   Since I see not a one will help me
   Against her who destroys and upsets me.   30
   I despair of them all, distrust them all,
   For I know very well that they're all like that!

5. And so My Lady's acting like a "woman"
   (And I blame her for it!),
   For she doesn't want what a man ought to want   35
   And whatever a man forbids, she does.
   I've fallen into very foul grace.
   I've carried on like the fool on the bridge,
   And I don't know why it's happened:
   Did I climb too high on the hill?   40

6. All grace is lost—it's true—
   (And I never even tasted it!)
   Since she who ought to have it most
   Has none; where will I find it?
   O! how bad it seems (if you see her)   45
   That she who owns this longing slave
   Who'll never have anything good without her
   Lets me die, won't lend me her aid.

7. Since prayers, thanks, and the rights I own
   Can't help me gain Milordess,   50

And she doesn't care a bit
That I love her, I'll never tell her of it.
No, I'll leave her. I'll give her up.
She's murdered me. As a corpse I speak.
I'm going away since she won't retain me   55
Downcast, to exile, I don't know where.

8. Tristan, you'll get nothing more from me.
   I'm going away, downcast, I don't know where.
   I'm through with songs. I'm giving them up.
   I'm hiding myself from love and joy.   60

[66¹⁴]

Tant ai mo cor ple de joya

1. I have a heart so filled with joy
       Everything changes its nature:
   Flowers white, crimson, and gold
       Seems the frost,
   For with the wind and the rain   5
       My fortune keeps on growing;
   Ah yes, my worth keeps mounting,
       My song's improving too.
   I have a heart so full of love
       And joy and sweetness,   10
   That the ice appears to me a flower,
       And the snow lies green.

2. I can go out without my clothes,
       Naked in my shirt,
   For fine, true love will keep me safe   15
       From wintry blasts.

¹⁴ Secular parody of Christian "contempt for the world" (cf. No. 5). Rhyme:
ababababcccb.

But a man's a fool to lose measure
   And not to toe the line,
And so I've taken special care
   Ever since I fixed on   20
The most pretty love who ever lived,
   From whom I expect great honor.
For in place of the wealth of her
   I'd not take Pisa.

3. She can cut me off from her friendship,   25
   But I rest secure in my faith
That at least I've carried away
   The beautiful image of her.
And I have for my own devices
   Such a store of happiness   30
That until the day when I see her,
   I'll feel no anxiousness.
My heart lies close to Love and
   My spirit runs there too,
Though my body's anchored here, alas!   35
   Far from her, in France.

4. Still I have steady hope from her
   (Which does me little good),
For she holds me as if in a balance
   Like a ship upon the waves,   40
And I don't know where to hide myself
   From woes besetting my senses.
All night long I toss and I turn
   Heaving upon my mattress:
I suffer greater torment in love   45
   Than that archlover Tristan,
Who underwent so many pains
   To gain Isolde the Blonde.

5. O God! Why am I not a swallow
   Winging through the air,   50

Coming through the depths of night
   There inside her chamber?
My good, joy-bearing lady,
   Your lover here's expiring.
I'm afraid my heart may melt   55
   If things go on like this.
Lady, because of your love
   I join my hands and adore:
Beautiful body with healthy hues,
   You make me suffer great woe.   60

6. There isn't any affair of the world
   That can occupy me more
Than the mere mentioning of her;
   Then my heart leaps high
And light suffuses my face, and   65
   Whatever you hear me say of it,
It will always appear to you
   That I really want to laugh.
I love that woman with such good love
   That many a time I cry,   70
And to me my sighs contain
   A far better savor.

7. Messenger, go on the run:
   Tell to my pretty one
The pain, O yes the grief   75
   I bear—and torment.

[67[15]]

Lo tems vai e ven e vire

1. The seasons come and turn and go
   Through days and months and years,

[15] For Ebles in line 23, see note to Number 59. Rhyme: *ABABCCD*.

And I, alas! have nothing to say,
For my desire is always one.
It's always one; it never changes: 5
I want the woman I've always wanted,
The one who never gave me joy.

2. Because she never ceases mocking,
I'm rewarded grief and loss,
For she made me sit at such a game   10
That I've been the loser, two to one;
Yet this kind of love soon is lost
When only one side maintains it,
Unless somehow a pact is reached.

3. I should stand my own accuser   15
Indicting myself with every right,
For never was man of woman born
Who served so long, yet all in vain.
And if she doesn't punish me for it,
My folly will keep on doubling still,   20
For a fool never fears till he's taken.

4. Never again shall I be a singer
Nor part of that school of Lord Ebles,
For all my songs aren't worth a jot,
Nor my voltas, nor my melodies.   25
And not a single thing I do
Or say would seem to work me well:
No, I see no improvement there.

5. Even though I make show of joy,
My heart is filled with wrath.   30
Who ever displayed such penitence
Before he even committed a crime?
The more I beg her, the harder she is,
But if she doesn't soon relent,
We'll come to a parting of the ways.   35

6. And yet it's good that she should bend me
   And make me subject to her will,
   For even if she dallies wrongly,
   Soon, I'm sure, she'll pity me.
   For so declares the Holy Scripture: 40
   A cause that has a happy outcome
   Makes the day worth a hundred more.

7. Never would I part from my life
   As long as I am safe and sound,
   For after the bran has blown away,   45
   The straw keeps fluttering a long, long time.
   And even if she isn't hot yet,
   Never would I take her name in vain
   If, from now on, she mends her ways.

8. Ah, my good, my coveted lover,   50
   Body well-shaped, delicate, smooth,
   Lively features all rosy-hued,
   Which God created with his very hands,
   All this time I've desired you,
   And nothing else has pleased me.   55
   No other love do I want one bit.

9. Sweet and well-instructed creature,
   May he who formed you grant to me
   The happiness I long for.

[68¹⁶]

Chantars no pot gaire valer

1. A song cannot in any way have value
   If the singing doesn't spring from heart,

¹⁶ Rhyme: *ABACCDD.*

And the singing cannot well from breast
Unless its source is fine, true love.
And so my verse looms high,   5
For I have joy from love, devoting there
My mouth and eyes, my heart and mind.

2. Dear God, I pray: never grant the might
To ward away this rage for love.
And if I knew I'd never have a thing,   10
And every day would bring worse ill,
Still I'd have my good heart at least;
For I have much more enjoyment:
Yes, good heart, and the strength to strive.

3. Foolish folk in their ignorance curse   15
The work of love; yet no loss!
For love is not about to crumble,
Unless it's that "vulgar" kind;
For that's not love; it's acting
With the name, it's sheer pretense;   20
There nothing's loved except what's grabbed.

4. And if I wanted to tell the truth,
I know from whom comes all this deceit:
From ladies who love for mere possessions,
Who are nothing but common whores.   25
I should be a liar—yes, false,
But instead I speak the truth shamefaced,
And I'm worried that I can't tell lies.

5. In mutual pleasure and in common will
Resides the love of two fine lovers.   30
And nothing good will ever come
If the desire is not an equal thing.
And he's a natural-born idiot
Who reproaches love for what it wants
And asks for a thing that's not quite right.   35

6. I know I've rightly placed my hope
   Whenever she shows me a cheerful face,
   The one I desire, want most to see,
   That noble, sweet, true, faithful one
   By whom even a king would be saved: 40
   The lovely, gracious, perfectly shaped
   Who raised me from nothing into wealth.

7. I've nothing dearer, fear no one more,
   And there's no task that's burdensome to me
   If it should please my lady master.   45
   That day will seem like Christmastime
   When she gives me one sure look
   With those beautiful, those spiritual eyes—
   So slow, that day will last a century.

8. The verse is polished; it's natural too,   50
   And good for the man who gets it all,
   And better for him who expects his fun.

9. Bernart de Ventadorn has made the plan;
   He spoke and made it; he expects his fun.

[69¹⁷]

Lo gens tems de pascor

1. The sweet season of rebirth
   With its freshening green
   Draws for us flower and leaflet
   With many a different hue;

¹⁷ The *"pascor"* of the opening line means either spring or Easter. Heavy mono-rhyme.

And therefore every lover   5
Is gay and full of song—
But me, I cry and clamor
Without a taste of joy.

2. To all I lament, good men,
   About Milordess and Love,   10
   For I placed my faith in them—
   Those ever treacherous two—
   And they've turned my life to grief;
   And the good and all the honor
   I have rendered to the fairest   15
   Counts for nothing, gives no aid.

3. Pain and grief and damage
   I've had, and I have a lot;
   And yet I've borne it all.
   And I don't even think they're harsh,   20
   For you've never seen any other lover
   Offer better without deceit:
   No, I don't go around changing
   The way those women do.

4. Since we both were children,   25
   I have loved her, courted her well,
   And my joy goes ever doubling
   Through each day of every year.
   And if she doesn't offer me
   A welcome-look and her love,   30
   Then when she's aging, let her beg
   Me to offer my desire then!

5. Woe's me! What good is living
   If I can't see day by day
   My fine, true, natural joy   35
   In her bed, stretched under a window,
   Body pure white from head to toe

Like the snow at Christmastide,
So that we two lying together
Can measure each other's sides?!   40

6. Never was loyal lover seen
   Who enjoyed a worse reward;
   For I love her with sincere love,
   And she says: "What do I care?"
   In fact, she says that's why   45
   She shows me her deadly rage,
   And if she hates me for this cause,
   Then *she's* guilty of a mortal sin.

7. Surely there'll some day be a time,
   My lady beautiful and good,   50
   When you can pass me secretly
   The sweet reward of a little kiss:
   Give it only on the grounds
   That I am taken with desire.
   One good is worth two others   55
   If the others are gained by force.

8. When I behold your features,
   Those gorgeous eyes full of love,
   I can't help wondering to myself
   How you can answer me so vilely.   60
   And I consider it high treason
   When a person seems honest and pure
   And turns out puffed with pride
   In places where he is strong.

9. Pretty Face, if my above-all   65
   Didn't stem from you alone,
   I'd long ago have left my songs
   Through the ill of the evil ones.

[70¹⁸]

Can la frej'aura venta

1. When biting breezes blow
   Out of your demesne,
   It seems to me I feel
   A wind from Paradise
   Because of my love for the noble one   5
   Toward whom I bow my head,
   To whom I pledge my will
   And direct my feelings;
   From all other ladies I part:
   So much she pleases me.   10

2. Even if she only gave me
   Her beautiful eyes and noble face,
   And never granted further pleas,
   Still she'd have conquered me.
   Why should I lie about it?   15
   (For in no way am I sure.)
   Hard it would be to show repentance
   After that time she told me
   That a good man gathers his strength
   While a bad one crouches scared.   20

3. The ladies, it seems to me,
   Are making a big mistake
   Because in no way at all
   Do they love their sincere lovers.
   I know that I shouldn't accuse them,   25
   Should say what they want to hear,
   But it pains me when a cheater gets
   Some loving out of sleight of hand,
   Or even more or just the same
   As a fine, true, noble lover.   30

¹⁸ Rhyme: *ababababba*.

4. Lady, what are you trying to do
   To me who love you so?
   For you see how I'm suffering
   And how I'm dying of desire.
   Ah! noble woman, debonair,   35
   Give me a pleasant look,
   One to lighten up this heart,
   For I'm racked with many woes
   And I shouldn't have to pay the price
   Just because I can't break free.   40

5. If it wasn't for evil people
   And savage smooth-tongued spies,
   My love would be guaranteed to me,
   But instead I'm tugged back.
   She is human to me in her comfort   45
   When time and place are right,
   And I know that underhandedly
   I'll get a lot, lot more,
   For the blessed man sleeps in peace,
   And the unlucky one in pain.   50

6. I'm a man who never scorns
   The good that God creates for him:
   For in that selfsame week
   When I parted from her side,
   She told me in clear, plain terms   55
   That my singing pleases her much.
   I wish every Christian soul
   Could have the same kind of joy
   That I had then and have:
   It's the *only* thing to brag of.   60

7. And if she guarantees me this,
   Another time I'll believe her;
   If not, never will I believe
   Another Christian lady.

RAIMBAUT OF ORANGE[19]

[71]

Escotatz, mas no sai que's es

1. Listen, lords! but I don't know what it is
   That I'm trying to say;
   It's not a love poem, not a satire,
   Nor an estribot; in fact, I can't find a name;
   And I don't know exactly how I'll carry it off   5
   If I don't know quite what it is,
      Because nobody ever saw such a poem written by a man or a
      woman in this century or any other gone by.

2. I know you think I'm a fool,
   But I just can't stop myself
   From telling you what I want.   10
   Nobody should blame me for it.
   But I don't care two little bits
   Except for what I can see
      And I'll tell you why (if I don't carry this thing through to the
      end, you'll be sure I'm mad): because I'd rather have six deniers
      in my fist than a thousand sous in Heaven.

3. I beg my lady friend not to worry   15
   That she'll do something to bother me.
   If she doesn't want to offer help right away,
   Then let her offer it after some waiting.
   Nobody else could deceive me
   As easily as she who's won me.   20

---

[19] Raimbaut of Orange (*ca.* 1144–1173). Lord of Orange and Courthézon, who squandered most of his patrimony in gambling, warring, and partying. Left about forty poems, mostly in the complex *trobar clus* style. This self-styled "I-Don't-Know-What-It-Is" ridicules the notion of genres, as well as religion. It contains prose endings for every stanza. An "estribot" in line 4 is a mixed song, with some satire. The Latin in line 28 says: "In the name of the Father and the Son and the Holy Ghost!"

I'm saying all this about a woman who makes me languish with a
few pretty words and long expectations—and I don't know why.
Do you think she'll be good to me, my lords?

4. Four months have passed by now—
Yes, and it seems a thousand years—
Since she guaranteed, she promised
She'd give me what's most precious to me.   25
Lady, since you clutch my heart,
Sweeten up this bitter love.
    O God help me, *in nomine Patris et Filii et Spiritus Sancti!* Lady,
    what will become of all this?

5. Because of you, I'm gay, yet full of grief;
Happy, sad, you make me sing;   30
And I've just left three women the likes of whom
The world has never seen—except for you.
And I'm such a good-mannered but mad singer
That people even call me a jongleur.
    Lady, do with me what Lady Emma did with the shoulder bone
    when she stuck it into her box whenever she wanted.   35

6. And so I've finished my Don't-Know-What-It-Is,
For so I'd like to baptize it!
Since I never heard the likes before,
Let everyone call it by this name.
And let them recite it by heart after learning it   40
Whenever they want to have pleasure.
    And if anyone asks who wrote it, answer: "A man who can do
    anything he wants, when he happens to feel like it."

[72²⁰]

Amics, en gran cossirier

1. Friend, I stand in great distress
   Because of you, and in great pain;
   And I think you don't care one bit
   About the ills that I'm enduring;
   And so, why set yourself as my lover   5
   Since to me you bequeath all the woe?
   Why can't we share it equally?

2. Lady, Love goes about his job
   By chaining two friends together
   So the ills they have and the lightness too   10
   Are felt by each—in his fashion.
   Yes, I think—and I'm no gabber—
   That all this deep-down, heart-struck woe
   I have in full on my side too.

3. Friend, if you had just one-fourth   15
   Of this aching that afflicts me now,
   I'm sure you'd see my burden of pain;
   But little you care about my grief,
   Since you know I can't break free;
   But to you it's all the same   20
   Whether good or bad possess me.

4. Lady, because these glozing spies,
   Who have robbed me of my sense and breath,
   Are our most vicious enemies,
   I'm stopping: not because desire dwindles.   25
   No, I can't be near, for their vicious brays

---

²⁰ Debate Poem (*tenso*) between Raimbaut and a nameless Lady, usually identified as the Countess of Dia, but without proof. See Number 73. The entire poem may have been written by Raimbaut.

Have hedged us in for a deadly game.
And we can't sport through frolicsome days.

5. Friend, I offer you no thanks
   Because my damnation is not the bit   30
   That checks those visits I yearn for so.
   And if you set yourself as watchman
   Against my slander without my request,
   Then I'll have to think you're more "true-blue"
   Than those loyal Knights of the Hospital.   35

6. Lady, my fear is most extreme
   (I'll lose your gold, and you mere sand)
   If through the talk of these scandalmongers
   Our love will turn itself to naught.
   And so I've got to stay on guard   40
   More than you—by St. Martial I swear!—
   For you're the thing that matters most.

7. Friend, I know you're changeable
   In the way you handle your love,
   And I think that as a chevalier   45
   You're one of that shifting kind;
   And I'm justified in blaming you,
   For I'm sure other things are on your mind,
   Since I'm no longer the thought that's there.

8. Lady, I'll never carry again   50
   My falcon, never hunt with a hawk,
   If, now that you've given me joy entire,
   I started chasing another girl.
   No, I'm not that kind of shyster:
   It's envy makes those two-faced talk.   55
   They make up tales and paint me vile.

9. Friend, should I accept your word
   So that I can hold you forever true?

10. Lady, from now on you'll have me true,
    For I'll never think of another.   60

COUNTESS OF DIA[21]

[73]

Estat ai en greu cossirier

1. I've suffered great distress
   From a knight whom I once owned.
   Now, for all time, be it known:
   I loved him—yes, to excess.
        His jilting I've regretted,   5
   Yet his love I never really returned.
   Now for my sin I can only burn:
        Dressed, or in my bed.

2. O if I had that knight to caress
   Naked all night in my arms,   10
   He'd be ravished by the charm
   Of using, for cushion, my breast.
        His love I more deeply prize
   Than Floris did Blancheflor's.
   Take that love, my core,   15
        My sense, my life, my eyes!

3. Lovely lover, gracious, kind,
   When will I overcome your fight?
   O if I could lie with you one night!
   Feel those loving lips on mine!   20
        Listen, one thing sets me afire:

---

[21] Countess of Dia (1150–1200?). Mysterious poetess often identified as Beatritz,
wife of Count William I of Valentinois (1158–1189), but without convincing proof.
See note to Number 72. Only four or five poems attributed to her.

Here in my husband's place I want *you,*
If you'll just keep your promise true:
   Give me everything I desire.

GUIRAUT DE BORNELH[22]

[74]

Reis glorios, verais lums e clartatz

THE COMPANION OUTSIDE:
1. Glorious King, true light and clarity,
  Almighty God, Milord, if it please thee,
  To my companion be a faithful friend;
  I haven't seen him since the night came on—
    And soon will come the dawn.   5

2. My dear companion, whether you wake or sleep,
  Rouse yourself up; it's time to vigil-keep;
  For in the orient—I know it well—
  I see the star that makes the day come on—
    And soon will come the dawn.   10

3. My dear companion, singing I call your name:
  Sleep no more, for I've heard the bird exclaim
  That goes in quest of day throughout the wood;
  And I fear the jealous one will make you pawn,
    For soon will come the dawn.   15

---

[22] Guiraut de Bornelh or Borneill (*ca.* 1155–*ca.* 1205). Considered in his own day "The Master Troubadour," but condemned by Dante and most moderns for his artificiality. This religious Dawn Song shows his skill. Of humble origin, perhaps from the hamlet of Bourneix in Dordogne, he traveled widely into Aragon and Navarre, leaving about eighty pieces. The last stanza is sometimes considered a crude interpolation and thus omitted.

4. My dear companion, open the window wide—
   Look at the stars waning in the sky!
   See if I bring a true picture to your eyes;
   If you don't rush, all hope will soon be gone,
      For soon will come the dawn.   20

5. My dear companion, since you parted from me,
   I haven't slept, haven't left my knees;
   No, I have prayed to God, St. Mary's Son,
   To let your loyal companionship go on—
      For soon will come the dawn.   25

6. My dear companion, here on the terrace stones,
   You begged me not to sleep, to lie alone
   And keep my watch all night into the morn.
   My song, my love are things you'd soon see gone—
      But soon will come the dawn.   30

THE COMPANION INSIDE:
7. Ah, dear companion, I now know such delight;
   I want to see no morn, I want the night.
   The loveliest lady on whom Sun ever shone
   Lies in my arms. I say—to Hell be gone
      Those jealous ones and dawn.   35

BERTRAN DE BORN[23]

[75]

Un sirventes on motz no falh

1. I've made a sirventes where not a word
   Will fail, and it didn't cost me an onion,

---

[23] Bertran de Born (*ca.* 1140–*ca.* 1214). Master of the witty, satiric sirventes.
Unfairly condemned by Dante as a sower of discord in *Inferno* XXVIII.113–142,
and re-created by Pound's monologues in *Personae*. Lord of the castle of Hautefort

And I've learned the art of living so
That with brothers, first and second cousins,
   I'll share an egg or a copper piece,   5
And if later they try to grab my share,
   I'll toss them out of the tribe.

2. All my thoughts I keep in my safe,
   Although they've caused me trouble galore
   Between Sir Aimar and Sir Richard;   10
   A long time they've watched me distrustfully,
      But they're making such a ruckus
   That their babes, unless the King parts them,
      Will get it in the guts.

3. William of Gourdon, a muted clapper   15
   You've attached there inside your bell,
   And I like you—God help me, yes!
   But as a lunatic and a fool
      They count you, those two viscounts
   Who made the pact; yet they yearn   20
      To lock you in their buddyhood.

4. Every day I'm struggling, I'm brawling;
   I joust, I beat back, I contend;
   And they light my land and they burn it,
   And they turn my orchard to a pile of twigs,   25
      Blending my barley with my straw,
   And there's not one coward or diehard
      Who's not assailing my door.

(Altafort) in the Limousin-Périgord region, shared with his brother Constantine, who had acquired it through marriage. His outcries against Richard the Lion-Hearted, Philip Augustus of France, various Spanish lords, and the local barons reflect the historical turbulence shown in this poem. About forty poems survive, many of them preceded by prose explications (*razos*), which I omit. Here the primary contestants are Aimar (Ademar) V of Limoges, Richard, Elias VI of Périgord (nicknamed Talleyrand); affairs best dated in 1182. In the last line, the peacock warned the daw not to surpass the limits of nature. Rhyme: *AABBCBC*.

5. Every day I resole, I regird,
   I recast those barons, I heat them up   30
   For I want to send them hot to war.
   Yet I'm a fool even to consider it
       Because their workmanship's worse
   Than the chains that bound St. Leonard;
       A man's a damned fool to bother!   35

6. Talleyrand can't leap, he can't trot,
   And he can't even move from Arenalh;
   He can't pitch a lance or a dart:
   No, he's living like a Lombard
       So stuffed up with inertia   40
   That when other folks splinter away,
       He just stretches out and yawns.

7. At Périgueux, up to the wallwork
   As far as a man can throw with mace,
   I'll come armed on my horse Bayard,   45
   And if I find some paunchy Poitevins,
       They'll find out how this sword cuts,
   For I'll cover their heads with mud
       And mix their mail with brains.

8. Barons, God save you, God watch out,   50
       And help you, see you all wax hale;
   And may he tell you to tell Lord Richard
   What the peacock said to the daw.

[76²⁴]

Be·m platz lo gais tems de pascor

1. How I like the gay time of spring
   That makes leaves and flowers grow,
   And how I like the piercing ring
   Of birds, as their songs go
   Echoing among the woods.   5
   I like it when I see the yield
   Of tents and pavilions in fields,
   And O! it makes me feel good
   To see arrayed on battlefields
   Horses and horsemen with shields.   10

2. And I like it when the scouts
   Make people with property flee,
   And I like it when I see the rout
   Of a swarm of opposing armies;
   And O! how my spirits adore   15
   The sight of strong castles attacked
   With barricades broken and hacked
   And troops waiting on the shore
   That's completely encircled by ditches
   With strong-staked rows interstitched.   20

3. And likewise I like a lord
   Who's the first man out in the fray,
   On horse, armed, fearlessly forward,
   Inspiring his men to obey
   With his valiant deeds;   25
   And when the battle's fierce
   Everyone's prompt to pierce
   And freely follow his lead,

²⁴ Pleasure Song, with war as theme. Doubtfully attributed, but the style is
Bornesque if not de Born's.

For a soldier is soon forsaken
Unless he's given many blows, and taken.   30

4. Maces, swords, helmets—colorfully—
   Shields, slicing and smashing,
   We'll see at the start of the melee
   With all those vassals clashing,
   And horses running free   35
   From their masters, hit, downtread.
   Once the charge has been led,
   Every man of nobility
   Will hack at arms and heads.
   Better than taken prisoner: be dead.   40

5. I tell you: no pleasure's so large
   (Not eating or drinking or sleep)
   As when I hear the cry: "Charge!"
   Or out of the darkened deep
   A horse's whinnying refrain,   45
   Or the cry: "Help! Bring aid!"
   As big and little in turn cascade
   Into ditches across the plain,
   And I see, by the corpses whose sides
   Are splintered, flags unfurling wide.   50

6. Barons, put up as pawns
   Those castles, cities, and villas well-stored
   Before bringing each other war!

[77²⁵]

Miei sirventes vuolh far de·ls reis amdos

1. About two kings I'll write half-a-sirventes,
   For shortly we'll see which one has more knights:

²⁵ Self-styled "Half-A-Sirventes." Richard the Lion-Hearted's opponent was Alfonso VIII of Castile. Dating difficult.

Brave Alfonso of the Castilian throne
Will come to look for hirelings, if I hear right.
Richard will let his gold and silver fight   5
By the bushel and peck; to him's no great fuss
To lavish and spend; who cares about trust?
Why, war's more to him than a quail to a kite!

2. If both these kings prove strong and hale,
   Soon we'll see strewn among our fields   10
   Helmets, swords, shields, and mail,
   And bodies, spear-split from belt to brain,
   And stallions running unmounted, unreined,
   And many a lance through thigh and chest,
   With tears and joy, sorrow and happiness.   15
   The loss'll be great; greater still the gain.

3. Trumpets and drums, banners and flags,
   Standards and stallions of every hue
   Soon we'll see as our great age drags
   The holdings from every usurious Jew.   20
   Down no highway will go no laden mule
   Trusting the day, no burgher unaskance,
   Nor any merchant heading out from France.
   No, he'll be rich who grabs as he chooses.

4. If Alfonso comes, I'll put my faith in God: 25
   Either I'll live or lie hacked on the sod.

5. And if I live, great will be my bliss;
   And if I die, thank God for what I'll miss!

[78[26]]

Bel m'es quan vei chamjar lo senhoratge

1. Ah, how I like to see great power pass
   As young men gather in the estates of old
   And everyone, with babies by the mass,
   Bequeaths hope for a leader brave and bold.
   Then I think that the age will soon renew   5
   Better than any flower or bird's refrain,
   For knowing that certain lords and ladies are through,
   We allow the young to take up hope again.

2. You can tell a lady's old by her balding hair;
   She's old, I say, when she hasn't any knight,   10
   Or if she takes her lovers by the pair,
   Or if she takes a lover full of spite;
   Old she is if she loves in her estate,
   Or if she uses magic as a crutch.
   I call her old when jongleurs irritate   15
   And certainly she's old if she talks too much!

3. A lady's young when she values noble rank
   And likes good deeds whenever good's been done;
   I call her young if her heart is fine and frank
   And she casts no evil eye on valor won.   20
   She's young if she keeps her body well looked after,
   Young if she knows exactly how to behave;
   I call her young if gossip brings her laughter,
   And if she can keep herself with her lover safe.

4. A man is young if he'll risk his hard-won hoard,   25
   He's young if he's ever suffered need or want.
   I call him young if he spreads an expensive board
   Or if his gifts approach the extravagant.

[26] Self-styled "Young-Old Song," conceived partially in the genre of the Pleasure Song.

He's young when he burns all his chests and treasure
And wars and jousts and hunts and rambles.   30
He's young if he knows every woman's pleasure,
And young he is if he yearns to gamble.

5. A man is old when he's scared to take a dare
   And stores away his bacon, wine, and wheat.
   I call him old if he offers eggs and Gruyère   35
   On days when he and his friends are allowed meat.
   He's old when he shivers under both cape and cloak,
   Old, if he rides on a horse he hasn't tamed;
   Old, if a day of peace doesn't seem a joke,
   Or if he runs away from a gory game.   40

6. Arnold, jongleur, take my song "Young-Old"
   To Richard, let him watch it, see it's sung:
   Let him not care a damn for gold that's old,
   But only prize his treasures when they're young!

[79²⁷]

Ieu m'escondisc, domna, que mal no mier

1. I apologize, lady; I deserve no ill
   For what the glozing spies have said of me;
   And mercy I beg: may no man confuse
   The fineness of your loyal, noble form,
   Humble yet frank, refined and pleasure-bearing,   5
   Nor say, lady, I spoke of it with lies.

2. At first throw let me lose my sparrow hawk;
   Let common falcons pounce on for the kill
   And swipe him off, and let me see him plucked
   If ever my longing for you did not surpass   10

²⁷ Complaint.

My yearning to possess another woman
Who'll give her love and keep me for repose.

3. Now I shall take an even stronger risk
   (I couldn't pray against greater unpleasantness):
   If ever I fail you—even in my thoughts—   15
   When we're alone in chamber or in bower,
   Then may my potency flag with other companions
   In such a way that they can't help me out.

4. And if I sit down to tables to gamble,
   I hope I never catch a single coin   20
   Nor, with all the chips taken, even begin;
   And always may my throws come out snake-eyed
   If ever another lady I woo or seek
   Except you whom I love, desire, hold dear.

5. Let me be lord of a castle split in shares,   25
   And let me live in the tower with three peers,
   And let us all hate each other's guts,
   And may I always need a good crossbowman,
   A doctor and serf, watchmen and porters too,
   If ever I've heart to love another lady.   30

6. May Milady desert me for another knight
   And let me not have any idea where I am:
   May the wind fail when I'm far out at sea;
   In the court of the king, may porters trounce me,
   And in the battle's press, may I flee first,   35
   If he didn't lie who told you all those tales.

7. Lady, if I own a good, duck-hunting hawk
   Who's fine and molted, good at catch but tame,
   Who can handle every other kind of bird—
   Swans and cranes, white herons, black ones too—   40
   Why would I want a mangy chicken-chaser,
   Fat and fidgety, who doesn't know how to fly?

F

8. You lying, jealous, poison-tongued flatterers,
   Since you've caused Milordess all this trouble,
   I'll flatter you if you'll just leave us alone!   45

[80²⁸]

Domna, puois de me no·us chal

1. Lady, since your heat is not for me
   And you've drifted from my side
   Without the slightest reason,
   I don't know where to search,
   For never again   5
   Shall such rich joy be garnered
   By me; and if I can't find another
   Of the same kind who meets my liking,
   Worth the same price as you I've lost,
   Never again will I have a lover.   10

2. And since I'll never find your like,
   One who's both beautiful and good,
   Whose body's richly full of joy,
   With lovely manners
   And ever gay,   15
   Whose worth is wealthy and ever true,
   I'll go around subtracting
   One pretty feature from every girl
   To make my Lady Self-Conceived,
   Who'll last me till I have you back.   20

3. That healthy, fresh complexion
   I'll take, pretty Cembelis, from you,
   And also that sweetly loving look;
   And yet there's superabundance

---

²⁸ Often referred to as "The Song of the Self-Conceived Lady."

Of things I leave,   25
For pretty things you're never lacking.
Milordess Aelis, from you I beg
Your graceful mode of conversation,
For you could give Milady help;
Never will she be fool or mute.   30

4. And I wish the Viscountess of Chalais
   Would give me in full possession
   Her throat and both of her hands.
   And then I'll direct my career
   Without false turn,   35
   Flinging myself straight to Rochechouard
   To ask Milady Agnes' hair,
   For even Isolde, beloved of Tristan,
   Who is celebrated for all her parts,
   Never owned locks of higher praise.   40

5. And Audiart, though she wish me ill,
   I hope she'll give me a feature, too,
   For she's put together in a noble way:
   No, she hasn't any fault,
   For her loving   45
   Never faltered, never turned bad.
   And from my Better-Than-Good I beg
   Her young, upright body of highest price,
   So fine that one can see in a glance
   How wonderful to hold her nude!   50

6. And also from my Lady Faidida
   I'd like that gorgeous set of teeth,
   Her welcome and that gentle response
   She bestows so generously
   In her abode.   55
   My Beautiful Mirror, I bid she grant
   Her gaiety and her beauty fair:
   She always knows how to maintain

Good standing; she's most informed:
Never does she twist or change.   60

7. Pretty Lord, from you I ask naught:
   No, I'm as desirous of the one
   Who's self-conceived as I am of you:
   I feel a very avid
   Love being born   65
   Which has seized my entire heart;
   But I'd rather just keep asking you
   Than clench another with a kiss.
   Why does Milordess refuse me thus,
   Since she knows I love her so?   70

8. Papiols, take this song of mine
   And run to my Lady Magnet:
   Tell her love here's no longer known,
   But has fallen from high to humble.

[81²⁹]

Si tuit li dol e·lh plor e·lh marrimen

1. If all the grief and sorrow, the strife,
   The suffering, the pains, the many ills
   That men heard tell of in this woeful life
   Assembled, they would count as nil
   Compared to the death of the young English King,   5
   Who leaves behind youth and worth in tears
   In this dark world beset with shadowy fears,
   Lacking all joy, abounding in doleful spite.

²⁹ Lament for the Young King: Prince Henry of the Short Mantle, son of Henry II
of England and Eleanor; he died of fever at the age of twenty-eight in France.

2. Grievous and sad, sensing the bitter wrong,
   Stand his noble soldiers, left behind;   10
   His troubadours, his jongleurs sing no song,
   For death's bereft the warrior from mankind:
   Still they salute their young English King,
   Who makes the generous seem steeped in greed.
   He never did, nor will he now, take heed   15
   To repay this wicked world its tearful spite.

3. O boundless death, abounding yet in pain,
   Brag, brag you've got the finest cavalier
   Who ever stalked upon this broad terrain,
   Who, needing nothing, never knew his peer,   20
   For peer there never was to that English King.
   God, it's more just, if ever you would grant:
   Let *him* live, instead of all those tyrants
   Who never pay with worth—just doleful spite.

4. Since Love now flees this jaded age, downweighed   25
   By grief, I consider all its joys a lie,
   For nothing lasts that doesn't pass away,
   The way tomorrow feels today slip by.
   Let everyone admire the young English King!
   Who in all the world of valiant men was best.   30
   It's gone—that body full of lovingness,
   And all that are left are grief, discord, spite.

5. You who desired to counter all this pain
   By entering this world with its many snares,
   And suffered death that we might live again—   35
   We cry out in your just and humble name:
   Show mercy upon our young English King!
   Pardon, if pardon pleases, toward this end:
   That he may stand among his honored friends
   There where grief never goes—nor spite.   40

PEIRE VIDAL[30]

[82]

Ab l'alen tir vas me l'aire

1. With every breath I draw to me the air
   That wafts upon me over from Provence,
   And all that comes to me is wondrous fair,
   And each report of excellent provenance
   Sets me listening with an inner glow;   5
   Yes, from a single word I want much more:
   It's beautiful when all is going well there.

2. There is no haven more surpassing fair
   Than from the banks of Rhone to alpy Vence;
   There is no joy abounding anywhere   10
   Like that between the sea and blue Durance.
   And there among the people good and kind
   I've left my heart ajoying still behind
   With her who sets the wrathful folk adance.

3. No man could call that day an evil one   15
   When he of her has a happy souvenir,
   For she is source and cause of earthly fun,
   And whoever whispers flattery in your ear
   Will just be telling truth, not packs of lies,
   For she's the best—I'll brook no bold reprise—   20
   The fairest in the world, without a peer.

[30] Peire Vidal (*fl.* 1170–1204). Popular troubadour with a simple style, who attracted many legends: supposedly dressed himself in wolfskins to woo Loba (She-Wolf) de Pennautier, and was almost torn apart by her dogs; reputedly married the daughter of the Byzantine Emperor on Cyprus and assumed imperial pretensions, including the royal title. Probably the son of a furrier in Toulouse, he visited many dignitaries in Spain and Italy; served Count Raymond V of Toulouse. Fifty poems survive.

4. And anything I do or ever say
   I owe to her, for she's the one who imparts
   The knowledge and the skill to guide my way,
   And therefore I am gay, and so songs start.   25
   And anything I do that finds good end
   Is inspired by the sweet body of my friend,
   Including all reflections of good heart.

RICHART DE BERBEZILH[31]

[83]

Atressi com l'olifanz

1.   Just like the elephant
        Who, when he falls, can't rise
        Till others have upthrust him
        With their cranelike cries,
        I'll take up his custom: 5
   I know my troubles are pachydermally heavy
   And if that Court at Puy with its tycoon
   And all its loyal-loving lords and ladies
   Don't lend a hand, I'll wallow in my swoon.
   Lords and ladies, get pity for my pain   10
   From her who makes laments and logic vain!

2.   If you fine noble lovers
        Can't help my joy come back,
        Then poetry—I'll spurn it.
        It just can't fill my lack.   15
        Or else I'll become a hermit

---

[31] Richart de Berbezilh or Rigaut de Barbezieux (*fl.* 1170–1207). From Saintonge;
attached to Marie of Champagne, daughter of Eleanor. Only ten poems remain,
this one with fantastic conceits drawn from bestiaries. Two short *tornadas* (final
refrains) omitted.

Alone with no companion (for whom I'm burning).
My life's too full of misery and despair.
Joy's turned to grief, happiness to mourning.
My God, I'm not in any way like the bear!   20
When I'm abused or clubbed with a heavy bat,
I don't thrive, don't prosper—don't get fat.

3.   O I know Love's strong enough
        To help the tried but true man
        (Even if my love's more than "nice").   25
        Still, I never carried on like Simon
        Pretending to be Christ!
Wanting to soar to the very heavens above,
But shoved the other way for his sinful pride.
My pride is such a simple thing—just love.   30
Ergo, let pity give what love's denied,
For there's a place where reason conquers pity.
The place where reason fails is not so pretty.

4.   I'll shout to all the world
        About myself, prolix, profuse.   35
        If I could only imitate
        The phoenix (O what's the use?),
        Who burns himself to procreate,
Then I'd burn all this misery and be purged.
I'd even burn those poems, bald untruths.   40
Then, in a chorus of sighs and tears I'd surge
Up where all virtue, loveliness, all youth
Reside—where pity's never in absentia,
Where all good forces hold annual convention.

5.   Song, be my middleman   45
        Over there where I dare not go
        Nor even look, except cross-eyed.
        My penning-in's so thorough
        That no one's on my side.
Better-Than-Woman, I ran from you two years   50
Wildly, like a deer running at chase.

Now I've come back, brimming over with tears,
Ready to die from the shouts of your huntress face.
Deerlike I come to you, lady, for your grace.
Do you care? Is love's memory so soon erased?   55

ARNAUT DANIEL[32]

[84]

L'aura amara

1. The bitter breeze
   Makes branchy canopies
   Rise light
   That softened wafts once leafed,
   And the trilling   5
   Bills
   Of fowls aflutter
   Makes mumble, stutter
   With mates,
   Celibate.   10
   And thus I've the might
   To endow, to endite
   Delight
   For men, for the maid
   Who made me rise sky-high   15
   Will make me die
   Unless pain strains a sooner good-bye.

---

[32] Arnaut Daniel (*fl.* 1170–1210). Primary exponent of *trobar clus,* the hidden or abstruse style, as here. A native of Ribérac near Périgueux, he was a poor jongleur until he won acclaim from Richard the Lion-Hearted and various lords of Aragon and Italy. Hailed by Dante in *Purgatorio* XXVI.115 ff. as "the better craftsman of our maternal tongue," thus preferring him to Guiraut de Bornelh. Translated by Ezra Pound. The rhyme in this poem proceeds from stanza to stanza rather than within the strophes, as I have been forced to render it. Sense difficult in many places.

2. Not askance
   Was that first glance
   When eyes   20
   Felt the heart capitulate;
   Two sous
   I give you
   For hush-hush billet-doux;
   Rare   25
   Is the prayer
   To another proffered;
   But comfort's offered
   Whenever I hear
   Good cheer,   30
   Good words without a bitch
   About her; then I itch
   To serve her so:
   I'm hers from head to toe.

3. Love, look!   35
   You've got me hooked;
   And I fear
   To hear, if you kiss me off,
   That I'll give in
   To sin—   40
   Ah, better you run for cover!
   Yet I'm a true lover,
   Dear,
   Won't veer,
   Though my heart firm-pitched   45
   Makes me ditch
   Much verse.
   O, if she's perverse,
   I'll need a kiss piping hot
   To bring heart calm—   50
   No good any other balm.

4. So she renders
   (To whom I surrender)

Some ease,
Since she's the capitol of worth,   55
Answering pleas
Tranquilly
That I've inside in rows;
Soon I'll expose
Hot   60
My thought:
O I'd be dead,
But on I'm led
By hope;
And I pray right away   65
She'll make me happy, gay;
Elsewhere grappled,
Joy isn't worth an apple.

5. Sweet gal, you
Are the source of all value: 70
I'll abide
Even your overweening pride,
For you're whole-
ly the goal
Of all my fantasies   75
Which worked me long
Wrong;
Yet mockery
Never made me walk away
Or leave   80
Grieved,
For I never aimed
For anything less vain:
I want your bod
More than the monks of Doma God.   85

6. And so prepare
Some verses and an air
Complete
To the King that you cultivate.

Honor High's   90
Dry
Here, but there is double-priced;
They also prize
Givin',
High Livin'—   95
Ah, go joyin' there!
Watch that king
Raise up his ring!
I'm not gone
A day in haste from Aragon   100
But I'd be home;
Yes, but now they're calling me to Rome.

7. The pact is signed:
   I see in mind
   Each night   105
   The lady that I tout—
   I, the partnerless Arnaut;
   Any other thought
   Will end complete at naught.

[85³³]

Lo ferm voler qu'el cor m'intra

1. The fervent will that my heart enters
   No beak can scratch, nor can tear the nails
   Of lying spies who through gossip lose their souls;
   Because I dare not bat with stick or rod
   (Except on the sly), there where I have no uncle   5
   I'll find joy: in the orchard or the chamber.

---

³³ Sestina, a form that relies on the repetition of the end-words of stanzas rather than upon internal rhyme. The Virgin is alluded to in line 25. Stanza 7 brings all six end-words together in a compressed form.

2. O when I recall that chamber
   Where I know to work me ill no man will enter,
   But everyone will be more than brother or uncle,
   All of my limbs start trembling, even my nails,   10
   Like some little kid about to face the rod:
   Such fear I have she'll be too much for my soul.

3. Would she were of body and not of soul!
   And would agree to hide me inside her chamber!
   She wounds my heart more than a switch with a rod   15
   Because this slave, where she is, dare never enter;
   Forever I'll be with her in flesh and in nail,
   And never trust the chastising of friend or uncle.

4. Even the very sister of my uncle
   I never loved more or as much as her, on my soul!   20
   I'd like to be as near as the finger to the nail,
   If it pleased her, there deep inside her chamber.
   This love can treat me (which in my heart now enters)
   More at its will than a strong man with weak rod.

5. After the fruition of the Dried-Out Rod,   25
   After Sir Adam, there never moved nephew or uncle
   With the fine true love that into my heart enters:
   I don't think it's been contained in a body or soul.
   Wherever she is—in the plaza or inside her chamber—
   My heart is clinging, as if it had fingernails.   30

6. Yes, thus it hangs with its nails,
   My heart gripping her, like a bark around a rod;
   Of joy she is my tower, palace, and chamber;
   So much I never loved brother, father, or uncle;
   And in Paradise joy will double for my soul   35
   If ever a man through good love there should enter.

7. Arnaut sends over his Sestina Uncle-Nail
   For the pleasure of her from the rod down to the soul,
   His Desired One, whose worth in the chamber enters.

THE MONK OF MONTAUDON[34]

[86]

Molt mi platz deportz e gaieza

1. Ah, how I like fun and fooling around,
   Good eats and gifts and men who have some guts;
   Girls who are straight, but dig the high-class ways
   And know how to give a comeback that's just right;
   And I like the rich who are not always up-tight   5
   But are genuine bastards toward their foes.

2. And I like a guy who talks to me nice
   And gives me presents without any catch;
   Rich kooks who aren't always going around bitching;
   And I swear I like a good, intelligent hassle,   10
   And a snooze when it thunders and lightnings,
   And a big fat salmon in the midafternoon.

3. And I like to stretch out in summertime
   Along the banks of a river or a brook
   When the fields are green and the flowers ripe   15
   And the birds are piping their little peeps
   And my girl friend sneaks up on the sly
   And gives it to me one time quick!!

4. And I like a guy with wide-open arms
   But without that faggot two-facedness;   20
   And I like the cool of my little pal,
   Her smooches—and everything I can get.
   And if my enemies all go to Hell,
   I like it—yeah! when I give the shove.

[34] The Monk of Montaudon (*fl.* 1180?–1215?). Rollicking poet whose actual identity is masked. His vida claims that he came from Vic in the Auvergne and that he became the Prior of Montaudon (although the name varies widely in the manuscripts). Sometimes identified as the Prior of Vic, known as Peire of Vic. His poems include a debate with God and arguments among the saints. Genre: Pleasure Song.

5. And O how I like my buddies   25
   When they're sitting there with my foes
   And I hear someone call for my theme
   And they clap and they shout and they yell!

RAIMBAUT OF VAQUEIRAS[35]

[87]

Gaita ben, gaiteta del chastel

1. Watchman from the castle wall, guard well,
   When I've what I most deeply prize
       Here in my arms—until the dawn.
   Let the day come! But never, never tell.
       New games arise   5
   To snatch away the dawn, the dawn, O yes, the dawn.

2. Watchman friend, wake and shout "Oyé!"
   O I'm rich and what I want I own.
       My only enemy's—the dawn.
   And the ruthless havoc of the risen day   10
       Makes me moan
   More than the dawn, the dawn, O yes, the dawn.

3. But guard yourself, watchman on the tower,
   From that jealous man—your evil lord—
       Who envies more than does the dawn.   15
   And softly, softly, speak of Love's great power.
       Fear comes toward
   Us only from the dawn, the dawn, O yes, the dawn.

[35] Raimbaut of Vaqueiras (*ca.* 1155–*ca.* 1210). Born to a poor knight in a castle
near Orange. Spent much time in Spain and Italy, serving Boniface II of Montferrat,
whom he followed on the Fourth Crusade in 1202. Believed to have died in Salonika.
More than forty poems extant in a variety of styles; here, a Dawn Song.

4. Lady, good-bye! I'm sorry I can't stay!
It hurts me, but I simply have to leave.   20
   O it pains me so—that dawn—
As I watch its slowly rising ray.
   Deceiver!
That's all he is, the dawn, the dawn, O yes, the dawn.

[88³⁶]

Altas undas que venez suz la mar

1.   High waves who ride upon the sea,
Rolled by the will of the wind in every way,
Bring some news of my belovéd to me;
He's never come back after that farewell day.
   And the God Amór, O!   5
One hour gives me joy and then gives sorrow.

2.   O gentle breeze blowing over there
Where my good friend lives and sleeps and lies,
Carry me one breath from his body fair!
Send me a draught to make this desire die.   10
   And the God Amór, O!
One hour gives me joy and then gives sorrow.

3.   Wrong loving makes him vassal in foreign lands,
And so I weep as I think of his games, his smile.
I never thought I'd be parted from my man,   15
For I always gave whatever could beguile.
   And the God Amór, O!
One hour gives me joy and then gives sorrow.

³⁶ Imitation of a Galician-Portuguese *cantiga do amigo,* love song from a woman
to a man.

FOLQUET OF MARSEILLE[37]

[89]

Vers Dieus, el vostre nom et de Sancta Maria

1. In the name of Saint Mary, in yours, True Lord,
   Let me awake as the morning star moves toward
   Me from Jerusalem, lending me these words:
      Rise up, up and away,
      All who the Lord obey,   5
      For the morning's under way
      As the night expires.
      May the Lord be praised
      And adored in every way
      As together we pray   10
      For peace, our lives entire.
      Day comes, Night flies
      The clear, tranquil sky
      As the dawn's not shy
      But comes in full attire.   15

2. Lord God, born of Mary the pure,
   To restore us to life with death's cure,
   To harrow Hell, that the Devil thinks secure,
      O Cross-wise raised,
      Thorn-crowned, abased   20
      By the bile's taste—
      Lord, honored men desire
      Their sins erased,
      Knowing your mercy chaste

---

[37] Folquet of Marseille (1150–1231). Son of a rich merchant of Genoa, he lived in southern France, squandering his patrimony in riotous living. Renounced secular life and in 1205 was installed as Bishop of Toulouse. Played a harsh role in persecuting heretics during the Albigensian Crusade. Defended Simon de Montfort at the Lateran Council of 1215. Died in seclusion in 1231, hated by most South French. However, stories of his miracles were common, and Dante awarded him with a place in his heaven of love: *Paradiso* IX. Genre: religious Dawn Song.

Pardons sin's waste.   25
Amen, Lord, may it transpire!
Day comes, Night flies . . .

3. O you ignorant of prayer, be diligent!
   Listen to what I say; grasp my intent:
   Lord, to you, beginning of all events   30
     I offer thankful praise
     For that love and grace
     You've offered me always,
     And pray, Lord, pity inspire
     You to guard my days   35
     From wrong-taken ways:
     O keep the Devil at bay
     With his subtle fire!
     Day comes, Night flies . . .

4. God, grant me wisdom and sense to apprehend   40
   Your holy laws, to heed, to comprehend;
   Grant mercy to nourish me and to defend
     From worldly ways,
     From sin-fall safe!
     Lord, I believe, I praise   45
     You as you rightfully desire.
     In a sacrifice's place
     Accept my faith.
     So offering, I beg grace:
     O make me, torn, entire!   50
     Day comes, Night flies . . .

5. To glorious God who gave his body for sale
   To buy us life, I pray: over us veil
   That Holy Spirit, over all evil prevail:
     Let me be raised   55
     To the ranks of the saved
     And there, where you hold sway,
     Live beneath the pavilion's spire!
     Day comes, Night flies . . .

PEIRE CARDENAL[38]

[90]

Tartarassa ni voutor

1. Not a buzzard, not a vulture
   Can smell the stink of rotting flesh
   Like those clerics and those preachers
   On the sniff for earthly wealth.
   Right away they're rich men's servants,   5
   And when they sense disease's swipe,
   Then they cozen out bequeathings:
   The relatives have nothing left.

2. The Franks and the clergy get the praise
   For evil, since they're masters there;   10
   And the usurers and the traitors
   Own the age about half and half;
   For with their lying and their cheats
   They have so upset the world
   There's not a religious order left   15
   That hasn't mastered the lesson too.

3. Know what happens to all that loot
   Belonging to those who get it ill?
   Up there springs a mighty robber:
   Nothing will he leave behind.   20
   Name is Death; O how he beats them!
   In just four ells of linen cloth
   Off he rolls them to his mansion
   Where they find other evils galore.

[38] Peire Cardenal, Cardinal (*ca.* 1185–*ca.* 1275). Greatest poet of the Albigensian Period, with some seventy songs surviving, mostly *sirventes*, as here. Born in Puy Nôtre-Dame, he attached himself to the courts of Raymond VI and VII of Toulouse. Also worked for James I of Aragon and Alfonso X of Castile. "Died at about one hundred years of age," claims his vida-writer, who is more reliable than most.

4. Man, why perpetrate such folly,   25
   Why transgress those commandments
   Of God, who is your rightful Lord
   And formed your body out of nothing?
   He who battles against his Master
   Would sell a good sow in the marketplace;   30
   Yes, his earnings will be those
   Won by that other villain, Judas.

5. Our true God, who is full of sweetness,
   Master, be our guarantor!
   Keep us from the hellish tortures,   35
   Hold us sinners from torment safe;
   Unravel those out of the evils
   In which they're caught, in which bound:
   Yield them then your truthful pardon
   In return for their true confessions.   40

[91³⁹]

Una ciutatz fo, no sai cals

1. There once was a city (I know not which)
   Where rain had fallen in such a way
   That all the inhabitants of the town
   Who were touched went suddenly mad.

2. They all went crazy, except for one: 5
   That one escaped (there was no more)
   For he was safe inside a house
   Asleep when all this was going on.

3. When he woke up after his sleep
   And saw that the rain had gone away,   10

³⁹ Fable Poem. A few final lines omitted.

Outside he went among the folk.
They all were acting completely mad.

4. One wore a cloak, another was nude;
   Another was spitting up at the sky;
   One threw stones, and another sticks;   15
   Another stood tearing at his gown.

5. One was striking, another hit back;
   Another was acting like a king
   And held himself regally in the hips;
   Another leaped through the market stalls.   20

6. One was threatening, another cursing;
   One was swearing, another laughed;
   One spoke, and didn't know what he said;
   Another made constant startled looks.

7. And the man who still had his wits   25
   Was wondrously struck by these fits
   And saw that they all were crazy,
   And he looked up, and he looked there,

8. To see if one wise man existed,
   And yet he could not spy a single one.   30
   And so he stood gaping at them all.
   And they showed greater wonder at him,

9. Amazed by his tranquillity.
   They thought he must have lost his mind
   Because he wasn't aping them,   35
   For to them it all appeared

10. That they were wise and full of wit
    And that he was utterly deranged.
    One strikes his cheek, the other his neck:
    He couldn't keep himself from tumbling.   40

11. One man presses, another shoves:
    He thinks he's going to flee the mass,
    But one man tears, another pulls;
    He takes the blows, rises—falls.

12. Then, lifting up with giant strides,   45
    He rushes home on double time,
    Muddy and battered and halfway dead,
    And glad to be out of their clutches.

13. This little fable concerns this world:
    It's like the people you meet today.   50
    This age of ours is that very town
    That's full to the limit with lunatics.

14. For the greatest reason man can have
    Is to love and fear his God,
    And to hold to his commandments;   55
    But now that sense is wholly lost.

[92⁴⁰]

Un sirventes novel vuelh comensar

1. I'd like to start a sirventes that's new,
   One I'll recite upon the Judgment Day
   To him who made me, formed me from the void.
   And if he plans to hold me in account,
   And if he wants to cast me to devilhood,   5
   Then I'll reply: "Master, mercy! no!
   For in a wicked age I groaned my years.
   And guard me now, I beg, from all those torturers."

---

⁴⁰ Complaint to God.

2. Then I shall make his court all stand in awe
   As they attend the pleading of my case: 10
   For I'll say he's the guilty party then
   If he plans to cast his own to hellish pain.
   For he who loses the things he ought to gain
   Rightfully wins a lack for his vileness;
   For he should be sweet, as well as generous,   15
   In holding on to souls who have transgressed.

3. Those devilish types he ought to dispossess
   And then he'd have a running stock of souls,
   And the clearing out would gladden all the world,
   And he himself could give himself his pardon: 20
   Yes, willingly could he destroy them all,
   Since everyone knows he owns the absolution.
   "Beautiful Master Lord, go and dispossess
   Those enemies who are vicious and are vile.

4. "Never should you deny the open door,   25
   For Peter, who is porter there, receives
   Shameful remarks: instead, every soul who treads
   Past those portals should walk in with a grin.
   For never was there a court one calls complete
   Where one man laughed and yet another cried.   30
   And though you are monarch powerful and bold,
   Unless you open, I'll issue a complaint.

5. "I have no wish to voice you my despair;
   Instead, I place in you all of my faith
   In hope that you defend me from my sin: 35
   It's *your* burden to save me, corpse and soul.
   Now let me offer you a pretty choice:
   Either send me back where first I saw the day
   Or pardon me for the wrongs that I have wrought.
   Never would I have sinned had I not been born.   40

6. "If I suffer evil here and more in Hell,
   By faith! that would surely be a sinful wrong,

And I'd have a rightful reason to reproach you,
For I've a thousand sufferings for every good."

7. —"Mercy I beg of you, Holy Lady Maria: 45
Offer good witness for me unto your Son,
That he may lift this father and his children
And place them there in grace beside St. John."

SORDELLO[41]

[93]

Planher vuelh en Blacatz en aquest leugier so

1. I want to mourn for Lord Blacatz with this lighthearted sound,
With a heart that's sad and sore beset, for there are reasons for it:
In him I lost a good, true friend and a worthy lord,
And all the manly virtues are gone with him.
Ah, the loss is deadly! for I think I'll never see   5
A return of any goodness, unless it comes just so—
Let everyone split up his heart—yes, let those barons eat!
For they're all heartless men who could stand a cordial treat!

[41] Sordello (*ca.* 1215–*ca.* 1270). Most famous Italian who wrote in Provençal.
Born at Goito near Mantua; became notorious for abducting the beautiful Cunizza,
sister of the powerful Ezzelino da Romano, away from her husband, Rizzardo di
San Bonifazio. Abandoning her later, he went to Spain and finally Provence, where
he was patronized by Blacatz, lord of Aups, who died between 1235 and 1240. In his
Lament for Blacatz, Sordello summons the following to eat his lord's heart, in
respective order: Emperor Frederick II, Louis IX of France, Henry III of England,
Ferdinand III of Castile, James I of Aragon, Thibaut of Navarre (see No. 149),
Count Raymond VII of Toulouse, and Count Raymond Béranger of Provence.
Returned to Italy with Charles of Anjou in 1266. Fought at the battle of Benevento
and in Sicily; was rewarded with some land in the Abruzzi region, where he died.
Dante made him guardian of his Vale of Princes (*Purgatorio* VI, VII), and he
appealed to Browning and Pound because of his intense energy and fierce scorn for
corruption.

2. Ah, number one comes the Emperor of Rome, a man
   Who needs some hearty food if he wants to overtake   10
   Those Milanese by force, for they think he's a loss—
   He's got no inheritance, even with his friendly Germans.
   And after him let the King of France step up to the banquet,
   For he wants to win back Castile that he lost through foolishness:
   But let him think of his mother; she won't touch a piece—   15
   No, she's too dignified to do anything that distasteful!

3. I like that English King, for he's a man of little heart,
   And if he'll just sample some, he'll be valiant and good,
   And he'll win back the land snatched by the King of France,
   Who knows he's a good-for-nothing and leaves him in disgrace.   20
   And that Castilian King! I think he should eat for two!
   For he holds two domains, and is not good enough for one!
   But if he wants a nibble, he should eat secretly,
   For if his Mamma catches him, she'll flail him with her rod.

4. And the King of Aragon should have a taste, I do believe,   25
   For it will help to purge him of the shame
   That he gets over here from Marseille and from Millau,
   For he gets not a jot of honor for anything done or said.
   And next I want the Navarrese King to step up to the feast,
   For he was a worthy count before he was crowned, I hear.   30
   It's terrible when God helps a man to mount in wealth
   And then weakness of heart makes him tumble in price.

5. The Count of Toulouse needs a good big bite of heart
   If he thinks of what he had and what he has now;
   For if this new infusion doesn't help him recoup his losses,   35
   It's lost for good with that old heart in his breast.
   And the Count of Provence should eat if he'll recall
   How a man who's disinherited isn't worth a damn
   And although he fights and defends himself with guts,
   He still should dine on this heart for the burdens he bears.   40

6. The barons will curse me for the evil I've said here,
   But they know I think they're as low as they think me.

7. Beautiful Restorer, in you alone I may find my grace,
   And I scorn every man who won't hold me as his friend.

[VI]
ITALIAN SONGS

Italian literature is remarkable for its sudden flowering in the thirteenth century, without any visible antecedents. Yet the appearance is fully understandable in terms of literary connections with Provençal. The troubadours were born wanderers, and many of them ventured into northern Italy, especially after the Albigensian Crusade impoverished the nobles at home and dictated an exodus. Sordello, who is grouped with the Provençals, was an Italian, as were many others who wrote in Old South French.

When literature written in Italian did at last appear, it naturally bore a strong trace of its southern French heritage. The first group of writers in the native tongue was the so-called Sicilian School, which flourished from the time of the coronation of Emperor Frederick II (1220) to his demise (1250). Frederick was reputedly himself a poet, but the few bland works that come down with the notation "King Frederick" are now usually ascribed to his son, Frederick of Antioch. Still, the Hohenstaufen Emperor did support poetry, and it flourished from Naples to Palermo. Each of the five poets in Numbers 95 to 99 is believed to have worked for him: Pier was his right-hand man and Re Enzo, or King Heinz (to use the German equivalent), was Frederick's bastard son. Thus the antipapal, freethinking, heretical emperor casts his shadow over the early development of Italian song.

The differences between Provençal and Italian lyrics are as obvious as the likenesses. For one thing, the *canso* form (in Italian, *canzone*) yields very fast in popularity to the more abbreviated, more epigrammatic *sonnetto* (sonnet), which is totally lacking in Provençal literature. No one knows why or how this form became so widespread—was it a reflection of popular songs?—but a look at Petrarch's output will attest to the eventual dominance of the genre.

If one had to theorize, he might say that the genius of the Provençal lyric lay in its continual exploration of the poet's mind, with emphasis upon the madness of love and playful disorder. The Provençals placed great stress upon wit, gaiety, and the casual things of life: "I'll write a poem, then take a nap" (No. 52). The Italians, on the other hand, are often deadly serious. Giacomo's poem (No. 95), perhaps the world's

oldest extant sonnet, states a proposition somewhat whimsically: he would
like to see his lady in heaven. When he is called to account for this
proclamation, he does not retract. In fact, he insists upon putting her
there, just as Dante places his Beatrice in the final circle of the blessed in
the company of Mary, Jesus, and the saints. Similarly Guinizelli in Number
105 is challenged by God for his pretensions, and although many feel
that he withdraws completely, one can read the last stanza of his poem in
a semidefiant way: "*You* take the blame for making my lady so beautiful."

The fact that the term for "my lady" in Italian can be *madonna*, the
epithet of the Virgin, no doubt promotes this equation of the holy with
the profane. Imagistically, the Italians seize upon the rose and other
accouterments of Mary, even in the earthy *Contrasto* (Debate Poem) of
Cielo d'Alcamo, Number 96. Italian lyrics are filled with expressions that
might have been drawn from a laud to the Perfect Lady. It is not at all
surprising that a Tuscan poetess appears with that very name, although
some consider her a fiction (No. 102). In sum, Italian poetry is far
more metaphysical than courtly in its tone and diction. Perhaps the fact
that the literature begins with the loving St. Francis of Assisi, who saw an
easy correspondence between the human and the divine (No. 94), establishes the ethos from the start. To an Italian like Iacopone da Todi (No.
100), the Virgin is a warm, dramatic, living mother, not a remote abstraction. Religion in Italy is either conveyed very movingly as in the Umbrian
School, which includes St. Francis and Iacopone, and which was the
product of the Papal States, or it is contested frankly, as in Rinaldo
d'Aquino's Complaint Against the Crusade (No. 98) or in the work of
the important Tuscan School, which dominated the period after 1260.

This last great movement was fathered by Guido Guinizelli, whose
famous *Al cor gentil* (No. 105) was the poetic manifesto of Dante's
circle and succeeding generations. A term often used to describe this
poetry is *dolce stil nuovo* or "sweet new style," which is taken from the
mouth of Bonagiunta da Lucca in Dante's *Purgatorio*. It is difficult to
stipulate the exact doctrines of this school, but Dante tells Bonagiunta
that his mode of composing was as follows:

> . . . I am one who
> When Love breathes on me, take note, and in the mode
> He dictates to me inside, I go making meanings.
> (XXIV. 52–54)

Bonagiunta replies:

> O brother, now I see the knot
> That held Guittone and the Notary and me
> From gaining the sweet new style that I hear.
> I see well how your pens ran straight
> Behind the great dictator, and certainly
> That was not the case with ours.
> If anyone else looks further carefully
> That is the only difference between our styles.

The passage seems to indicate that freshness of conception and adherence to a guiding structure (following the dictator) are the features that made Guinizelli, Cavalcanti, and Dante great. These were lacking in the self-conscious, rhetorical work of Bonagiunta and Guittone d'Arezzo, both of whom are omitted from this collection precisely for these reasons.

Certainly there is freshness in Guinizelli. His Numbers 103 and 104 approach the woman with a beautiful blend of natural imagery—the morning star of Venus, the green banks of pastoral poetry—along with an insistence upon an ideal system that the woman suggests, a system that is clearly Christian-Neoplatonic. The famous correspondence of the lady-angel is made in *Al cor gentil* in such a way that we can see the whole structure of the *Divine Comedy* emanating from the work. In fact, in the *Vita Nuova* Dante freely acknowledges his debt to the first Guido in his imitative canzone "Love and the noble heart are a single thing" (No. 117). In his other poems from that early work (Nos. 116, 118) one can see Beatrice entering the realm of God, where Guinizelli's lady might well have feared to tread. My selection of Dante's work emphasizes the point to which he takes his woman beyond Guinizelli, for Dante is properly the epic poet. No collection of lyrics can express his achievement, which was to make his love for Beatrice mesh with his love for the divine.

Cavalcanti, however, is a mystery. This "second Guido" was Dante's best friend, as we are told in the *Vita Nuova*. It was he who persuaded Dante to compose in Italian, not Latin. When Dante put Cavalcanti's father in his Circle of Heretics in *Inferno* X, he was perhaps giving us a clue about this rather enigmatic poet. For the difficult *Song of Love* (No. 111) does not present love in the optimistic, idealized treatment established by Guinizelli. Love is an accident, a movement in substance (not a miracle or divinely motivated occurrence). It is analyzed psychologically and even physiologically rather than theologically: "Love is not virtue. . . ." Furthermore, Cavalcanti's love does not lead to heaven: "his pleasures/ Last but a little, for he stays not long." Still, Guido insists, love is responsible for whatever good is done on earth, and even without access to a metaphysical system, it is the antecedent of virtue.

In his less difficult poetry, the objective, realistic side of Cavalcanti can be seen. His Pastourelle (No. 106) is a frank representation of the sexual act as a precursor to a magic vision. In this brilliant evocation of the sensual, one feels the door to the refined new paganism of the Renaissance opening. Lest we align Cavalcanti with the rationalists as opposed to the idealists, we must mention Numbers 107 to 109, which show his kinship with the writers of the *dolce stil nuovo*. Number 107 shows the gradual stages whereby the natural is transformed into the supernatural; it is like Diotima's speech in Plato's *Symposium* set to music.

Number 110, however, reestablishes the tragic tone that runs throughout much of Cavalcanti's work, where love is as often disaster as triumph, death or suffering more than redeeming vision. In the poignant Farewell Ballata (No. 112), perhaps written before his untimely death in Sarzana on the Ligurian coast in 1300, the woman seems more like the abstract goddess Wisdom, a handmaid of art, than an actual woman of Tuscany. In his *Decameron* VI.9, Boccaccio describes Guido as having been "one of the best logicians and natural philosophers in the whole world." The emphasis on humanistic values is explicit in his work.

Aside from writing the masterpiece of the Guinizelli tradition, Dante wrote some poems which fascinate because of their strangeness. His Invitation to Guido and Lapo (No. 114) to embark on a magic ship shows a skillful blend of the romantic with the mystical: Merlin rubbing shoulders with Plato. His Sestina of the Rock Lady (No. 115) is utterly baffling unless one interprets her as the Dark Lady antithesis to Beatrice. It is an early poem and shows perhaps a wavering on the poet's part; he is still in the dark wood with which the *Comedy* opens. Lastly, the *Tenzone* or Debate Poem with Forese Donati (No. 119) shows the virulent, choleric side of the poet that is often concealed under the role of the timid Everyman in the epic poem. He slashes Forese so mercilessly here and in other poems that he apologized later by placing his victim among the redeemed in *Purgatorio* XXIII.

The ·brawling, boisterous side of Italian literature—what we expect when we move from a southern French castle to a Tuscan city bursting with energy—is continued by the man of Siena, Cecco Angiolieri. He puts Dante down in the witty sonnet, Number 123, and establishes his general hatred of man and life in Number 120, saving most of his invective for women (Nos. 121, 124) and especially for his particular woman, the crude, lowly born Becchina (No. 121). As the Black Mass accompanies the true one, so Cecco and Becchina accompany Dante and Beatrice to complete the medieval world view.

Other poets of the period include Folgore of San Gimignano, who wrote a beautiful sequence of sonnets on the twelve months of the year, showing a fine handling of realistic detail. Lapo Gianni and Cino da Pistoia are two other members of the *dolce stil nuovo* who were capable of writing verses that stand out from the rather vague, abstract poetry of many of their peers.

Francesco Petrarca is, of course, the culminating genius of the Italian lyric tradition of the Middle Ages. In him the sonnet found the hands of the master shaper, for he made it the vehicle that was most appealing to the poets of the Renaissance. To assess Petrarch's intellectual achievement is not easy, however. He was acquainted with the work of most of the foregoing writers, as well as with the troubadours, yet he managed to strike an original style. His poems written to Laura depart from those of the *dolce stil nuovo* because of the way in which he portrays her realistically and insists on singing about the unhappiness of love, as well as the joy. After Laura's death (see No. 135), the *Canzoniere* or *Songbook*, the collection of his sonnets and other poems, tells about his moving away from earthly preoccupations to the divine.

Throughout the *Songbook*, which he called in Number 129 his *Rime Sparse* (Scattered Rhymes), Petrarch creates the persona of the lover as a wandering, melancholy figure. Putting aside humor entirely and reducing metaphysical overtones to rhetorical conceits (usually with paradox), he found the medium that proved fascinating to later generations. To many moderns, such as Ezra Pound, Petrarch seems contrived, self-serious, and even morbid; yet he did catch the figure of the brooding poet, alternately at home with and displaced in nature, who marks the change from medieval romance to later romanticism.

G

ST. FRANCIS OF ASSISI[1]

[94]

Canticle of the Creatures: Altissimu, onnipotente Bon Signore

1. Most mighty and most powerful, Good Seigneur,
   Thine be the praise, the glory, and the honor
   And every blessed word.
   Thou alone, Most Mighty, canst all claim,
   And no man is worthy to speak thy name.   5

2. Praise to thee, Milord, with all thy creatures,
   Especially Messér my brother Sun,
   Who day makes and who lights us all alone,
   And he is beautiful and shiny with great splendor;
   Thy meaning, Mighty, to mankind he doth render.   10

3. Praise be thine, Milord, for sister Moon and all the stars;
   In Heaven didst thou cut them precious and pretty and shining far.

4. Praise be thine, Milord, for brother Wind
   And for Air and Cloud, Fair Weather and for Rain,
   By which thou givest creatures what doth sustain.   15

5. Praise be thine, Milord, for sister Water,
   Who is precious and chaste, thy useful, humble daughter.

6. Praise be thine, Milord, for my brother Fire,
   By whom thou lightest the night;
   And he is handsome and happy, full of vigor and might.   20

[1] St. Francis of Assisi (1182?–1226). Founder of the Franciscan Order. After a spoiled youth, he was converted to Christianity in his twenties, espousing the cause of the poor. Granted his order by Innocent III. Received the stigmata on his limbs in 1224. Reportedly composed the *Canticle* before his death at San Damiano. Life recounted by Thomas of Celano and St. Bonaventure.

7. Praise be thine, Milord, for sister Our Mother Earth,
   Who doth rule us and yield us from her girth
   And to fruits with colored flowers and grasses doth give birth.

8. Praise be thine, Milord, for those who pardon with thy love
   And bear infirmities and tribulations;   25
   Blessed are they who will suffer in peace,
   For by thee, Most Mighty, they shall be crowned.

9. Praise be thine, Milord, for our sister Bodily Death,
   Whom no living man can ever outrun.
   Woe to those who in mortal sin take their last breath,   30
   But blessed those living in thy most holy will,
   For a second death shall never work them ill.

10. Men, praise and bless My Lord, and in servility
    Work for him, and thank him with humility.

GIACOMO DA LENTINO, THE NOTARY[2]

[95*]

Io m'agio posto in core a Dio servire

I've put it in my heart to serve my Lord
So that I may rise into his Paradise
To that holy place where, so I've heard,
Are games and laughter, everything that's nice.
Without Milady I would not wish to go there,   5
For without her I could find no delectation—

___

[2] Giacomo da Lentino or Iacopo da Lentini, nicknamed The Notary (*fl.* 1230–1245). Considered the father of the sonnet, of which this may be the oldest extant sample. Worked for Frederick II as *notarius* and *scriba* in 1233 and 1240.

* Original text appears in Section X, p. 392.

She with the shining face, the golden hair—
Sad would I be at my lady's separation.

But I'm not saying this to take a dare
And commit a voluntary mortal sin,   10
As if I had to have her bearing fair,
Her visage lovely from the brow to chin—
Still, it would prove great solace for my care
To see my lady stand in full glory there!

CIELO D'ALCAMO³

[96]

Rosa fresca aulentissima

HE:
1. Fresh, sweet rose, my summer sprout,
   Adored by virgins—and missuses too—
   I'm in hellish fire. Pluck me out!
   Lady, I know no peace night or day
   Because my thoughts all turn your way.   5

SHE:
2. Buzzing around this rose is insanity.
   Go plow the ocean. Harrow it with seed.
   Hoard the age's wealth (match your vanity!)
   I'll never be yours in earthly life.
   I'd rather be God's shaven wife.   10

HE:
3. If you were a nun, I'd ask Death's pardon.
   No, life couldn't hold another charm.

---

³ Cielo d'Alcamo, Ciullo dal Como (*fl.* 1230–1250). Unknown Sicilian poet. His *Contrasto* (Debate Poem: the usual word in Italian is *Tenzone*) is dated from its mention of the coins *augustali* (translated "ducats" in line 22). Translation very free.

O when I see you, rose of the garden,
You give me pleasure every hour.
Why not let our love burst into flower?   15

SHE:

4. I don't care a hoot for flowering love.
Listen, if my daddy sees you here,
He'll pluck *your* little flower from above.
Well, you found access to my door.
Pray your exit's lucky as before.   20

HE:

5. Bah! if he finds me here, who'll bother?
My defense is twenty thousand ducats.
Would my properties in Bari escape Father?
Thank God the Emperor's in health!
Sweetheart, never underestimate wealth.   25

SHE:

6. Lord, how you pester me night and day!
Why, I've got francs and twenty-carat gold.
Give me all the Sultan's tucked away
And double the loot of the Mussulmans—
Still, I'll never undergo your hands.   30

HE:

7. Women have heads carved out of stone
But men can still persuade them.
The chase is hot. The catch comes home.
Who wants to be a lonely quarry?
Don't resist, dear. You'll be sorry.   35

SHE:

8. Me sorry? Why I'd rather be slain
Than disgrace all womankind. Last night
Why'd you prowl around here half-insane?
Go home, troubadour. Sit.
I don't like your talk one little bit.   40

HE:

9. O me! it's not the first time I felt the lash.
   I feel it every day when I make my rounds.
   No other girl ever made me act rash
   Like you do, envied rose sublime.
   I still think Fate will make you mine. 45

SHE:

10. If *that's* my fate, I'll leap off a cliff
    Rather than waste my beauty in your hands.
    I'll cut my hair, if that's destiny's drift,
    And really become a nun
    Before I'll give you your little fun. 50

HE:

11. If you're a nun, girl of the shiny face,
    I'll go to your convent and be a priest.
    I'll get you. Who cares about disgrace?
    And stay with you each waking hour.
    I've simply got to have you in my power. 55

SHE:

12. O God, poor me! What fate could be worse?
    Almighty Jesus, you're mad at me,
    Pitting me against a man like him—perverse!
    Go see the world. It's big enough.
    You'll find some girl with better stuff. 60

HE:

13. I've hunted Tuscany, Calabria, Lombardy,
    Apulia, Constantinople, Pisa, Syria,
    Germany, Babylonia, and all of Barbary,
    But never found a girl so modest.
    That's why I want to make you my goddess. 65

SHE:

14. Well, you worked hard. Why not promise this?
    Go ask me from my mother and my father.

Then to the church—if they say yes—
And marry me before our folks.
That's the only way I'll bear your yoke.   70

HE:

15. My life, your proposition's a useless thing.
No, I know the gist behind your talk.
Ruffle your feathers. Down fall angel wings
When I give girls an earthly shove.
Or, if you think you can—keep your love!   75

SHE:

16. Don't try to make me cower at your stick.
I'm as gloriously strong as any fortress.
You know, sometimes you talk like a boy of six.
Get up, get out, go home to bed.
Sometimes I almost wish you'd drop dead.   80

HE:

17. Aha, my life, you'd hang me up to shoot!
Well, I can be hacked or even killed
But I won't leave till I've got that fruit
Dangling in your garden of delight.
That's what keeps me hungry day and night.   85

SHE:

18. My fruit's not purchased by knights or counts
Though it's wanted by many marquises and lords.
It's not for you, no matter how you flounce.
Listen carefully to what I say:
Your money's just a needle in the hay.   90

HE:

19. O I've lettuce, but not for you those stocks!
Don't scoff till you've toted up the sum.
Ill winds turn proud prows upon the rocks.
Remember my words, though brief:
This stubbornness causes me much grief.   95

SHE:

20. If grief made you totter off your feet
    And people rushed in here on every side,
    Yelling: "Help this poor man!" Me, I'd retreat.
    You couldn't offer your hand with hope,
    Not if you were Sultan—or even Pope!   100

HE:

21. Life, if God willed my death in your house,
    I'd be consoled by daily hauntings.
    People would shout: "See that lying louse
    Keeping a dead man in her room!"
    With words alone, you can seal my doom.   105

SHE:

22. If you don't take away your curses,
    My brothers'll find you in our mansion.
    I warn you, handsome, life *could* be worse!
    You came to preach all by yourself
    Without any friends or relatives to help.   110

HE:

23. True, I've no relatives to aid me.
    I'm all alone among your gentle clan.
    It's now a year since I first saw you, lady,
    Stepping out in your party dress.
    Beautiful, that was the start of my distress.   115

SHE:

24. Ah yes, you fell in love, traitor Jude,
    With all my purple, scarlet velvets.
    Swear on the Gospel: say you'll be true:
    You'll never in this life own *me*.
    I'd rather pitch myself into the sea.   120

HE:

25. If you jumped in the sea, my lady grand,
    I'd swim the breadth of all the ocean.

I'd drag your corpse up on the sand
And end where I'd like to begin:
Locked with you even in death—in sin.   125

SHE:

26. Forgive him, Father, Son—St. Matthew too—
    I swear I never heard those evil words.
    He's no heretic—no son of a Jew.
    Lord, when a woman's dead and done,
    She can't offer a man any fun!   130

HE:

27. Now, life, you know just where I stand.
    If you won't help me, I'll end my song.
    Lady, I fail. Help! You know you can!
    I love you even unloved, forsook:
    You've caught me. I'm a fish upon your hook.   135

SHE:

28. I know you love me. To me, you're just a Moor.
    Get up and go. Come back tomorrow morning.
    Do what I say. It's you that I adore.
    I promise this without fail:
    I'm yours. Yes, you've got me in your jail.   140

HE:

29. Dear, I still can't go. Please, I beg:
    Take this knife. Slit me down the gullet.
    Do it quicker than you can fry an egg.
    Beautiful, grant what I implore:
    My heart and soul wage constant war.   145

SHE:

30. I'm sure your soul's as hot as your body looks.
    Well, I know only one cure for this disease.
    Why not swear you're mine on the Holy Book?
    Look, you could even cut off my head:
    I'm not going to go just *anywhere* I'm led!   150

HE:

31. Sweet, I have that book in my pocket.
   (I took it when the father wasn't looking.)
   I'll swear upon it. God, I'd never mock it.
   But show your love here in my arms.
   Lady, my soul has so many gentle charms.   155

SHE:

32. Sir, since you've sworn, I've no defender.
   Your burning body's setting me on fire.
   I wronged you, but—mercy! I surrender.
   Now quick! upstairs let's wend
   And give this long, long talk a happy end.   160

PIER DELLA VIGNA[4]

[97]

Amore, in cui disio ed ho speranza

1. Love, by which I have desire and hope,
   Has given me, beautiful, a reward from you,
      And now I'm waiting till my happiness comes,
   Firmly expecting a good time in good season.
      Like a man at sea who's hoping to ride the swells,   5
   And the time is right, and out he flings his sails,
   And the hope he has is true with no betraying—
   Just so am I, my lady, as I move toward you.

2. Ah, if I could reach you, loving lady,
   Like some thief asneak, and not be seen!   10
      If Love would grant me just this little gift,

---

[4] Pier della Vigna (*ca.* 1182–1249). Close counselor to Frederick II and secretary of the imperial chamber. Studied at Bologna; assumed imperial duties after 1220. Disgraced and imprisoned in 1249; committed suicide. Movingly described by Dante in *Inferno* XIII.

I'd think that I had grasped some good-omened joy.
Ah, I would speak with you graciously, my lady,
And tell you how I've loved you this long while '
More sweetly than Pyramus whispered to his Thisbe,   15
And I'd love you for as long as I have life.

3. Your love it is that holds me in desiring
   And gives me chance for hope with some great joy,
       For I don't care if I grieve or if I suffer,
   For I'll remember the hour I came to you;   20
       And if I delay too long, I think I'll perish,
   O perfumed breath! and you will lose me too.
   And so, my beauty, if you wish me well,
   See that I don't die in my hope for you.

4. In hope of you I live, my lady fair,   25
   And still my heart goes on in quest of you,
       And it seems to me the hour is getting longer
   That true love spends in sending me to you;
       And I'm searching for a time that will be right
   To loose my sails in your direction, rose,   30
   And anchor in a port where I'll repose
   With heart intent upon your mastery.

5. Go, little song, and carry these laments
   To her who holds my heart within her power;
       Go, count for her the pains that I have felt   35
   And tell her how I'm dying with desire,
       And let her send a message back to tell
   How I can console this love I bear for her;
   And if I ever did a thing debased,
   Let her give me penance as she wills.   40

RINALDO D'AQUINO[5]

[98]

Giammai non mi conforto

1. Never again that comfort,
   Never that joyous heart.
   The ships down in the harbor
   Are straining to depart.
   Away all the people run   5
   To lands across the sea.
   But me—poor weeping thing—
   What shall become of me?

2. Away, away he'll run,
   Fade quietly out of sight,   10
   Leaving me here alone.
   All day, all the night
   Many will be the sighs
   That assail me constantly.
   Not in heaven, not on earth   15
   Will life exist for me.

3. O Holy, Holy Savior
   Who from Mary came our way!
   Watch, protect that lover,
   Since you're taking him away.   20
   O reverenced and feared
   Power from above!
   In your hands I place
   My tender love.

---

[5] Rinaldo d'Aquino (*fl.* 1235–1279?). Aristocrat from the Campagna, possibly a brother of St. Thomas Aquinas. Perhaps the imperial falconer of Frederick II. Wrote this Complaint Against the Crusade (of 1227–1228).

4. O cross that saves mankind,   25
   You plummet me to error,
   Twisting my grievous mind
   Beyond all hope of prayer.
   Why, O pilgrim cross,
   Why this bitter turn?   30
   Bowed beneath my loss,
   I kindle; O I burn.

5. The Emperor who rules the world
   In his peaceful sway
   Ravages poor little me   35
   By taking my hope away.
   O reverenced and feared
   Power from above!
   In your hands I place
   My tender love.   40

6. When he took up the cross,
   I didn't know the end was this:
   Whatever love he gave me
   I repaid him kiss for kiss.
   Now I'm thrust aside—   45
   Yes, condemned to prison—
   Now I'm forced to hide
   In lifelong derision.

7. The ships are in their moorings.
   Soon they'll depart.   50
   With them and that rabble
   Sails my heart.
   O Father, O Creator,
   Guide them to holy haven.
   By your sacred cross   55
   They're all enslaven.

8. And O Darling, I beg you:
   Take pity on my hysteria

Write me a little sonnet.
Send it to me from Syria!   60
Night and day I'll know
Only this bitter strife.
In lands beyond the ocean
Lies my whole life.

RE ENZO (KING HEINZ)[6]

[99]

Tempo vene che sale a chi discende

Time comes for one descending to ascend,
A time for standing mute, a time for speech,
A time to listen for one who would intend,
A time for looking out for many things.
There is a time for vengeance if one offends,   5
A time to put aside a fear of threats,
A time to obey if another reprehends,
A time to make pretense that one can't see.

And thus I hold him a wise and knowing man
Who guides himself always with his reason   10
And knows how to conduct himself with the time,
And with the people stands always in good season,
And never offers any grounds for doubt
That might let his deeds be suspect of any treason.

[6] Re Enzo or King Heinz, Heinrich (*ca.* 1220–1272). Bastard son of Frederick II
from an unknown mother. Married Adelasia in 1238, thereby claiming rights to the
Kingdom of Sardinia. Captured by the Bolognese at the battle of Fossalta (May 26,
1249) and imprisoned in the Central Square of Bologna, where his castle quarters
still stand; never freed. This poem, attributed also to Guittone d'Arezzo, based on
Ecclesiastes 3:1–8.

IACOPONE DA TODI[7]

[100]

Donna de paradiso

MESSENGER:
Lady of Paradise,
Your Son's in custody,
The blesséd Jesus Christ.
Run, Milady, and see:
They beat him mercilessly!   5
He'll die, it seems to me,
The whip so cruelly bites!

VIRGIN:
Tell me, how can it be?
He never acted wrongly.
Did they bind him strongly—   10
O my one hope, Christ!

MESSENGER:
For a thirty-denier dole,
Milady, Judas sold,
Betrayed for the love of gold—
That was his heavy heist!   15

VIRGIN:
Help, my Magdalene!
Suddenly I've pain!
O God, hè goes on rein—
As someone once prophesied.

---

[7] Iacopone da Todi (1236–1306). Born in the Umbrian city of Todi of wealthy
parents. Renounced the world for Franciscan orders after the sudden, tragic death
of his wife at an elegant ball. This Dialogue Poem is part of his *Lauds* to Christ
and Mary. Number 19 formerly attributed to him.

MESSENGER:
Help, Madonna, quick!   20
Look! the people spit!
They shove, won't let him sit!
Now he's at Pilate's side.

VIRGIN:
O Pilate, don't allow
My Son to suffer now.   25
I can show you how
All his accusers lied.

CROWD:
Crucify, yes crucify
This "King" who tries to falsify
The laws that we all live by,   30
And Rome he has defied!

VIRGIN:
Please, O please attend me!
See how this grief will end me . . .
A change of heart would lend me
A little peace of mind.   35

CROWD:
Let's drag the thieves outside,
Companions for homicide.
A crown of thorns there'll be
For the self-claimed monarchy!

VIRGIN:
O my Son, my Son, my Son!   40
Lovely lily, amorous one!
Son, who can make languish
This heart now filled with anguish?
Son, with eye ever dancing,
Son, why aren't you answering?   45

Son, why have you pressed
Away from this suckling breast?

MESSENGER:
Milady, look! they bring
The Cross of suffering
On which the Light of Things   50
Will be hanged high.

VIRGIN:
What are you doing, Cross?
Snatching him to my loss?
What charges do you toss?
No sin he ever tried.   55

MESSENGER:
Help, grieving mother of worship—
Your Son is being stripped.
The nails are next—the whips—
For they will crucify.

VIRGIN:
O if they tear off his clothes,   60
That body will disclose
Those cruel and brutal blows—
The blood I'll have to spy.

MESSENGER:
Lady, they're lifting his hand—
Now on the Cross it stands.   65
The pounding they command—
Straight to the board he's plied.
The other hand they're snatching—
Out on the Cross it's stretching.
His face his pain is etching,   70
And that's now multiplied.
Lady, his feet now go,
Nailed on the wood down low.

They wrench and maul him so,
His joints are gaping wide.   75

VIRGIN:
Ah, I begin my lament.
Son, my one true enjoyment,
Who ordered your life spent?
My one delicate pride.
Better if they had pressed   80
This heart out of this breast
Than I should see you trussed
And agonized—

CHRIST:
Mother, and are you there?
You're causing me even more care   85
With all of this despair
That grips you in its vise.

VIRGIN:
Son, do you cast me blame?
Husband and father in name,
Son, who will make you lame?   90
Who has bared your hide?

CHRIST:
Mother, why now complain?
I want you to remain
And serve the friends I've gained
Through the world wide.   95

VIRGIN:
Son, this is not to ask!
Son, I refuse the task!
Son, with you I'll pass,
Until my breath's expired.
A single grave will mark—   100
Son of a mother made dark—

The place where we both embark,
Choked by this homicide.

CHRIST:
Mother with heart perplexed,
I want you to stand erect   105
With John, who is my elect,
As your new son he'll abide.
John, take my mother there;
Hold her with great care;
Her heart has felt a tear—   110
So hold her tender and tight.

VIRGIN:
Son, your soul's departed.
Son of one brokenhearted,
Son of a woman martyred,
Son who was mortified.   115
Son who is rosy and fair,
Son beyond all compare,
Son, where for me? where?
Son, have you left my side?
Son who is blond and white,   120
Son with a face of delight,
Why did the world show spite,
Son, why were you despised?
Son who was pleasant and sweet,
Son of a woman with grief,   125
Son whom the masses treat
In a wicked wise.
Now, my new son, John—
Your belovéd brother is gone;
The knife for him was drawn,   130
As was long prophesied,
Which killed both Son and Mother,
Cruel death did them smother
Lying wrapped round each other
In each other's arms gripped tight.   135

[101]

Senno me par e cortesia

1. To me it seems sense and nobility
   To worship Messiah with imbecility.

2. It seems to me great intelligence
   To worship God by losing your sense;
   In Paris you will never see   5
   Such a great philosophy.

3. Who for Christ becomes all mad
   Seems afflicted, troubled, sad;
   But a master he will be
   Of nature and theology.   10

4. Who for Christ acts all hazy
   Seems to the people utterly crazy;
   He who hasn't known insanity
   Thinks divine madness is all inanity.

5. He who wants to enter this school   15
   Will have to learn a new set of rules;
   Unless you experience madness directly
   You can't practice it correctly.

6. He who wants to join this dance
   Will witness love in great abundance;   20
   A hundred days' pardon is the fee
   For all who curse him wickedly.

7. But he who puts ambition above
   Will not be worthy of Christ's love;
   For Jesus dangled willingly   25
   With thieves accused of villainy.

8. He who seeks with true humility
   Will arrive with great agility;

Go no more to Bologna University
To master doctrines of perversity.   30

THE PERFECT LADY OF FLORENCE
(LA COMPIUTA DONZELLA DI FIRENZE)[8]

[102]

Lasciar voria lo mondo e Dio servire

I want to go away from vanity
And leave the world and serve my God
Because I see on every side of me
Madness and unchecked evil and great fraud:
Sense and courtesy are still expiring   5
And fine value and goodness of every kind;
And so I want no husband, want no sire;
Leaving the world is all that's on my mind.

When I recall how man with ill's adorned,
I suddenly am disdainful of all the race   10
And toward my God all of my body's turned.
My father makes me stand with pensive face.
He turns me away from service to my Christ.
What man will come to claim my dowry's price?

[8] The Perfect Lady of Florence, La Compiuta Donzella di Firenze (latter 1200s).
Otherwise unknown poetess often considered a construct of the male poets of the day.

GUIDO GUINIZELLI[9]

[103]

Vedut'ho la lucente stella diana

I have seen the blazing morning star
Appear before day hands us dawn,
Shaped like a woman standing afar,
More splendid than any other one—
Snow-white face with scarlet glow,   5
Gay, sparkling eyes, full of love for earth;
No worldly Christian girl I know
Can match her beauty and her worth.

By the love of her I'm so assailed
With a battle of sighs that rages fierce,   10
Before her I'd stand by fear impaled:
O if she knew how desires pierce
And, wordlessly, would get me some gain
From the pity she should pass upon my pain!

[104]

Io voglio del ver la mia donna laudare

I truly wish to give my lady praise
And liken her to lily and to rose:
Brighter than morning star she comes and glows
And makes me think of all that heavenly blaze.
Green banks I compare with her, I compare the skies,   5

[9] Guido Guinizelli, Guinicelli (*ca.* 1230–1276). Acknowledged father of the *dolce stil nuovo*. Judge in Bologna, descended from wealthy Ghibellines; driven into exile after the Guelph victory in 1274. Died near Padua. Immortalized by Dante in *Purgatorio* XXVI, where he introduces Arnaut Daniel.

Flowers of every color, yellow and green,
Azure and gold, the richest jewels to be seen;
Through her even Love feels his value rise.

She passes in the streets, noble, adorned;
She humbles the pride of any with her greeting,   10
And skeptics to believers quickly are turned;
No wicked man with her would risk a meeting;
And still I say: her powers are even keener.
No man thinks evil once that he has seen her.

[105*]

Al cor gentil rempaira sempre amore

1. Love always repairs to the noble heart
      Like a bird winging back into its grove:
   Nor was love made before the noble heart,
      Nor did nature, before the heart, make love.
   For they were there as long as was the Sun,   5
      Whose splendor's ever bright;
   Never did love before that shining come.
   Love nestles deep inside nobility
      Exactly the way
   One sees the heat within the fiery blaze.   10

2. Fire of love in noble heart is caught
      Like power gleaming inside a precious stone.
   The value does not come down from the stars
      Until the Sun has blenched the stone all pure.
   Only after the might of the Sun   15
      Has drawn out all that's vile
   Does the star bestow its noble power.

---

* Original text appears in Section X, p. 393.

Just so a heart transformed by nature pure,
    Noble and elect,
A woman starlike with her love injects.   20

3. Love for this reason stays in noble heart
    Like a waving flame atop a burning brand,
Shining, its own delight, subtle and bright;
    It is so proud, it knows no other way.
Yet a nature which is still debased   25
    Greets love as water greets the fire,
With the cold hissing against the heat.
Love in noble heart will find a haven
    Like the shine
Of a diamond glinting in ore within the mine.   30

4. Sun beats against the mud the livelong day;
Mud it remains; Sun does not lose its ray;
The haughty one says: "I am noble by my tribe."
    He is the mud; Sun is the noble power.
Man must never believe   35
    That nobility exists outside the heart
In the grandness of his ancestry,
For without virtue, heart has no noble worth;
    It's a ray through a wave;
The heavens retain the sparkle and splendor they gave.   40

5. Shines among the powers of heaven
    God the creator, more than Sun in our eye;
Each angel knows the Maker beyond its sphere,
    And turning its circle, obeys God's noble power.
And thus it follows at once: 45
    The blessèd tasks of the Master transpire.
In the same way, in all truth, the beautiful lady
Should behave, for in her eyes reflects the desire
    Of a noble man
Who will turn his every thought to her command.   50

6. Lady, God will ask me: "Why do you presume?"
    When my soul stands before his mighty throne.
"You passed the heavens, came all the way to me,
   \ And cheapened me in the light of profane love.
To me is due all the praise   55
    And to the Queen of the Royal Realm
Who makes all fraudulence cease."
I'll tell him then: "She had an angel look—
    A heavenly face.
What harm occurred if my love in her was placed?"   60

GUIDO CAVALCANTI[10]

[106]

In un boschetto trova' pasturella

1. Once within a little grove
   A shepherdess I spied;
   More than any star of sky
   Beauteous did she prove.

2. Ringlets she had, blonde and curly locks,   5
   Eyes filled with love, a face of rosy hue,
   And with her staff she led her gentle flocks,
   Barefoot, with their feet bathed by the dew.
   She sang, indeed, as if she were enamored;
   She had the glamour   10
   Of every pleasing art.

---

[10] Guido Cavalcanti (*ca.* 1255–1300). Florentine member of the rich merchant classes: Guelph and White in politics; banished to Sarzana in Liguria, where he contracted malaria; died in August, 1300. His mistress, Giovanna (Vanna), is mentioned in the *Vita Nuova,* where Dante tells us that her secret name was Primavera or Spring (see No. 107, line 2). The heroine of this Pastourelle is a simple peasant girl.

3. I greeted her, and asked her then at once
   If she had any company that day;
   She answered sweetly: "For the nonce,
   Alone throughout this grove I make my way."   15
   And added: "Listen, but when the bird's
   Gentle song is heard,
   A friend should have my heart."

4. And when she told me of this state of mind,
   And suddenly I heard birdsongs in the wood   20
   I said to myself: "This surely would be time
   To take from this shepherdess what joy I could."
   Grace I requested—just to kiss her face—
   And then embrace
   If she should feel like me.   25

5. She took my hand, seized with love's old power,
   And said she'd give me her heart too;
   She led me then into a fresh green bower,
   And there I saw flowers of every hue.
   And I was filled so full of sweetened joy   30.
   Love's godlike boy
   There too I seemed to see.

[107]

Fresca rosa novella

1. Fresh newborn rose,
   My beauteous Spring,
   Through field, by river,
   Gaily singing,
   Your noble worth I set   5
      In nature.

2. Your truly noble worth
   Renews itself with joy
   In agéd man or boy
   With every setting forth;   10
   Birds chant to it their vows,
   Each in his own Latin,
   From vespers into matins,
   On their greenish boughs.
   The whole world's now with song,   15
   Since it's your season,
   And, with proper reason,
   Hymns your majesty,
   For you're the most heavenly
       Of creatures.   20

3. Heavenly features
   In you, my lady, rest;
   O God, how wondrous blessed
   Now seems my desire.
   Lady, your glad expression,   25
   Whenever it comes and passes,
   Nature and custom surpasses
   In wonderful expression.
   Together women admire
   Your truly godlike form,   30
   For you are so adorned,
   Your beauty's not transcribed,
   For can't it be described:
       Beyond nature?

4. Beyond our human nature   35
   God made your excellence
   To show by its very essence
   That you were born to rule.
   Now, so your noble face
   May stay forever near,   40
   To me keep ever dear
   Your most abundant grace,

And if I seem a fool
To set you as my queen,
Know that I don't blaspheme,   45
For Love makes me courageous
Which still no force assuages
   Nor measure.

[108*]

Chi è questa che ven, ch'ogn'om la mira

Who is it comes whom every man admires,
Who sets the air with clarity atremble?
Bringing Love too, so no man dare dissemble,
By speech, but each can only now suspire?
O how to catch her from the eye's swift gyre?   5
Love tells me: "No, you'd only bumble,
Because of women she's so far most humble
That any other you must then call 'ire.' "

No one could count her many charms, though modest,
For toward her bends every noble power;   10
Thus Beauty sets her forth to be her goddess.
Still my mind is not so high and grand,
Nor have I felt the grace at any hour
To encompass her and say, "I understand."

   * Original text appears in Section X, p. 394.

[109]

Avete 'n vo' li fior' e la verdura

You have in you the flowers and the verdure
And all that's light or beautiful to sight,
So far outshining Sun, that nurture
No man knows who knows not your delight.
In this world live no other creatures   5
So full of beauty or of countless pleasures;
Whoever fears Love needs but view your features,
To rest assured of all his many treasures.

The ladies who now lend you company
Much please me because of their respect for you,   10
And so I beg them, for their courtesy:
Whatever they can, that much honor show
And hold with love your loving mastery;
Because of all the rest, you are the best.

[110]

Noi siàn le triste penne isbigotite

We are the pens, saddened and dismayed,
The scissors and the sorrowing knife
Who formed these words of woeful strife
Your eyes have just now surveyed.
We'll tell you why we've camped apart   5
And come to you, reader, now and here:
The hand that formed us felt great fear—
Ah, fearsome forms beset his heart!

Forms which had him so unmanned
And forced him almost to his very end   10
That he had nothing left but sighs.

And now we beg you, strongly as we can:
Please try to think of us as loyal friends;
Just let us see one pair of pitying eyes.

[111¹¹]

Donna me prega, per ch'io voglio dire

1. A lady asks me; therefore, I'd explain
   An accident that often fiercely smarts
   And is so high it claims Love for its name.
   Now who'd deny, let him hear its fame,
   Though I can't hope to teach a lowly heart;   5
   I'd reach some men with knowledge in their brains,

2. Who bring to reason some intelligence.
   Because without a bit of natural science
   I have no will or wit to try to prove
   Where Love is born, or who created Love,   10
   What is his virtue or his potency,
   How he might move or what his essence be,
   His delights which by "to love" are known
   Or if Love's ever to men's sight been shown.

3. In that part where memory has its locus   15
   He takes his state and there he is created,
   Diaphanous by light, out of that dark
   That comes from Mars and then takes lasting focus;
   And once he's made, he has a name sensate,
   Taking desire from heart, from mind his mark.   20

¹¹ *The Song of Love (Canzone d'Amore)*. Difficult text, edited by Mario Casella, *Studi di Filologia Italiana*, 7 (1944), with emendations by J. E. Shaw, *Guido Cavalcanti's Theory of Love* (University of Toronto, 1949). An "accident" in stanza 1, line 2, is a Scholastic term meaning "a movement in a substance." In stanza 10, the "one who to truth is sworn" is his unnamed philosophical source: Aristotle, Albertus Magnus, Averroes?

4. He comes from an image seen and comprehended
   That's apprehended in the Possible Intellect;
   There he waits in subject, without wandering,
   And in that part his vigor has no force,
   For Love's never from pure quality descended;   25
   And yet he shines, himself his own effect,
   Without delight, unless it's that of pondering,
   Because he cannot breed from his own source.

5. Love is not virtue, but he takes his course
   From what we call perfection—   30
   Not rational but emotional, I say:
   Outside of health he steers his judgment's force,
   Lets ecstasy gain reason's predilection,
   Choosing poorly friends to vice's way,
   Pursuing his power often to death's end.   35

6. Yet if by chance his power is turned aside
   To guide instead along the other way,
   He was not made by nature to go astray:
   However far from the perfect good he bend,
   By that much is the lover life denied: 40
   Stability can fail the mastery it's gotten;
   Love can't prevail when reason's all forgotten.

7. Love comes to be whenever desire's so strong
   It can't keep bearing nature's measures;
   Then leisure can't long please, and so Love veers,   45
   Changing complexions, turning smiles to tears,
   Twisting the face with fear; his pleasures
   Last but a little, for he stays not long.

8. And yet you'll find him most in men of worth
   Where his new qualities create new sighs   50
   And make men gaze at uncreated spaces,
   Arousing ire to burn in fiery faces
   (No man can imagine it until he tries).
   Love does not move, though arrows whistle forth;

He does not twist to find his jests at all;   55
Nor does he search for great wisdom, or small.

9. Like looks and tempers attract their kindred parts,
   And make Love's pleasures then appear the surer.
   No man can ever cower from his spear.
   Never was nymphlike Beauty like his darts,   60
   For coyer passions expire in such furor.
   Still, a reward awaits the spirit speared—

10. Though not a trace appears on the lover's face.
   For Love's no object, neither black nor white;
   Look at a lover; you find no form for seeing   65
   Unless some emotion from Love's form takes its being.
   Outside of color, likewise cut off from space
   This form out of darkness sheds faint light;
   Beyond all fraud, says one who to truth is sworn,
   So that only by this Love is true compassion born.   70

11. Go now, my song, where you aspire,
   Securely, for I've so upraised
   You, you'll be praised
   Most highly for your sense
   By all who own intelligence: 75
   To stand with others you have no desire.

[112¹²]

Perch'i' no spero di tornar giammai

1. Because I never hope to go once more,
     Ballata, into Tuscany—
  You go soft and gently

---

¹² Commonly called the *"Farewell Ballata,"* probably written in exile at Sarzana
shortly before death. Adapted by T. S. Eliot in "Ash Wednesday."

H

Straight to my lady's door,
And she, from her high courtesy,   5
Will do you honor.

2. Go, and carry with you tales of sighings,
    Filled with long pain and grievous fear;
Beware only of hostile spyings
    From those who hold nobility not dear.   10
    For certainly from my estate so low,
        To see you ill-dispatched
        Or by cruel hands snatched,
    Which cause me now so many anguished breaths,
        Would cause me after death   15
    Grief and fresher woe.

3. You feel, Ballata, now how death
    Forces me to put my life behind;
You feel my heart pounding with every breath,
    Sensing the end of every reasoning mind.   20
    Now my body's so totally torn apart
        That pain's not even fervent;
        If you would be my servant,
    I ask: take my spirit with you
        (And this I beg you too:)   25
    Soon, when it leaves my heart.

4. Alas, Ballata, to your kindly company
    This soul that trembles I too recommend:
Take it along, out of your piety,
    To that sweet lady where I send.   30
    Alas, Ballata, say with sighings more
        When you've at last drawn near,
        "I am your servant here,
    And I have come to stay
        From one who's gone away,   35
        But was Love's servant long before."

5. You, my voice, now weakened and dismayed,
   Which issues crying from this saddened heart,
With soul, and with this song that I have made,
   From ruined mind now reason wide apart.   40
   You'll find that lady pleasing to the sense
     For her sweet intellect;
     And out of charmed respect
   You'll always stand before her;
     Spirit, you too adore her   45
   Forever for her excellence.

[113[13]]

Guata, Manetto, quella scrignutuzza

Look, Manny, at that little hunchback,
And think a while how it could happen
She's misconstructed, all misshapen:
Just watch her bunch those shoulders back.
If she was dressed like a gentlewoman,   5
With a pretty hat and a muslin veil,
And there should follow in her trail
A company of elegant, gentle women,

You wouldn't feel that hardened bile;
You wouldn't suffer love's torment   10
Or stay all pent up in sadness' sway:
No, risking death, instead, you'd smile
Because that smile from heart was sent.
Otherwise you'd die—or run away.

[13] Satiric Sonnet about a hunchbacked woman.

DANTE ALIGHIERI[14]

[114]

Guido, i' vorrei che tu e Lapo ed io

Guido, I wish that you and Lapo and I,
Spirited on the wings of a magic spell,
Could drift in a ship where every rising swell
Would sweep us at our will across the skies;
Then tempest never, or any weather dire   5
Could ever make our blissful living cease;
No, but abiding in a steady, blessèd peace
Together we'd share the increase of desire.

And Lady Vanna and Lady Lagia then
And she who looms above the thirty best   10
Would join us at the good enchanter's behest;
And there we'd talk of Love without an end
To make those ladies happy in the sky—
With Lapo enchanted too, and you and I.

[115[15]]

Al poco giorno e al gran cerchio d'ombra

1. To slender daylight and a vast circle of shade
   I've come, alas! and to whitening of the hills,
   Where all the coloration is lost from the grass;
   And yet my desire has thus not lost its green,

[14] Invitation to Guido Cavalcanti and Lapo Gianni.
[15] Sestina of the Rock Lady.

For it is founded on a hard, hard rock   5
Which speaks and hears as if it were a woman.

2. Similarly this most extraordinary woman
   Stands frozen like the snow beneath the shade;
   She's never moved, unless it's like a rock,
   By the sweet season that heats up all the hills   10
   And makes them turn from whitening into green,
   Because it covers them with flowers and grass.

3. Whenever she wears a garland hat of grass
   She draws attention from every other woman,
   Because the blend of curly gold and green   15
   Is beautiful; Love stands within their shade,
   And locks me in between these little hills
   More tightly than the limestone locks the rock.

4. Her beauty exerts more power than magnetic rock,
   And her blows cannot be cured by any grass;   20
   For I have fled through fields and over hills
   To try to escape the clutches of such a woman;
   And yet her light won't grant me any shade,
   Under mound or wall or any frond of green.

5. I've seen her already dressed up in her green   25
   So stunningly that she would have moved a rock
   With the love I offer even to her shade;
   And so I've wanted her in a pretty field of grass
   To fall in love like me, like any woman,
   Surrounded by a circle of the highest hills.   30

6. But the rivers will run upward to the hills
   Before this wood that's dewy and is green
   Takes fire, as would any pretty woman;
   I'd take my life and sleep out on a rock
   And go around pasturing on the grass   35
   Just to see where her garments cast their shade.

7. Whenever the hills cast down a blackened shade
   In a fair green this youthful woman makes them
   Disappear, like a rock that's hidden under grass.

[116*]

Donne ch'avete intelletto d'amore[16]

1. Ladies who have intelligence of love
   With you about my lady I'd discourse,
   Not that by talk I'd reckon up her worth,
   But speech can often ease the burdened mind.
   I say: whenever her worth looms high above,   5
   Love makes me feel his presence sweetly, so
   That if I didn't gradually lose his glow,
   I'd teach the entire world to feel her love.
   And yet I should not be talking overmuch,
   For later fear will make me vilely quake;   10
   No, I shall treat her most genteel estate,
   Compared to what she is, with light-handed touch
   In talk to you, my loving ladies and lasses—
   It's not a thing for sharing with the masses.

2. An angel proclaims to the divine intellect,   15
   Saying, "My Master, upon the earth I heed
   A miracle in act that now proceeds
   Out of a soul which this far casts its splendor."
   Heaven, which has suffered no other defect
   Except the lack of her, to its Lord exclaims   20
   And every saint cries out in mercy's name.
   Pity is my only staunch defender,
   Saying in God, who my lady comprehends,
   "Delights of mine, suffer now in peace,

* Original text appears in Section X, p. 395.

[16] Canzone from the *Vita Nuova*.

For although your hope is one that can only please,   25
Still there's a man who's waiting for her end
And he will say in Hell: 'O spirits hexed,
These eyes have seen the great hope of the blessed.' "

3. My lady is desired in highest Heaven.
   Ladies, become acquainted with her power: 30
   I say: she is the gentle lady's endower,
   So go with her whenever she passes by.
   Love casts a frost upon hearts which are craven,
   And every thought then icily petrifies;
   But he who can stand and fix on her his eyes   35
   Will become a noble thing—or else, will die.
   Whenever she finds a man who shows his worth
   For seeing her, he experiences her grace;
   She humbles him, all injuries to erase,
   And changes into happiness all that hurts.   40
   For even more grace God has given a donation:
   Certain salvation after her conversation.

4. Love says about her: "How can she possibly be
   A mortal thing, since she's beautiful and pure?"
   He looks at her and inwardly is sure   45
   God wants to set her forth as something new.
   Almost the color of pearl she has, to the degree
   A woman should, certainly within measure;
   She has all good that lies in nature's treasure;
   Her very existence proves that Beauty is true.   50
   Out of her eyes, whenever she moves them round,
   Issue spirits of Love encased in blaze
   Which strike the eyes of all who on her gaze
   And penetrate till the heart of each is found:
   Love you will see upon her visage painting;   55
   No one dare look there long or he'll be fainting.

5. Song, I know that talking you'll make your way
   To many ladies, once I've set you free.
   Now I admonish: I've reared you up to be

A little daughter of Love, sweet and simple,   60
And wherever you go, you must always say:
"Show me the road; for I am being sent
To one whose praise explains my embellishment."
And if you don't want to act like an imbecile,
Stay away from people who are base,   65
Contriving, if you can, to show true grit
Only to ladies and to gentlemen of wit
Who will guide you quickly over the straightaways.
When you find Love and her in his company,
Never forget to offer greetings from me!   70

[117¹⁷]

Amore e 'l cor gentil sono una cosa

Love and the noble heart are a single thing
(So said wise Guinizelli in his rhyme):
One without the other can have no fling,
As reason and soul are joined forever in time.
Nature creates them when with love it abounds.   5
Love is the sire, his mansion is the heart;
Deep inside he lies in sleep wrapped round;
Sometimes a long time, sometimes soon he starts.

Beauty appears as a lady seeming wise,
Wakening desire from his heavy sleep,   10
Striking the heart through windows of the eyes.
Desire then lasts so long within the deep
It rouses the spirit of Love as best it can.
Thus too a lady is acted on by a man.

¹⁷ Sonnet from the *Vita Nuova*. Strongly indebted to Guinizelli.

[118¹⁸]

Oltre la spera che più larga gira

Beyond the sphere that circles us most wide
Passes a sigh that issues from my heart.
A new intelligence that Love imparts
With tears will be its upward guide.
When it arrives where it most desires,   5
A lady receiving honor it will see,
Shining with a splendor so dazzlingly
The pilgrim spirit will marvel at her fire.

Such he sees. But when he crosses the breach,
I can't comprehend; he talks with subtlety   10
To my mourning heart, which demands his speech.
I know only: he describes that noble lady
Because he often utters, "Beatrice . . ."
That, my dear women, is one thing I can reach.

[119¹⁹]

Ben ti faranno il nodo Salamone

Solomon's knot will soon be wrapping you in,
Bicci Junior, with those precious necks of quail.
Those expensive cuts of mutton will make you wail
Your sins duly recorded on the dead sheepskin.
Your house'll be even closer to St. Simon's Jail,   5
Unless, of course, you make a quick getaway.
But now (I fear) it's just too late to repay
Those debts—unless that appetite should fail.

¹⁸ Final Sonnet of the *Vita Nuova,* affirming the ascension of Beatrice into Paradise.
¹⁹ Debate Poem (*Tenzone*) with Forese Donati. "Solomon's knot" is a symbol of usury. The last line is freely rendered.

They tell me, though, you've got a clever hand.
Well, if it's true, maybe you'll be like new   10
Because you can make a hoist of some thousand grand.
Perhaps this art will ease your gluttony's grief:
You'll pay your debts, and stay in Florence too.
What's better, Bicci? To be glutton or be thief?

CECCO ANGIOLIERI[20]

[120]

S'i' fosse fuoco, arderei 'l mondo

If I were fire, I would burn the world.
If I were wind, I'd buffet it wide.
If I were sea, I'd drown it in swirls.
If God, I'd boot it on the Devil's side.
If I were Pope, what a gay thing I'd be!   5
I'd toss all those Christians into jail.
If Emperor, know what would pleasure me?
To slice off every head from every tail.

If I were Death, I'd go to visit Papa;
If I were Life, I'd bid him fond adieux.   10
And frankly I'd do the same for dear ole Mamma.
If I were Cecco, as I am and cannot choose,
I'd snatch the chicks who are young and happy too,
And all the old ugly broads I would leave to you.

[20] Cecco Angiolieri (*fl.* 1281–1312). Cynical poet of Siena. Member of an important family. Military deeds documented from 1281; known dead in 1313. Wrote only sonnets. Figures as a duped character in *Decameron* IX.4.

[121]

Becchin' amor!

"Becchina, my love!"
                    "What do you want, you lout?"
"Pardon me!"
                    "You don't deserve it a bit."
"Please! O God!"
                    "You're looking all washed-out."
"I'll serve forever—"
                    "What do I get for it?"
"My good faith."
                    "Ha! That you've got in droves."   5
"Always for you."
                    "Peace! I know what's fraud."
"How'd I go wrong?"
                    "A bird told me in the grove."
"Tell me, my love!"
                    "Go! in the wrath of God!"
"Want me to die?"
                    "It'd take a thousand years."
"Ah, you talk bad."
                    "*You* want to teach me the good?"   10
"No. I'll just die."
                    "God, you're a screw-up, dear!"
"God pardon you."
                    "O hell! go—like you should!"
"Ah, if I could . . ."
                    "Shall I lead you by your seat?"
"You've got my heart."
                    "And with torment that I'll keep."

[122]

La Stremità mi richer per figliuolo

Misery calls out to me: "Hi, Sonny!"
I answer back: "How goes it, Mother, there?"
I was bred by a stud named Grief—not funny!—
And Melancholy delivered me from the mare.
My swaddling clothes were woven from a thread   5
That's called Disaster by the common folk.
From the bottoms of my soles up to my head
There's not a thing in me that's not a joke.

When I grew up, to make a restoration,
They gave me a wife; she's the one who yells   10
As far as the starry heavens feel vibrations:
Her yap's a thousand tympanums with bells.
A man whose wife is dead enjoys purgation:
He who takes another goes straight to Hell.

[123²¹]

Dante Alleghier, s'i' so' buon begolardo

Dante, if I'm a big loud-talking cuss,
It's 'cause you've got your sword against my guts;
If I have lunch with someone, you have dinner;
I feed on fat, while lard-sucking makes you thinner;
If I shear out the cloth, you squeeze the carder;   5
If I run at the mouth, you gallop harder;
If I play gentleman, then you're downtrod;
If I'm the man of Rome, then you're a Lombard.

²¹ Debate Poem with Dante.

Okay! thank God at least we know we two
Are both to blame, me as much as you.   10
It's misery or bad sense that makes us run.
But if you want to carry on this fun—
Dante, I'll go until you're in the box;
For I'm the gay gadfly, and you're the ox.

[124]

Accorri, accorri, accorri, uom, a la strada

"Run, run, run, man, out in the streets!"
"Son of a gun, what's wrong?" "I'm robbed."
"Who did it?" "A girl who cuts as neat
As a razor, and leaves you feeling lopped."
"Why didn't you give it to her in the guts?"   5
"Who? Me?" "O hell, man, are you nuts?"
"No! You don't think—" "That's the way it looks.
She might as well have blinded you, you kook.

"Just look at what happens to men with sense!"
"Say it! You're torturing me." "O go with God!"   10
"I'm going—but slow. I'm mourning my expense."
"You're going how?" "With spirit all downtrod."
"Well, take your loss, and worse wherever you go!"
"Who killed me?" "How the hell should I know?"

FOLGORE OF SAN GIMIGNANO[22]

[125]

I' doto voi nel mese de gennaio

In the month of January I will bear
Courtyards with the snap of kindled hay,
Warm rooms with beds of the loveliest array:
Silken sheets and coverlets of vair,
Asti spumante, sugared nuts, and sweets,   5
The finest clothes from Arras and Douai
To ward the chill and bitter blasts away
Of winter wind and rain, of snow and sleet.

We'll go out sometimes in the course of day
And toss some glistening, shiny snowy balls   10
At the little girls who'll follow on our way;
And when we're tired of all those skids and falls,
Back to the court we'll troop in disarray,
And with fine friends make restful festival.

[126[23]]

D'April vi dono la gentil campagna

For April I offer the gentle countryside
All flowering with blossoms bright and fresh,
Fountains of water that never can depress,
Maids and ladies over whom you can preside;

---

[22] Folgore of San Gimignano (*fl.* 1300–1332). Born Giacomo di Michele, but called Folgore (The Splendor) because of his luxurious life-style. Cited for military successes in 1305, 1306. Sonnet to January.

[23] Sonnet to April.

Stallions from Spain, chargers which boldly prance,   5
Company coutured in the latest Parisian style,
Instruments from Germany, lutes and viols
For tunes of old Provence and for the dance.

And all around lie gardens by the score
Where everyone can lounge or wander on,   10
And each will bow with reverence and adore
The noble girl I place the crown upon
Which shines with finer jewels than does the hoard
Of Prester John or the King of Babylon.

LAPO GIANNI[24]

[127]

Amor, eo chero mia donna in domino

Love, I want my lady in my keeping,
The Arno River with finest balsam sweeping,
Silver encrustations on Florentine walls,
Rutted roads paved with finest crystal,
Battlemented citadels looming tall   5
And every Italian sworn to be my friend;
Roadways secure, world peace without an end,
Neighbors who have helping hands to lend,
Weather in every season moderate,
A thousand maids and ladies standing ornate,   10
With love their leading standard against wrong,
Ready both night and morn to join in song;
And gardens of great compass full of fruit,
With every kind of winged thing which toots,

---

[24] Lapo Gianni (*fl.* 1298–1328?). Cited in Number 114, as well as in the *De vulgari*, as one of Dante's closest friends. His lady was Lagia (Alagia or Adalasia). Probably held juridical and political posts.

With quiet canals and places where I can shoot;   15
This way I would be as blessed as Absalom
Or like great Samson or even Solomon;
I'd choose mighty barons for menial things:
All my songs would be sung to viols and strings;
And then to make my heavenly entry sure,   20
I'd ask a life young, healthy, happy, secure,
To last as long as this world of ours endures.

CINO DA PISTOIA[25]

[128]

Io guardo per li prati ogni fior bianco

Through all the fields I search for flowers white
In memory of what caused me such delight
That even sighing I go inquiring for more.
I still remember the white orbs with their sheen
Blending with a cut of brownish green   5
That Love himself once wore
At that time when with Mars and Venus gazing,
His keen-whittled arrow came blazing
Into the middle of my core;
And now when the wind has set the petals swaying,   10
I think of the whiteness of her lovely eyes
Which ignites this excitement that never dies.

[25] Cino da Pistoia (*ca.* 1270–*ca.* 1337). Native of Pistoia who studied law with
Francesco d'Accursio in Bologna and taught in Siena, Perugia, Naples. His legal
writings survive along with numerous poems. Praised by Dante in *De vulgari*.

PETRARCH[26]

[129]

Voi ch'ascoltate in rime sparse il suono

You who hear in scattered rhymes the sound
Of sighs with which I nurtured once my heart
As youthfulness in error made its start—
A different man in part from this man now—
In many styles I weep and turn in mind   5
Among vain hopes and sadness also vain;
If there is one experienced in love's pain,
His pity with his pardon I would find.

Ah, to the masses I see I was but a name
They mouthed for quite a time, and yet   10
Within me now this thought arouses regret:
The fruit of all my vanity is shame,
And penitence, for now the knowledge gleams
That all that delights the world are just brief dreams.

[130]

Padre del ciel, dopo i perduti giorni

Father in heaven, after the squandered days,
After the nights misspent in vanity
With that desire always burning fiercely,
Looking at limbs shaped beautifully to craze—
With your light, may it please that I now turn   5

---

[26] Petrarch: Francesco Petrarca (1304–1374). Italy's most famous medieval lyric poet. Biographies by Morris Bishop and Ernest Hatch Wilkins. Number 129 is the Introduction to the *Canzoniere* or *Songbook*, and the poems follow in chronological order.

To a different life, to tasks of a nobler kind
And leave the nets spread out in vain behind,
Showing the Adversary that he's been spurned.

It's going, Master, into the eleventh year
Since I was bent beneath the yoke of cruelty   10
That heaps on the submissive a direr loss.
My restless thoughts to a better place please steer;
Take pity on my suffering, though unworthy;
Remind me how you hanged upon the Cross.

[131]

Chiare, fresche e dolci acque

1. Waters clear and sweet and fresh
   In which those limbs would lie
   Of her alone who to me was a woman;
   The gentle trunk where she would press—
   Ah, memory's sigh!—   5
   Her flank against it as a column.
   Flowers and grasses as a dress
   Would lightly press
   Against her angel breast;
   The holy air forever at rest   10
   Where Love opened my heart to her loveliness—
   All of you, lend credence
   To these final words of grievance.

2. If it should be my fate
   (And Heaven should enter in)   15
   That Love should close these eyes now welling,
   May some great act of grace
   Bring you this body full of sin,
   While soul runs naked to its place of dwelling.
   Death will seem less distorted   20

If this hope is transported
Into that pass that is ever full of doubt;
A soul that's all worn out
Can find no port with any greater comfort
Or grave with greater quiet   25
To flee the trouble of bones and flesh's riot.

3. The time may yet return
   When that lovely one who's wild
   Comes tamely back to the haunts of former days;
   There on a blesséd morn   30
   Where she first beguiled
   My eyes, let her turn with a fond, desirous gaze
   Searchingly; and, mercy!
   Seeing me stretched adversely
   Among the stones, may Love inspire   35
   Sighs of soft desire
   So that she will get a little pity for me,
   And against Heaven prevail
   As she dries her eyes with her beautiful veil.

4. From pretty branches tumbled   40
   (Sweet to memory)
   A rain that filled her lap with gentle flowers;
   She sat there humbly
   Yet radiant in glory,
   Wearing a coverlet of that loving shower.   45
   Some flowers hemmed her dress,
   Some lay on a golden tress
   Like polished gold with pearl,
   Not seeming the hair of a girl;
   Some fell on earth and some the pool caressed;   50
   One drifted in a twisting disarray,
   Turning, as if to say: here Lord Love holds sway.

5. How many times I heard
   My fearful tongue repeat:
   "This one was born in Paradise for certain!"   55

Her face, her every word,
The sound of her laughter sweet,
Had weighted me with a very heavy burden
Of forgetfulness that brings
Division from tangible things,   60
Hearing myself muttering again:
"How did I get here? When?";
Believing myself in Heaven, not at that spring.
The grass gave such release
That nowhere else can I find an equal peace.   65

6. Song, if you had the embellishments you want,
   You'd bolt with great fastness
   Out of these woods, and run and join the masses.

[132]

Di pensier in pensier, di monte in monte

1. From thought to thought, from mountain unto mountain
   Love guides me; and every road with signs
   I find contrary to a tranquil life.
   On solitary slope, by brook or fountain
   Where shadowed vale between two hills reclines,   5
   There the soul quiets itself from strife,
   And as Love then invites,
   It laughs or cries or fears or feels assured,
   And face, which follows soul wherever it guides,
   Shows upset, which subsides   10
   And in one state of being seldom endures,
   So that one who to such living is inured
   Would say: "He burns. His life is all unsure."

2. Through highest mountains, thickets wild with thorns,
   I find repose; every inhabited place   15

Remains a mortal enemy to my sight.
With every step a novel thought is born
About my lady; the torment is replaced,
Which I forever carry, by delight;
Scarcely have I the might 20
To change this life alternately bitter and sweet
When I say: Love's keeping you in wait
For a time propitiate;
You hate yourself, yet another you will please.
And in this pass I sigh and on I go: 25
"When? And how? And is this really so?"

3. Wherever a hillock or high pine casts its shade
   I sometimes stop, and on a rocky mass
   I shape her lovely face within my mind.
   When I come to myself, my breast is bathed 30
   From passion, and I cry out: "O! alas!
   What have you come to? What have you left behind?"
   But as I hold inclined
   My thoughts upon the image I first made,
   With steady gazing my own self disappears 35
   And then as Love comes near
   The soul in its own delusion is swept away.
   Everywhere the beautiful one I adore
   I see; if this is error, I want nothing more.

4. Many a time (although now who will trust me?) 40
   I have seen her image upon the water appear,
   In the trunk of a beech, or where the grasses sway,
   Or in a white cloud, so that Leda would agree
   Her daughter Helen's beauty could not come near,
   Like a star that Sun eclipses with a ray 45
   The wilder the place
   Or the more deserted the strand where I chance to be,
   The more beautiful I cast her forth enshrouded.
   Then when the truth's unclouded,
   The sweet deception, I sit continually 50

As cold as stone, dead rock on living rock,
Shaped like a man who thinks and weeps and talks.

5. Where the shadows of other mountains never reach,
Ever upward toward the greatest, highest peak
A strong desire pulls which I can't resist;   55
Then as my eyes begin to measure the breach
Of losses, I cry, but even as I weep
I lighten this heart beset with its heavy mist;
My thoughts will not desist
From dwelling on the space that separates me,   60
For she is always far, yet ever near.
Softly within I hear:
"What are you up to now, wretch? It could be
That somewhere too your absence she is grieving."
And with this thought, my soul begins its breathing.   65

6. Song, go beyond that mount
Where the sky lies in happy serenity;
You'll see me by some flowing fount
Where the air wafts fragrantly
From the fresh-scented laurel tree.   70
There is my heart, and she who stole it from me;
Here you will see just a mere effigy.

[133]

S'amor non è, che dunque è quel ch'io sento

If love is not, what is this then I feel?
But if love is, O God, what then is he?
If good, where come these mortal jabs of steel?
If bad, why then this wondrous misery?
If I burn freely, why all this lamenting?   5
If it's forced on me, what can cries avail?

O living death, delight that quickly pales,
How can you master me without consenting?

And if I do consent, I wrongly feel the pain.
On contrary winds I sense the frail bark's terror   10
Blown out on open seas without a rudder,
Light in my knowledge, heavy in my error,
Myself not knowing what it is I'd gain:
The winter warms me; in midst of summer I shudder.

[134*]

Or che'l ciel e la terra e'l vento tace

The earth and wind are quiet now, the sky,
Sleep bridles beast and bird without a sound,
Night leads his starry chariot on its round
And Ocean waveless in his bedding lies:
I see, I think, I burn, I also cry   5
As sight of my upsetter brings sweet woe;
War is my steady state, with wrathful throe;
Only the thought of her will pacify.

Thus from a limpid, living fountain's poured
This fare of bittersweet on which I feed;   10
The same hand heals that causes laceration.
Still that this martyrdom move ever forward,
A thousand times a day I'm born, I bleed;
So far am I removed from my salvation.

* Original text appears in Section X, p. 397.

[135²⁷]

Rotta è l'alta Colonna, e'l verde Lauro

The Column's broken, the Laurel laid to rest
That granted shade upon my weary mind;
I've lost the thing I never hope to find
From Boreas to Auster, East to West.
Death, you've taken away my double treasure   5
That made me walk happily, head ever higher;
No oriental gem, no land or empire
Can bring her back—no, nor golden measure.

But if great destiny has given consent,
What can I do except keep feeling low,   10
Eyes forever wet, head forever bent?
O life of ours, so beautiful in show,
How speedily in one morning lies expired
Gain for many a year with pain acquired!

[136]

Gli occhi di ch'io parlai sì caldamente

The eyes of which I spoke with such warm love,
The arms, the hands, the feet, the very face
That caused a half of me to stand apace
And set me from the masses in remove;
The golden, curly hair that once she tossed,   5
The angelic sparkle as she smiled in mirth
That made for me a paradise on earth
Are now just dust, with all sensation lost.

²⁷ Sonnet on the deaths of Laura (the Laurel), April 6, 1348, and of his patron,
Cardinal Giovanni Colonna (the Column), July 3, 1348.

And yet I live. This rouses grief and wrong,
For I'm without the light I love so well,   10
A craftless raft cast upon fortune's swell.
Well, let this be an end to romantic song.
Dry is the vein where once my genius surged;
Turned is my zither into the key of dirge.

[137]

Quel rosignuol che sì soave piagne

The nightingale who now so soft complains
Perhaps the deaths of children or a mate
Makes sky and field with sweetness reverberate
With the sound of her poignant, pity-filled refrain.
All the night long it seems she's at my side   5
And my sad fate she utters with each breath;
To myself alone my sorrow I confide,
For I thought goddesses were exempt from Death.

How easy to fool oneself who feels secure!
Those two pretty lights, sunlike as they penetrated—   10
Who thought they'd ever lie like earth, obscure?
And now I realize my savage fate
Wills that I live and learn with bitter tears:
Nothing down here endures and still endears.

[138]

I'vo piangendo i miei passati tempi

I go weeping my time that now is past
Which I squandered in the love of a mortal thing,

Without rising to flight, though I had the wings
Perhaps to cut some example that would last.
You who survey my vile, worthless evil,   5
King of the heavens, deathless, invisible,
Help this soul unsettled and too fragile,
And all its lacks with your great mercy fill,

So that if I suffer warfare or a tempest
I'll die in peace and port; and if my stance   10
Was vain, at least my ending will be blessed.
In my little life that's left, I pray: advance
Your hand to me, as even in death I grope.
You know full well in others I have no hope.

GIOVANNI BOCCACCIO[28]

[139]

Or sei salito, caro signor mio

My most dear lord, now you have arisen
Into the realm where every soul awaits
Selection to be one of God's consecrates,
After departing from this earthly prison.
You're in the place desire pulled you toward,   5
Where you can cast your eyes on your Lauretta,
Who's sitting with my beautiful Fiammetta
Basking in the company of the Lord.

With Cino and Sennuccio and with Dante
You're living now, assured of eternal rest,   10

---

[28] Giovanni Boccaccio (1313–1375). Author of the *Decameron;* the first real master
of Italian prose. Lament on the Death of Petrarch, in sonnet form. Fiammetta was
Boccaccio's lady. Line 9 refers to Cino da Pistoia (see No. 128), and Petrarch's good
friend Sennuccio del Bene.

Studying things for us too far above.
If I was dear in this world where value's scanty,
O draw me after! let me too be blessed
With the sight of her who kindled my first love.

[VII]
NORTH FRENCH SONGS

In northern France, lyric poetry took a very different turn from that in Italy. From the start the North French had a vital tradition of songs of the people: anonymous Spinning Songs, Workers' Songs, Spring Dances, and Songs of the Ill-Married. This popular bent, with its emphasis upon things of this world, is an important element in North French literature from the early folk songs to the writings of François Villon.

When formal love poetry was written, as by the *trouvère* or troubadour Gace Brulé, the imprint of Provence was strong upon it, for the South French tradition had already developed fully. The basic situation of a suffering lover, an almighty and often uncooperative lady (and sometimes, but not always, a jealous husband) is the same in both. Unlike the Provençal poems, however, the North French lyrics tend to be devoid of metaphysical overtones. If service is mentioned, it is the service for a lady-lord and not for a lady-goddess; if joy is mentioned, it is usually secular fun and not religious ecstasy. In Number 147, for example, the situation is clearly social. We can see the girl in stanza 2 aligned with great demeanor, good company, beauty, and good sense; she is opposed to villainy. The reference is clearly courtly. Furthermore, we can detect a movement toward secular abstraction. One could easily capitalize the qualities cited above and create a social war, a *psychomachia* of the court, exactly as Jean de Meun and Guillaume de Lorris did in their *Roman de la rose*. In France the court takes precedence over the cathedral; the Gothic spirit of organization overcomes Romanesque suggestibility; and the madame of high society is more evident than the Madonna of another world.

Unfortunately the worldliness of North French poetry tended to work against its development. Rutebeuf stands out for his vigorous, Marcabrun-like morality, but the poets around him, who are not represented here, are jaded and effeminate. In the 1300s a revival took place under the leadership of Guillaume de Machaut and Eustache Deschamps. Although both men are greater musicians than poets, they kept the lyric alive by casting it in the highly musical form of the *rondeau*, as well as in the ever-popular ballade or chanson. Deschamps' indictment of Bohemia or his lovely praise of the city of Paris are sudden intrusions of realism into a highly artificial poetic world. When compared to her male counterparts, for example, Christine de Pisan sounds vigorous.

The dissolution of the tradition can best be seen in Charles d'Orléans, whose poetry is both graceful and fragile. Although his melancholy is tempered by the elegant form in which it is cast, it nevertheless verges upon morbidness. The artificial is so apparent in his work that nature itself seems almost man-made: the scenes in Number 163 are tailored by a designer of high fashion; the landscape in Number 164 is laid out by interior decorators. In short, the *haut monde* is omnipresent. Even religion is reduced to social terms in the graceful and brilliant Number 170. Yet at this point, despite the skill and mastery, one feels that the medieval sensibility is exhausted. We are ready for a change.

This shift occurred in the writings of François Villon. His *Last Will* presents the brawling, tumultuous world of Paris outside the elegant salon and the dining hall. When we put Charles and François side by side, we see the stirrings of future revolution: Charles's poetry, on the one hand, is aristocratic, far removed from the people and their needs; François', on the other, is a howl of the lower classes who are verging on degradation. For all that he may sound like a Renaissance humanist, Villon is as medieval as Duke William of Aquitaine. He writes prayers for his mother, as well as love songs to his whore-mistress; even in the face of death, he does not despair, but prays movingly to his God.

North French literature never produced the crowning achievements of medieval culture that were created in Italy, but in its adherence to the human condition, it helped to prepare the way for the modern world.

ANONYMOUS[1]

[140]

Voulez vous que je vous chant

1. Would you like it if I sing
   A song of love enchanting?
     One never made by a churl,
   No, but by a knight off parade
   In the spangled olive tree's shade   5
     In the arms of a little girl.

2. She wore a little kirtle of linen
   And a tunic made of white ermine,
     And a silken gown.
   Shoes were shod out of mayflower,   10
   Stockings came from an iris bower
     Tumbling tightly down.

3. She wore a beltlet made of leaf
   That grew all green when the rain was brief,
     With golden buttons riven;   15
   Her little purse was made of love,
   Flowers dangled down from above—
     For love it had been given.

4. She went on a mule that slowly trod,
   Whose feet were all with silver shod,   20
     His seat with gold inlaid.
   On his crupper in the flanks
   Were three rose trees arranged in ranks
     To bring her shade.

---

[1] Reverdie, a song with fantastic imagery, probably related to May Day or spring rites.

I

5. Thus she travels throughout the land;   25
   Chevaliers wait everywhere on her hand,
      Saluting with gentility!
   "Pretty girl, where were you born?"
   "I am from France, whom no man scorns,
      And from nobility.   30

6. "The nightingale gave me siring,
   Who on the branch is always choiring
      In the dells deep.
   A siren-mother gave birth to me
   Whose cry rings over the salty sea   35
      On a cliff steep."

7. "Beautiful, you have a very great line!
   Your parentage is truly fine,
      Your pedigree.
   To God our Father above, I pray   40
   That you may be given some day
      To marry me."

[141²]

Trois sereurs seur rive mer

1. Three sisters down by the side of the sea
      Are singing clearly;
   The youngest one has brownish hair and
   Cares for a brownish man:
   "I am dark, so naturally   5
   A darkish man should go with me."

2. Three sisters down by the side of the sea
      Are singing clearly:

---

² Spinning Song (*Chanson de toile*).

The smallest one is sobbing
For her boyfriend Robin   10
  In despair:
"O in the woods
You got my goods—
O take me there,
  Take me there."   15

3. Three sisters down by the side of the sea
   Are singing clearly;
The eldest one declares:
"A man should always put
His tender maiden up above,   20
And always take good care
To guard her love."

[142³]

Quant vient en mai, que l'on dit as lons jors

1. When the time is May, and the days are lengthening,
The Franks of France ride from the court of the King;
Raynáud rides in the front ranks, up in the fore,
And passes beneath the mansion of Erembor;
He doesn't deign to glance to the rail above—   5
  Ah, Raynaud, my love!

2. Fair Erembor in the sunny window glowing
Holds on her knees her colored bits of sewing;
She sees coming from the court of the King the Franks
With Raynaud astride in the foremost of the ranks.   10
She breaks into speech, cannot restrain the mind:
  "Ah, Raynaud of mine!

³ Spinning Song.

3. "Raynaud my love, I've already seen the day
   When if you passed our tower on your way
   Without some word from me, you'd have been all sad."   15
   "Yes, emperor's daughter, but you've been bad.
   You took another man; you gave me the shove."
       Ah, Raynaud my love!

4. "Raynaud, good sir, now listen to my complaint:
   I swear on a hundred virgins, by all the saints,   20
   With thirty women who with me will take their stand—
   Never, except for you, have I loved a man.
   Here, take this oath-pledge; then a kiss from me.
       Ah, Raynaud ami!"

5. The Count Raynaud now mounts upon the stair.   25
   Blond and tightly curling was his hair;
   His shoulders were broad, and yet his waist was slim;
   No land had ever seen a lusty man like him.
   When he sees Erembor, he sheds a tear—
       Ah, Raynaud my dear!   30

6. The Count Raynaud has mounted to the tower.
   He sits upon a couch with colored flowers.
   Beside him sits the beautiful Erembor.
   Their love goes on again as it had before:
       Ah, Raynaud amor!   35

[143⁴]

Lou samedi a soir, fat la semainne

1. On Saturday eve, when the week was through
   Gayette and Orior, sisters two,
   Walked hand in hand to bathe in the spring.

⁴ Spinning Song.

The wind gusts, the branches bend;
All sleep well who have a friend.   5

2. On the road from the market comes Gerald the fair;
His eyes seize on Gayette standing there;
He grabs her in his arms, holds her tight.
The wind gusts, the branches bend;
All sleep well who have a friend.   10

3. "Draw your water, Orior. Take it home.
You know the path where we always come.
I'll stay with Gerald, who holds me tight."
The wind gusts, the branches bend;
All sleep well who have a friend.   15

4. Orior goes off, looking pale and depressed;
Her eyes are weeping; sighs pour from her breast,
For Gayette her sister isn't with her there.
The wind gusts, the branches bend;
All sleep well who have a friend.   20

5. "O no!" says Orior, "I was born to fail!
I have lost my little sister down in the dale!
Gerald the youngster will take her to his place."
The wind gusts, the branches bend;
All sleep well who have a friend.   25

6. Gerald the youngster and Gayette go down
The straight road that leads direct to the town;
They arrive there, and right away they are wed.
The wind gusts, the branches bend;
All sleep well who have a friend.   30

[144⁵]

Por quoi me bat mes maris

1. Why is my husband always whacking
   Poor little me?
   I never give·him lying quacking,
   Don't go around always squalling
   Except when my gentleman friend comes calling   5
   On the QT.
   Why is my husband always whacking
   Poor little me?

2. Why is my husband always whacking
   Poor little me?   10
   If he won't let me lead the life
   Of a good and trusted happy wife,
   Then I'll arrange for him the strife
   Of cuckoldry!
   Why is my husband always whacking   15
   Poor little me?

3. Ah yes, now the course is laid:
   With a vengeance I'll be paid:
   With my lover I'll parade
   Stark nakedly.   20
   Why is my husband always whacking
   Poor little me?

⁵ Song of the Ill-Married (*Chanson de mal-mariée*), which celebrates cuckoldry.

RICHARD THE LION-HEARTED[6]

[145]

Ja nuls homs pris ne dira sa raison

1. A man imprisoned can never speak his mind
   As cleverly as those who do not suffer,
   But through his song he can some comfort find.
   I have a host of friends, poor the gifts they offer.
   Shame on them if this ransoming should trail   5
       Into a second year in jail!

2. This they know well, my barons and my men,
   English, Norman, Gascon, and Poitevin,
   What I'd leave of my property in prison!
   O I'm not saying this to cast derision,   10
       But still I'm here in jail!

3. Here is a truth I know that can be told:
   Dead men and prisoners have neither parents nor friends,
   No one to offer up his silver and gold.
   It matters to me, but much more to my men,   15
   For after my death, they'll be bitterly assailed
       Because I'm so long in jail!

4. No wonder if I have a grieving heart
   When I see my land torn by its lord asunder:
   If he'll recall the pact in which we took part   20
   And remember the pledges we vowed we'd both live under,
   Truly within the year, without a fail,
       I'd be out of jail!

---

[6] Richard the Lion-Hearted or Coeur-de-Lion (1157–1199). King of England
from 1189 to 1199. Son of Henry II and Eleanor of Aquitaine. Played a dramatic
but disastrous role in the crusades; imprisoned in Germany, causing the payment of
an enormous ransom. Composed his Complaint from Prison in North French.
Swashbuckling and romantic, but ineffectual as a ruler. Killed in a meaningless raid
on a second-rate castle in France. Envoi omitted from poem.

5. This they know, the Angevins and Tourains,
   Those bachelors there who are strong and own a lot,   25
   While I'm encumbered here in another's hands;
   They loved me lots, but now they don't love a jot;
   Over the plains I don't see a piece of mail
       Although I'm still in jail!

6. I've loved and I love still my companions true,   30
   The men of Cahiu and the men of Porcherain,
   But tell me, song, if they still love me too,
   For never to them was I double-faced or vain:
   They're villains if my lands they now assail—
       Since I am here in jail!   35

GACE BRULÉ[7]

[146]

Grant pechié fait qui de chanter me prie

1. He who begs me to sing commits a sin,
   For it's not right at all that songs outpour,
   For not one day of my life would I begin
   A song unless Fine Love composed the score.
   Yet at their bidding, I will give them more,   5
   Acting like one whose habits make him callow.
   His singing is often slick, but very shallow.

2. I never said that Love had stealthily
   Departed my fine heart; why, dead I'd be
   But evil gossips and bastards full of envy   10
   Have worked me wrong, that's plain to see.

[7] Gace Brulé (*ca.* 1170–1212). Nobleman from Champagne, associated with Eleanor's daughter by Louis VII, Marie of Champagne. About seventy poems survive. A second envoi omitted from Number 147.

Often they make me remember tearfully.
God never invented any worse divorce
Than one from joy and sweet-hearted intercourse.

3. I know, indeed, that if my loyal friend   15
   Would grant one pretty look with joy replete
   Then in my heart suddenly would end
   Sadness and hurt; but a false, deceiving cheat
   Has kept me too long unpaid; she metes
   Only pain and grievance as her pay,   20
   But with some effort I've snatched my heart away.

4. When I recall that gentle company
   And all the joys that made me feel so well,
   Nothing in the world seems as bad off as me,
   For my heart has suffered everything it's felt;   25
   And so I say and think: ah, what the hell!
   For Love would like to lighten this sad person,
   But instead, every day the sorrows only worsen.

5. A fickle heart and a constant, shifting madness
   Have caused many loyal lovers agony.   30
   I used to think that after suffering sadness,
   I'd have her joyous presence and she'd have me;
   But those gossips seem to work so cleverly
   That my hopes they've totally busted
   Of ever getting the joy in which I trusted.   35

6. This outrage was wrought by Pride and Villainy ·
   Acting behind the most appealing face
   Which ever became a mortal's enemy:
   A woman abounding in beauty and great grace.
   It seems a marvel whenever I retrace   40
   That great beauty that caused my faith's withering.
   And with no comfort will she bring delivering.

[147]

De bien amer grant joie atent

1. Great joy from loving well I am awaiting,
   For this desire is very strong in me;
   And here's a truth that I find worth the stating:
   Love rules with such great majesty
   Double rewards it is always compensating   5
   To those who will treat it loyally,
   But a man who won't consent to serve
   Will find himself for nothing quite unnerved.

2. She is a person of great demeanor
   And she lends good company;   10
   She's wise among men who are meaner,
   The girl who seized control of me.
   Good sense and beauty in her are keener
   And she despises all villainy.
   The only thing that upsets my weal   15
   Is that she doesn't know how I feel.

3. Never did I commit a sin
   Against Love voluntarily.
   At its command, I have always been
   And will be until life ends for me.   20
   He is one of the most envious men,
   The one whom Love deserts completely.
   My lady has taught this lesson to me:
   Honor comes from loving loyally.

4. Great Love will never mortify;   25
   The more it kills, the better you get;
   I would much prefer to live and die
   Than one day simply to forget.
   Lady, you could grant easily
   The great joy for which I fret.   30

The only things that make me sigh
Are the jealous deeds the jealous ply.

5. Lady, none of the others is your peer.
   Pretty and good, rightful receiver of lauds,
   You should never bend your ear   35
   To those false and depraved bawds
   Who with lies and guesses engineer
   To make lovers all distraught.
   And afterward they don't even know
   Exactly where they ought to go.   40

6. Lady, from you I'd never conceal
   Any desire or any thought.
   I love you with a love that's real,
   More than any other creature wrought.
   I want to be your servant leal,   45
   And for this end I feel so fraught
   That, without some mercy, I'm all undone;
   Far away or near, I can't go on.

7. Cens de Blois, unless like this you love,
   You can never soar in value above.   50

LE CHÂTELAIN DE COUCY[8]

[148]

La douce vois du rossignol sauvage

1. The sweet voice of the nightingale in dells
   That I hear night and day in trilling call
   Softens my heart again and sends me calm;

[8] Le Châtelain de Coucy (d. 1203?). Probably Guy de Thurotte, who is said to
have died in 1203 en route to the Fourth Crusade.

Then I've desire in singing to outswell.
Truly I should sing, since it makes fervent   5
Her to whom my heart stands ever feal;
I should have great joy, indeed great weal
If she would let me join her as her servant.

2. Never to her have I proved fickle, untrue
   (A thing that should put me in good standing);   10
   I love and serve and worship without bending,
   And yet my thoughts are things I must eschew,
   For her beauty puts me in such disarray
   That before her language always ceases;
   And I dare not regard her gentle features,   15
   So much I hate to tear my eyes away.

3. Firmly I've set my heart upon her serving;
   I think of no one else—God grant me joy!
   For never did Tristan, that potion-drinking boy,
   Love as loyally without a swerving.   20
   I put all there: body, heart, desire,
   Feeling and knowing—maybe like one who's crazed,
   And still I fear that as I course my days
   My service to her and loving might expire.

4. I will not admit I acted foolishly,   25
   Not even if for her I had to die;
   For the world finds none like her, pretty or wise,
   No one else who can equally pleasure me.
   I love my eyes: they made me see her;
   After I saw her, heart as hostage lay   30
   In her keeping for a very long stay,
   And even today, it refuses to leave her.

5. Song, go with this message over there
   Where I dare not go or bend my steps,
   For I fear the wicked people's depths   35
   Who guess before things even appear

The goods of love. God give them ill,
For to many they show ire and spite,
And day by day I suffer this plight,
For I'm forced to obey them against my will.   40

THIBAUT IV, COUNT OF CHAMPAGNE, KING OF NAVARRE[9]

[149]

Por mau tens ne por gelee

1. Not for icy wind or storm
   Neither for the morning chill,
   Nor for anything yet born
   Will I ever abandon my will
       To love the thing that's mine   5
   For I love her much indeed
   With a love that's very fine,
           Valara!

2. She's pretty, blonde, and nicely hued;
   I like the way that she attracts.   10
   O God! the thing that I pursued
   You granted exactly as I asked!
       If she is ever denied
       To me, I'll beg and pray
       Until the day I die—   15
           Valara!

---

[9] Thibaut IV, Count of Champagne, King of Navarre (1201–1253). Acceded to the kingship through his uncle in 1234. Led an unsuccessful crusade. Many of his poems believed written for Blanche of Castile. About sixty works survive. The fifth stanza is omitted here.

3. Lady, in your bailey
   My body and life I've placed.
   By God, please don't assail me!
   Where fine hearts stand with pride effaced,   20
     Mercy and grace
     A man should find
     To bring him solace.
       Valara!

4. Lady, do me a courtesy!   25
   May it please you to impart
   These words for the sake of me:
   My pretty, gentle sweetheart,
     I dare to name you,
     For the love of another   30
     Will never defame you.
       Valara!

RUTEBEUF[10]

[150]

Empereeur et roi et conte

Emperors and kings and counts
And dukes and princes, who hear recounts
Of diverse tales for your delight
Of men who always seemed to fight
Way back then for the Holy Church,   5
Tell me now the way you'd work

---

[10] Rutebeuf (*ca.* 1230–*ca.* 1285). North France's moral poet. Left more than fifty pieces, including a play, *The Miracle of Theophilus,* with a Faustian theme. Rather prolix when compared to Marcabrun, whom he resembles. From Champagne, but lived in Paris and elsewhere. This selection from his Complaint for the Crusade omits several lines.

Your way into Paradise.
Those men before paid the price
Through martyrdom and through great pain,
If you listen to the epic strain,   10
That they suffered here as earthly men.
See now the time! God comes again
With outstretched arms, bloodily drenched,
God who for your very sake quenched
The fires of Hell and Purgatory.   15
Well, let's begin a brand-new story!
Serve your God with well-placed wrath,
For he is now showing you the path
Unto his kingdom and his realm,
Which are now being overwhelmed.   20
Therefore dispose all your affection
On avenging him and on protection
Of the Holy Blesséd Promised Land
Which in great tribulation stands
Almost lost (O God take heed!)   25
Unless to assist it, at once you speed. . . .

GUILLAUME DE MACHAUT[11]

[151]

De toutes fleurs n'avoit, et de tous fruis

1. There is no fruit within my bower,
   No flower except for a single rose;
   All the rest have been devoured

---

[11] Guillaume de Machaut (*ca.* 1295–1377). Master musician. Author of long *dits* or narrative poems that influenced Chaucer. Worked for John of Luxemburg, who was King of Bohemia, as secretary. Buried in the cathedral of Reims, where he served as canon. This poem is a ballade.

By Fortune, who now fierce opposes
   This sweet flower,   5
Its scent and color to overpower;
But if I see it picked or pressed,
Another one I'll never possess.

2. Ah, Fortune, you're a gulf, a pit,
   Which tries to swallow any man who thinks   10
He can follow your false law, for it
Is an ever unsure, deceptive thing.
   Your honor, laugh, and gladness
Are really nothing but tears and sadness.
If your deceits wither her rosiness,   15
Another one I'll never possess.

3. The virtue that my flower encloses
Does not stem from your fickle ways,
For Nature it is who makes the roses
And then donates them straightaway: 20
   I doubt your power
To kill the worth and value of my flower.
Let her be mine. But nonetheless—
Another one I'll never possess.

[152¹²]

Blanche com lys, plus que rose vermeille

White as a lily, redder than a rose,
More splendid than a ruby oriental,
Your beauty I regard; no equal shows
White as a lily, redder than a rose.

¹² Rondeau.

I am so ravished, my heart knows no repose   5
Until I serve you, a lover fine and gentle,
White as a lily, redder than a rose
More splendid than a ruby oriental.

[153¹³]

Se par amours n'amiez autrui ne moy

If for your love you took no one, not me,
My grief that's great would be a lesser thing,
For love creates a sure expectancy
Unless for your love you took no one, not me.

But when I see you love and you desert me,   5
It's worse than death. And so this word I bring:
If for your love you took no one, not me,
My grief that's great would be a lesser thing.

EUSTACHE DESCHAMPS¹⁴

[154]

O Socrates plains de philosophie

O Socrates, full of philosophy,
Anglus in practice, Seneca ethical,
Great Ovid in your poetry,

¹³ Rondeau.
¹⁴ Eustache Deschamps (1346–*ca.* 1407). Follower of Machaut, who may have been his uncle. Served Charles VI during the Hundred Years War. Wrote more than one thousand ballades like this Ballade to Chaucer, of which only one of three strophes is presented. Anglus in line 2 is an eponymous hero based on the French word for England, "*Angleterre.*" The sense in line 9 is difficult.

Lively in speech, wisely rhetorical,
Most high eagle who by your theory   5
Illuminate Aeneas' domain,
The Isle of Giants, Brutus' plain
Sown with your flowers and your rosy plants;
You taught those ignorant of romance,
Noble Geoffrey Chaucer, translator grand! . . .   10

[155[15]]

Qui aime bien, il a peu de repos

1. He who loves well has little peacefulness;
   Of his love he always stands in dread;
   He shakes and trembles, loses bone and flesh;
   Fright keeps his heart and mind in evil stead.
   He fears and groans, never knows peace in bed.   5
   This a true lover feels for his *amie;*
   Always he tracks, probes, and twists the head.
   Never did True Love live without Jealousy.

2. Still we must not give her an evil name,
   Not call her a false, old, greedy lout,   10
   As many do who foolishly hand her blame,
   For if she were proud and wouldn't suffer a bout,
   Love long ago would have snuffed her out;
   Instead, he holds her in his company
   As his shield, his loyal servant, and his scout.   15
   Never did True Love live without Jealousy.

3. Who doesn't love is always from her far,
   For no one cares for a thing he'd be without;
   Therefore Love and Jealousy are par;
   Lady and Lover—each the other doubts,   20

---

[15] Ballade on Jealousy.

And that's sure sign they're on the royal route
Of True Amour. For a hating man won't be
Full of Jealousy. Lovers, don't throw her out!
Never did True Love live without Jealousy.

[156¹⁶]

Poux, puces, puor et pourceaux

Lice and fleas and swine and reeks—
These are Bohemia's native stuff;
Bread and salt-fish, weather gruff,
Pepper, aging cabbage, and leeks,
Meat that's smoked till it's black and tough;   5
Lice and fleas and swine and reeks.

Twenty mouths from two bowls stuffed,
Drinking beer of a bitter brew,
Bedrooms with straw and dung astrew,
Lice and fleas and swine and reeks;   10
These are Bohemia's native stuff,
Bread and salt-fish, weather gruff.

[157¹⁷]

Quant j'ai la terre et mer avironnee

1. When you've circled earth and sea,
   And been wherever man can be,
   Jerusalem, Egypt, Alexandria,

¹⁶ Rondeau on Bohemia.
¹⁷ Ballade to Paris. Third stanza omitted.

Galilee, Damascus, Syria,
Cairo, Babylonia, Tartary, 5
   And all the ports they have there
Where sugars and all spices are sold,
Cloth of silk and drapes of gold,
Something better the Frenchmen hold—
   For Paris is beyond compare. 10

2. Crowned over other cities she reigns,
   Fountain of sense, center for brains,
   Nicely placed on the River Seine,
   With orchards, woods, and open plains,
   With every good that mankind claims 15
      And more than you can find elsewhere.
   Strangers love her the very first day
   Because she's always lighthearted and gay;
   They'll find no equal when they go away,
      For Paris is beyond compare. 20

CHRISTINE DE PISAN[18]

[158]

Se souvent vais au moustier

If I often go to chapel,
It's to see the Maiden who
Is as fresh as the rose that's new.

Why should those others babble?
Is it really some great news 5
If I often go to chapel?

[18] Christine de Pisan (*ca.* 1364–1431?). Native of Venice whose father was chief physician to Charles V of France. Grew up at the French court. Widowed at age 25, she supported herself by writing. Fond of feminist causes; idolized Joan of Arc. Died in a convent. Wrote rondeaux, as here, and ballades, which follow.

There's no road that I will travel
Unless she will advise me;
They are fools to criticize me
If I often go to chapel. 10

[159]

Ce mois de mai tout se resjoie

1. This month of May all is joy,
   Except for me, who am full of woe;
   For I don't have my long-held boy
   And I weep with a voice that's low.
   I had a love that made me glow, 5
   But now he's staying far from me.
   Alas! come back, come soon, *ami!*

2. In this month when all turns green,
   Let us go sporting in the park
   Or hear the nightingale who preens 10
   Or listen to the warbling lark.
   You know where. If you'll just hark
   To a voice that whispers lovingly,
   "Alas! come back, come soon, *ami!*"

3. For in this month Love's little boy 15
   Gathers in prey and he commands
   Every lover to find some joy,
   Every lady with her man;
   No one should linger with single hand,
   Night or day, it seems to me. 20
   Alas! come back, come soon, *ami!*

4. This heart of mine for your love grieves,
   Alas! come back, come soon, *ami!*

[160]

Ha! le plus doulz qui jamais soit formé

1. Ah, the gentlest man who was ever framed,
   In talk and conversation ever glad,
   The paragon by everyone acclaimed,
   The best lover a woman ever had!
   For my true heart, a repast to devour,   5
   Most savory desire of any I hold dear,
   My one beloved, my paradise, my bower,
   Most perfect pleasure upon which eyes can peer—
   Your sweetness only causes warlike havoc here.

2. Your sweetness truly in a havoc came   10
   Upon my heart which never thought to be
   In such a plight, but suddenly the flame
   Of great desire lit it so recklessly
   It would have died, had Sweet Thought not shown face.
   Souvenir too upon heart's couch appears.   15
   We lie and lock you round in thought's embrace;
   But when I realize that not one kiss is near,
   Your sweetness only causes warlike havoc here.

3. My sweet friend, whom I love with all my heart,
   There's not one thought of ever throwing away   20
   Your handsome look, which became a part
   Enclosed within; nothing could ever efface
   The sound of your voice or the gracious touch
   Of those gentle hands which I hold dear,
   That like to feel and to explore so much!   25
   But when I can't see you, when you're not near,
   Your sweetness only causes warlike havoc here.

4. Handsome and fine, who's come to make heart's seizure,
   Never forget me; that one wish I hold dear;

For when I can't look upon you at my leisure, 30
Your sweetness only causes warlike havoc here.

CHARLES D'ORLÉANS[19]

[161]

Dedens mon Livre de Pensee

Within the Book of My Meditation
I found my heart industriously
Writing Grief's True History
Complete with tearful illuminations,

Blotting out the once pleasant sketch 5
Of much beloved happiness,
Within the Book of My Meditation.

Ah, where did he find this theme?
Heavy drops of sweat now stream
Down from him as he keeps expending 10
Pain on this task that's never ending
Within the Book of My Meditation.

[19] Charles d'Orléans (1394–1465). Son of Louis d'Orléans, the brother of King
Charles VI. Captured by the British at Agincourt in 1415 and imprisoned in England
for twenty-five years, where most of his poems were written. Married Marie of
Clèves and spent his final years at Blois, where he entertained many poets, including
Villon. Master of rondeaux (Nos. 161–165, 167–169) and ballades (No. 166).

[162]

Allez vous en, allez, allez

O go away, away, away!
Melancholy, Grief, and Strife.
Think that you'll rule me all my life
The way you've done in other days?

I promise: thus it will not be.   5
Reason will gain the mastery.
Away, away! O go away,
Melancholy, Grief, and Strife!

And if you ever do come back,
I pray that God may send a pox   10
On all your wretched, cursed pack,
And stifle all that gives you life.
O go away, away, away!
Melancholy, Grief, and Strife.

[163*]

Le temps a laissié son manteau

Time has laid aside his cape
Of wind and cold and rain,
And puts on vestments once again
All in brilliant sunshine draped.

There is no beast, there is no bird   5
Who does not sing or cry these words:
"Time has laid aside his cape."

  * Original text appears in Section X, p. 398.

Rivers, brooks, and all the springs
Carry in lovely livery
Cuts of silvery jewelry,   10
Each dressed in his brand-new things—
Time has laid aside his cape.

[164]

Les fourriers d'Esté sont venus

The furnishing men of Summer have come
To ready up his dwelling place.
They've fastened all his carpets down
With flowers and grass interlaced.

His velvet rugs extended stand   5
In grassy green throughout the land,
The furnishing men of Summer have come.

A heart with sorrow wearisome—
Thank God!—will soon be hale and gay.
Take to the road, O go away,   10
Winter! you can no longer stay,
The furnishing men of Summer have come.

[165]

Les en voulez vous garder

Would you truly try to prevent
Running rivers from rushing by,
Cranes that circle in the sky
Would you gather into nets?

Just to dream of such a try 5
Causes me astonishment;
Would you truly try to prevent
Running rivers from rushing by?

Let the time go brushing by
At Lady Fortune's commandment; 10
And all those other steady events
You never really can turn awry
Would you truly try to prevent?

[166]

En la forest d'Ennuyeuse Tristesse

1. In the Forest of Troubled Sadness
   One day as I happened to pass alone,
   I met the Goddess of Loving Gladness,
   Who called to me, saying, "Where are you going?"
   I said that because of Fortune's throws 5
   I'd been exiled long among these trees,
   So that my name now could only be
   The Man Deranged Who Knows Not Where He Goes.

2. She laughed, and with great humbleness
   Replied: "My friend, if I just knew 10
   Why you've fallen into this distress,
   I'd gladly do everything I could for you,
   For I put you on the road a while ago
   Toward Every-Pleasure. Who sent you astray?
   It makes me unhappy now to survey 15
   The Man Deranged Who Knows Not Where He Goes."

3. "Alas!" said I, "my sovereign Princess,
   You know my story; what more can I tell?

It's Death who did it, making crude redress;
He took away that thing I loved too well   20
Who was the source of all my many hopes,
Leading me ever onward as my guide;
Nobody called me, with her at my side,
The Man Deranged Who Knows Not Where He Goes.

4. "I'm blind. The road, the road is—where?   25
I've wandered tipping, tapping here and there,
With just a stick, the pathway to disclose;
What a great pity this is the fate I bear:
The Man Deranged Who Knows Not Where He Goes."

[167]

Quant j'ay ouy le tabourin

Whenever I hear the tambour's cry
That tells me to run after May,
Back in my bed, without dismay,
My head deep in the pillow lies.

I say to myself: "It's early yet.   5
I'll get up later—by and by . . .
Whenever I hear the tambour's cry.

"The young ones can split up the cuts;
I'll be Nonchalance's friend.
He and I can share an end.   10
He's the neighbor I find most nigh
Whenever I hear the tambour's cry."

[168]

Est-ce tout ce que m'apportez

Tell me, is this all you bring
On this your day, Saint Valentine,
Only the butt of hope, the thing
For which all unconsoled men pine?

Briefly you bring encouraging   5
To be happy on this morning fine.
Tell me, is this all you bring
On this your day, Saint Valentine?

Nothing else except a greeting,
"Happy day" inscribed in Latin,   10
An ancient relic on ancient satin.
Such presents set you chuckling.
Tell me, is this all you bring?

[169]

Ne hurtez plus a l'uis de ma Pensee

At the doorway of my Thought, never knock again,
Worry and Care, or you will find your aches.
Thought is asleep; she does not wish to wake.
All the night long she has given over to pain.

She's still in danger; care must be maintained.   5
So cease, yes cease, let daylight on her break.
At the doorway of my Thought, never knock again,
Worry and Care, or you will find your aches.

Good Hope, to bring her a cure, maintains
A medicine will work that she brings as gift. 10
Thought's head from the pillow can't be lifted
Unless repose brings respite from her pain.
At the doorway of my Thought, never knock again.

[170]

On parle de religion

1. They talk about religion,
   With its strict governing;
   They talk of great devotion
   That causes suffering;
   But as far as I can discover, 5
   My intentions I will fashion
   Where I feel the most compassion:
   In the observances of lovers.

2. Always in contemplation
   They hold their hearts ravished in trance, 10
   So that they may pass by gradations
   To the high Paradise of Romance.
   Between hot-cold, thirst-hunger they hover
   Suffering with hope in many a nation;
   Such, you will find, are the observations 15
   In the observances of lovers.

3. Barefooted, they beg dispensations
   From Consolation; from Carefreeness,
   They do not ask for any rations,
   Except for Pity—a small redress 20
   In the sacks where Sustenance lies covered

For their very simple provisions.
Are these not holy conditions
In the observances of lovers?

4. With bigots I want no dealings;   25
   I've no respect for their feelings.
   My affection rests, all else above,
   In the observances of love.

FRANÇOIS VILLON[20]

[171]

The Last Will (Le Testament),
En l'an de mon trentiesme aage

In the thirtieth year of my age
I have now drunk deeply of shame,
Not all a fool, not all a sage,
And not without a little pain,
Most of which I was forced to meet
At the hands of Thibault d'Aussigny—
If he's a bishop blessing the streets,
Blessings he'll never bestow on me! . . .   8

I mourn the slipping days of youth   169
That more than other men I supped
For Age kept mum his awful truth,
Not saying time would soon be up.

[20] François Villon (1431–*ca.* 1463). North France's greatest medieval poet. Scholar and thief, imprisoned and condemned for thievery and murder; disappears after banishment in 1463. Wrote *The Last Will* in 1461 when despairing about his health. Reared by Guillaume de Villon, whom he mentions in lines 849 ff. The Pretty Helmress (*Belle Heaulmière* or Seller of Weaponry) was the mistress of Nicholas d'Orgemont, canon of Nôtre Dame (lines 453 ff.).

On foot he did not take his fling
Or horseback. No. How did he go?
Suddenly—in a burst of wings.
Not one souvenir did he throw.   176

He's gone. And here I sit
In learning weak, poor in sense,
Berry-black, sad, out of it,
Without an income, cash, or rents.
My lowest relative, I'm sure,
Steps up to utter he will quit me,
Forgetting even though I'm poor
Nature decrees that he admit me. . . .   184

It's true that I have loved enough   193
And willingly I'd love again.
But a belly that is seldom stuffed
One-third full and a heart with pain
Keep me away from those much-trod ways.
Ah well, somebody with bloated pants
Will profit from my absent place.
Out of the belly springs the dance!   200

Eh God! if only I'd hit the books
In the time when my youth ran riot
And tried to ape a gentleman's looks,
I'd have a home, soft bed inside it.
But no! School was a thing I abhorred,
Running away like a naughty kid;
Even now as I write these words,
Heart aches for the dumb things I did. . . .   208

Where are the gentlemen debonair   225
I followed in the days now fled,
Who sang so sweet, talked so fair,
Charming in all they did and said?
Some are stiff, and some are dead,

And some are almost completely bereft;
In Paradise may they find a bed,
And God save all of us who are left!   232

Yet some of them have well pursued
(Mercy God!) lives as lords and profs;
While others go begging totally nude,
Eying the butts of bread in shops;
Still others have entered into cloisters
To be Celestines or Carthusians,
Booted and gartered like fishers of oysters.
Ah, what is man's lot?—diffusion! . . .   240

From youth I've known just poverty   273
Stemming from humble generation;
My father never lived elegantly;
Horace was his dad's appellation.
Poverty follows us, tracks us down.
On all the tombs of all my tribe
(May God in Heaven gather them round)
You'll find no crown or scepter inscribed. . . .   280

I'm well aware that I am shoddy: 297
No angel's son with a diadem,
Crowned with a star or heavenly body.
My dad is dead. God quiet him!
As for his corpse, it's under the stone.
I've heard that Mother an end will find
And she's heard it too; the poor thing moans.
And Sonny—he won't lag far behind.   304

I'm positive that the poor and the rich,
Wise man and fool, the priest and lay,
Noble, churl, kindheart and bitch,
Big and little, grisly and gay,
Women with collars turned up high
From every heard-of social caste,
Strikingly hatted as they swirl by—
Death will snatch to the very last.   312

If Paris or Helen faces death
Or anyone else, he faces pain,
For that's what makes him lose his breath;
Poisons pour through every vein;
And then he sweats; O God, he shudders!
No doctor can the grief erase;
And there's no child, sister, or brother
Who'd volunteer to take his place. 320

Death has made him shivery pale.
His nose is curved; his veins gain height;
The neck swells out as limp flesh fails;
Joints and sinews puff out tight.
Body of woman, now so tender,
Polished, soft, and nicely leavened,
Must you to this woe surrender?
Yes! Or mount up straight to Heaven. 328

[171A²¹]

Dictes moy ou, n'en quel pays

1. Tell me where, in what domain
   Is Archipiades fair of Greece,
   Flora the Roman or that Thaïs
   Who in her looks was their cousin germane,
   Echo who always answered again
   By riverbank or by poolside clear,
   Whose beauty exceeded what was humane—
   But—where are the snows of yesteryear? 336

2. Tell me, where is wise Heloise
   For whom Pierre underwent castration?
   Love dealt him this great deprivation;

²¹ Ballade of the Women of Time Gone By. Pierre in line 338 is Peter Abelard.

K

He became a monk at St. Denis.
And where is that queen, O tell me please,
Who told them to bear old Buridan near
The Seine in a sack, and then to release—
But—where are the snows of yesteryear?   344

3. Where is Queen Blanche, the lily-white
Whose siren voice echoed through the palace,
Big-Footed Bertha, Beatrice, Alice,
Harembourg, who held the Maine tight,
Sweet Joan in whom Lorraine took pride;
In the English fires she disappeared.
Where, Virgin, where do they all abide?
But—where are the snows of yesteryear?   352

4. Prince, do not ask within this week
Or in this year when they'll appear;
The answer this one verse will speak:
"Where are the snows of yesteryear?"   356

* * * * * * * * * * * * * * * * * * *

And so for these poor little tricks   445
Who now are old without a cent;
When they see all the young slender chicks
Taking their places, how they lament
Inwardly as to God they demand
Why their time was not to their choosing.
The Lord is silent. As the matter stands,
He won't risk answering—and losing.   452

It seems to me that I can hear
The Pretty Helmress, who issued arms,
Wishing she had those girlish charms
And speaking like this loud and clear:
"Ach! Old Age—felon and fierce,
Why is it me you've so soon pierced?

What is it—what?—that turns aside
These blows that would bring me suicide?   460

"You've taken away that great franchise
That Beauty to me one day decreed
Over merchants, churchmen, and laity,
For never was man with a pair of eyes
Who wouldn't have given me his all,
Though repenting it later in a stall,
If only I'd give him for a fee
What beggars now scorn and won't take free.   468

"O many a man have I refused—
And for me it wasn't always smart.
Instead, I'd expend my finest arts
On the love of a tender kid with ruses.
Okay—to others I put on the screws,
But, on my soul, I loved that one true!
Yet later he made his crudeness felt
When I learned he loved me just for my geld.   476

"It's true he only knew how to sock
And kick me around. I loved him more.
He'd drag my carcass over the floor,
But I'd forgive all those cruel knocks
If he'd just ask me for a kiss.
That glutton, rotten down to his pith,
Would take me and—O! the devil's name!
What have I got now? Sin and shame.   484

"Now he's dead. Thirty years have gone,
And here I stand, ancient and gray.
Christ, when I think of yesterday,
The thing I was; what I've become!
When mirrors show my form paraded
And I see everything desiccated,
Sick and thin and withered and dry—
Into a sudden rage I fly!   492

"Where is that glance once so merry,
Those arched eyebrows, that long blonde hair,
Eyes that sparkled wide-set and fair,
With which I'd catch even the wary;
That splendid nose so perfectly shaped,
Those pretty ears that downward draped,
The flushed ripe cheeks, the dimpled chin,
Those beautiful lips of bright vermilion?   500

"Cute little shoulders jutting out,
Those long white arms, lithe fingertips,
Delicate breasts, high, rounded hips
Ready for any sudden bout
Handed down in the lists of love;
Good wide loins that flared above
The yoke where thighs sprout muscle-hardened,
Where pussy lay in her little garden?   508

"The brow has linings; the hair is gray;
Eyebrows have fallen, eyes grown blunt,
That used to laugh as they made the hunt
To snatch those devils and make them pay.
Hooking nose makes me look bossy;
Ears are drooping—yes, and mossy;
Complexion's pallid, dull as paste;
Chin is wrinkled, lips a waste.   516

"This is the end to which all beauty slumps.
Arms get short, and hands get gnarled.
Shoulders all in humps lie snarled;
Titties—what? yes, shrunken clumps.
And haunches fare no better than dugs.
As for that hidden treasure, ugh!
The thighs aren't thighs as vessels burst,
Resembling speckled cuts of wurst.   524

"And so for the good old days we call
Among ourselves, old silly twats,

As on our aged haunches we squat,
All hunched up in squalid balls,
Kept warm by little hempen trifles
Whose fire bursts soon, and then is stifled;
Ach, God! I was such a delicate wench
But . . . yes . . . it's happened to many a *Mensch*."   532

[171B²²]

Or y pensez, Belle Gantiere

1. It's time to think, my Pretty Glover,
   Who served apprenticeship with me,
   About your value as a lover,
   And you too, Blanche of the Bootery;
   Look to the left and look to the right.
   "Spare no man" is my declaration.
   Once old, they'll let you feel their spite,
   Like surplus coins cried out of circulation.   540

2. And you there, little Sausage-Cleaver,
   Who at the dance always moved faster,
   And you, Guillemette the Carpet-Weaver,
   Don't pretend that I'm not your master.
   The shop'll soon be bolted and leased
   As bloat declares its proclamation:
   You're fit now only for an old priest,
   Like surplus coins cried out of circulation.   548

3. Jeanneton the Bonnet-Bender,
   Watch that your lover doesn't cling;
   And Katherine the Wallet-Vender,
   Don't send your men out pasturing.
   Who isn't pretty shouldn't vex,

²² Advice of the Pretty Helmress to the Daughters of Joy.

But cause a constant exultation;
Foul old age must buy its sex
Like surplus coins cried out of circulation.   556

4. Girls, will you stop for just one bit
And try to grasp my great frustration?
I'm out of it totally now, I quit—
Like surplus coins cried out of circulation.   560

* * * * * * * * * * * * * * * * * * *

CLAUSE NUMBER ONE: This soul entombed   833
I trust to the Blessed Trinity,
To the hands of Our Beloved Lady,
Who chambered God within her womb.
And now I cry upon the love
Moved by the nine great orders above
That they may bear my soul with moan
Before the precious heavenly throne.   840

Item: My body I hereby leave
To our awesome mother, the Earth;
Because of long famine, there's a dearth
Of fat, which will cause the worms to grieve.
And let it be given with great dispatch:
From Earth it came; to Earth, go back.
Everything if I've rightly learned
Is always glad to make a return.   848

Item: To my more than father,
Master Guillaume, who gave me coddling
Like a child just risen from swaddling
In a way as tender as any mother
(He got me out of many a jam
Though none was worse than where I am)—
I beg him on knees to leave the joy
Of all this mess to his little boy;   856

To him I bequeath my library
With *The Romance of the Devil's Fart,*
Reproduced by a man with heart,
Who called himself Guy Tabarie;
It lies under the table in reams,
And the matter inside is more than it seems,
For although it looks like mere porno hack,
Its ideas will make up for other lacks.   864

Item: To my poor mother I leave
This hymn to offer the Mistress in praise
(She who suffered such bitter days
For me, God knows, and still will grieve).
No castle or fortress can I yield
Where body and soul could find some shield,
For evil fortune over me rolls—
You have nothing else, Mother, poor soul!   872

[171C[23]]

Dame du ciel, regente terrienne

1. Lady of heaven, regent over Earth,
   High empress of the infernal swampish plain,
   Receive me, a simple person of Christian birth,
   That I may be a part of your select domain,
   Although my life has been one of little gain.
   My goods from you, My Lady and My Mistress,
   Are so great that they dwarf my sinfulness,
   Goods by which the soul wins immortality
   And stays there. O God, don't think that I jest!
   By this faith I want to live and die.   882

[23] Ballade for His Mother to Pray to Our Lady. His name occurs anagrammatically
in stanza 4.

2. And tell your Son that I'm indeed his woman.
   By him my sins will all be washed away;
   Pardon me, as he did to the Egyptian
   Or the clerk Theophilus, who at last obeyed;
   You freed and quit him after he truly prayed,
   Although the Devil held him in his grasp.
   I pray: keep me from coming to that pass,
   O Virgin who never suffered man's lechery
   And bore the Sacrament we adore in Mass.
   By this faith I want to live and die.   892

3. Lady, I'm just a poor and ancient thing;
   One letter I cannot read; I'm completely lewd.
   I see in church where I do my worshiping
   Paradise painted; I hear harps and lutes;
   And Hell—the pot boils over with those brutes.
   One makes me fear, one gives me happiness.
   Give me the joy, O you highest Goddess,
   On whom every sinner must rely;
   I'll show my faith, no feints, no laziness,
   For by this faith I want to live and die.   902

4. Virgin, you carried, you, my worthy princess,
   Iesus, who'll reign until the earth shall fade,
   Lord Almighty, who took on human weakness,
   Leaving the heavens to come down to our aid,
   Offering to Death his precious youthfulness.
   Now him as Lord I promise to stand by:
   For in his faith I want to live and die.   909

* * * * * * * * * * * * * * * * * *

[171D*]

Se j'ayme et sers la belle de bon hait[24]

1. If I love and serve the one debonair   1591
   Will you say I pursue a vile, foolish life?
   She has every good for which I care,
   For her I gird on buckler and knife;
   When visitors come, I run for a pot;
   Scrambling for wine, I keep cool and mute;
   I hand out water, cheese, bread, and fruit,
   And if they pay me, I say, *"Bene stat;*
   Stop in, old fellow, when the load is great
   In this bordello where we hold our estate."   1600

2. Ah, then, the venom suddenly erupts
   When Margot climbs in without a sou.
   I can't look at her. I hate her guts.
   I grab dress and panties, girdle too,
   And shout, "I like this loot a lot."
   She handles her flanks: "You damn pariah!"
   She screams; she swears on the dead Messiah
   That she won't take it. A stick I've got
   To inscribe my message on her pate
   In this bordello where we hold our estate.   1610

3. Peace we make. A fart she bestows
   Like a puffy beetle on a heap of dung;
   Laughing, she twists her fist on my nose;
   "Bébé," she whispers, swats me on the bung;
   Like a log we sleep, drunk, shank to shank;
   We awake to hear her interior toot;
   She climbs on me, will not waste her fruit;
   I groan below, squeezed flat like a plank.

---

* Original text appears in Section X, p. 398.

[24] Ballade for Fat Margot. *Bene stat* in line 1598 means "It stands well; all right."

With steady strokes, my lust she abates
In this bordello where we hold our estate.   1620

4. Come hail or wind or ice, I've baked my bread.
   I'm horny; she has horns upon her head.
   Which one is worse? Well, the man once said:
   "Bad cat, bad rat"—an equal fate we rate.
   Garbage we love; garbage is all we've got.
   We run from honor; honor flees our lot
   In this bordello where we hold our estate.   1627

[171E²⁵]

Car ou soies porteur de bulles

1. Whether you carry papal bulls,   1692
   Hustle or shoot the dice in crap,
   Make your own money, blow your cool
   Like some neurotic about to snap,
   Are a lying traitor with faith to let,
   Guilty of thievery, rapine, and fraud,
   Where's it all go? Where, will you bet?
   All to the taverns and the broads.   1699

2. Rhyme, rail, jangle, or peck the lute
   Like any nutty, nervy clown;
   Act up, work magic, toot the flute,
   Perform in every city and town
   Farces, jests, moralities;
   Win at poker, quilles, and glic—
   Away it goes, just listen to me,
   All to the taverns and the chicks.   1707

²⁵ Ballade of the Taverns and the Girls. Line 1705 contains the names of three card games.

3. So stay away from this filthy stool;
   Go plow; trim your fields from weeds;
   Feed and groom your horses and mules,
   Even if you never learned how to read.
   If you take it easy, it'll all be okay.
   But if you scutch the hemp into rods,
   The labor won't hold; you'll throw it away
   All to the taverns and the broads.   1715

4. Doublets with spangles, even your pants,
   Frilly shorts and robes with furls—
   You could do worse than just to hand
   All to the taverns and the girls.   1719

[171F²⁶]

Icy se clost le testament

1. Here is closed the final will,   1996
   The end of poor François Villon.
   But his burial's waiting still;
   When you hear the carillon,
   Come in red vermilion dolled
   Because with a lover's death he ended.
   This he swore upon his balls
   As from this world his way he wended.   2003

2. And I believe he didn't fib
   For he was chased like a lowly peon
   Because of those hateful loves of his
   All the way down to Roussillon.
   There is no bramble, not a gully
   (For so he truthfully contended)

²⁶ Ballade to Close the Last Will.

      That did not try to strip him wholly
      As from this world his way he wended.   2011

3. That's how he went: violently, so
    That at his death he had just rags;
    He shuddered in those final throes
    Because love gave him spurring jabs;
    He could feel such pricks down under
    That make a buckler's blows seem tender;
    This is the thing that gives us wonder
    As from this world his way he wended.   2019

4. Prince, like a merlin straight and fine,
    Know what he did as his parting ended?
    Took a long swig of black, brackish wine
    As from this world his way he wended.   2023

[172[27]]

Je suis François, dont il me poise

I am François—a thing to weigh—
Born in Paris (that's out Pontoise way).
My neck will grasp as the rope descends
How much the ass weighs in the end.

[173[28]]

Freres humains qui après nous vivez

1. My fellow brothers, who after us will live,
    Don't let your hearts turn hard against our sins;

[27] Quatrain.
[28] Epitaph of Villon.

For if you find the pity to forgive,
Mercy from God the sooner you will win.
You see us here: five, six, hanging apart;   5
And flesh, whose care we always have allayed
Is battered now, devoured and decayed;
And we, the bones, are of dust and ash composed;
Yet God forbid you laugh our ills away
But pray that God salvation on us dispose.   10

2. And if we call you brothers, certainly you
   Must not show disdain, though we have been dispensed
   Through Justice. After all, you know it's true
   Not every man has always shown good sense.
   Excuse us, for we have now been sent   15
   To see the Virgin Mary's only son
   And may his grace forever on us run
   And may Hell's thunderbolt not dare come close;
   For we are dead; trouble's no longer fun:
   So pray that God salvation on us dispose.   20

3. Rain's washing we have felt; we have felt the scour;
   The sun has scorched, burned our flesh black and dry;
   Magpies and crows our eyeballs have devoured
   And plucked our beards, the brows above our eyes.
   We have not hanged one hour unagonized: 25
   Now here, now there, restlessly we are carried
   Wherever the constant, shifting winds have harried;
   We are left like pitted thimbles by the carrion crows.
   And so of this company of ours be wary,
   But pray that God salvation on us dispose.   30

4. Prince Jesus, who over us has mastery,
   Watch that Hell never around us close;
   May the Devil never deal with this company.
   Man, there is nothing here of mockery—
   But pray that God salvation on us dispose.   35

[VIII]
GERMAN SONGS

The German lyric tradition follows that of the French. Aside from some anonymous songs, the Middle High German lyric did not really flower until it felt the influence of the Provençal troubadours. Then the tradition of love poetry or *Minnesang* was born, in the twelfth century. Previously, in the Old High German period, literature existed, but it was largely composed of lays, riddles, or magic charms—certainly not songs of love. Once it joined the mainstream of the European tradition, German poetry adopted many of the conventions that were already established. For example, the notion of *Frauendienst* or "service to women" is a central part of the rhetorical strategy of the *Minnelied* or "love song." There is still much argument over the origin of the word *Minne* ("love"). Most people generally believe that the word is connected with the Greco-Roman words for "remember." The learned nature of the term suggests an esoteric import, just as much of the music of the Minnelieder was borrowed from the French.

We must not, however, suggest that the Germans were mere imitators. They adapted the Provençal tradition in a highly realistic way, unlike the poets of Italy. The woman in German songs is almost never an angel. She is a woman and, even more strongly than in her North French counterparts, an object who is possessable. Love in German poetry is never totally removed from sex. In the most famous of all the Minnesinger poems, Walther von der Vogelweide's *Under der linden* (No. 190), the act of possession is clearly stated. In fact, German poetry, more than that of any other European country, underscores realism almost to the point of naturalism. The nature setting in a North French poem often seems like a window dressing; in a German poem, it is a recurrent reminder of the natural life.

In keeping with this highly objective presentation, the German lyric tradition places strong emphasis upon poetic imagery. The linden tree (or lime tree, for Middle High German *linde* can be translated by either word) becomes a dominant symbol of the force of nature, complemented sometimes by the brooks and the meadows. Yet unlike the nature setting in other countries, the German landscape is frequently focused upon a bird, a flower, a tree, or a star, and does not move upward into another realm.

The realistic nature of German song is also conveyed by the fact that the lyrics frequently have a narrative at their base. Some of the poems that follow are clearly Dawn Songs (*Tagelieder*) or Pastourelles, and others suggest a story line indirectly (Nos. 178, 181, 186, etc.). As a result, German poetry avoids the danger of too much abstraction.

Furthermore, although much has been said about the so-called courtly-love movement in the poetry, one can see that the works which follow are not encumbered with didactic tropes or motifs, the way some of the inferior works in other countries are. The absence of a metaphysical overtone in much of the verse preserves a certain fresh, folk-sounding quality that prevents the selections gathered here from sounding repetitive or labored; the stifling "court" atmosphere is not at all evident.

German lyrics also have a rather somber, brooding tone that often asserts itself. With this melancholy goes an inclination toward meditation, but the thought is usually secular. See, for example, Walther's famous Number 191. Philosophy to the medieval German poet is frequently not theology, and the poetry itself is the key to the meditation.

Perhaps the major contribution of the Minnesingers was their music, which has been preserved much better than that in many other countries. Those who would like a detailed account of this development, along with a record, should consult B. G. Seagrave and W. Thomas, *The Songs of the Minnesingers* (Urbana: University of Illinois Press, 1966).

ANONYMOUS

[174]

Dû bist mîn, ich bin dîn

Thou art mine,
I am thine,
And like this we'll always be.
Thou art part
Of my locked heart,   5
And it's true I've lost the key.
So abide
Deep inside
For it's there thou'lt ever be.

[175¹]

Wære diu werlt alliu mîn

If the world were all mine
　　From the sea to the Rhine,
　　　　I'd throw it all away
If only the Queen of England lay
　　In my warm entwine.   5

¹ A German song from the *Carmina Burana*. See Numbers 32–50. The Queen is
undoubtedly Eleanor of Aquitaine, wife of Henry II.

THE KÜRENBERGER[2]

[176]

Ich zôch mir einen valken mêre danne ein jâr

I trained me a falcon for more than a year.
I trained him to heed every wave of my hand;
I bound up his feathers with fetters of gold;
He sprang up and flew to a distant land.

Since then I have seen that falcon flying free   5
With silken jesses dangling from his feet
And feathers shiny with their gold and red:
God grant that all who love each other meet!

[177]

Der tunkel sterne

Like a dark star
    That wants to hide,
You must, pretty lady,
    Stay from my side,
And always on others   5
    Rest those eyes
So no one discovers
    What between us lies.

[2] The Kürenberger (*fl. ca.* 1150). Probably an aristocrat from Kürnberg Castle near Linz, Austria. Small corpus survives.

[178]

Swenne ich stån aleine in mînem hemede

When I stand all alone
  In my dressing gown,
And I think about you,
  My knight of renown,
My color rises up in a flush   5
Like a blushing rose on a thorny bush,
And my heart lays claim to a mighty share
  Of desire and despair.

DIETMAR VON EIST[3]

[179]

Slåfest du, friedel ziere?

LADY:
Are you sleeping, tender lover?
They'll be coming to discover—
Ah! there's a bird just now
Striking a tune on the lime-tree bough.

KNIGHT:
I was snuggling in sleep's arms;   5
Now, love, you sound an alarm;
Loving unlabored cannot be;
I do what you order, Milady.

The lady began to moan:
"You ride. You leave me alone.   10

---

[3] Dietmar von Eist or Aist (*fl.* 1150–1170). Probably an Austrian born near the Eist, a tributary of the Danube. Numbers 179 and 180 are Dawn Songs.

When will you ever come back to me?
God! joy goes with your company. . . ."

[180]

Ûf der linden obene dâ sanc ein kleinez vogellîn

MAN:
Up above on a linden high
  I hear a little fowl;
At the forest's edge the cry
  Made my heart go on prowl
To a place where it had been before.   5
  I saw the blossoms of rose unfurl,
Which loosed the thoughts from memory's store
  About the beauty of a girl.

WOMAN:
It seems to me a thousand years
  Since in my darling's arms I lay;   10
Of any guilt I'm surely cleared
  If he's estranged these many days.
Since then, I've had no flowers to see
  And I have heard no bird in song;
Happiness has been short for me,   15
  And sorrow far too long.

[181]

Ez stuont ein frouwe alleine

There stood a lady all alone
Waiting upon a moor;
She wanted her own man to come;

She saw a falcon soar.
"O ho! you falcon, how you fly!   5
You go wherever desire flings.
You choose some bough away up high
And there you lower your wings.
Ah me—I share your wanderlust.
I chose a man whom I could trust.   10
I staked him out with my two eyes.
But ladies fair now envy my prize.
O God, when will my lover appear?
I never begrudged another her dear."

SPERVOGEL (THE SPARROW)[4]

[182]

Swer den wolf ze hirten nimt

He who asks the wolf to dine
    Is asking for a cause to whine.
No wise man ever overloads his trawler.
This is my wisdom. I am the scholar.
A husband who spends his every thaler   5
To buy rich clothes throughout the year
    Will soon have mighty cause to fear.
Her arrogance will grow and grow
    Till he gets a bastard *quid pro quo.*

[4] Spervogel, "The Sparrow" (*fl.* after 1150). Early master of the single-stanza *Spruch* or *sirventes.*

FRIEDRICH VON HAUSEN[5]

[183]

Mîn herze und mîn lîp diu wellent scheiden

1. My heart and my body would like to part
   Although they've journeyed together a good long time.
   My body wants to go fight against the heathens.
   My heart has chosen its contest in a girl,
   The best in the world. It's troubled me a while   5
   That the two of them don't get along together.
   My eyes have brought me often to great grief.
   Only God, I'm afraid, can settle this strife.

2. I thought that I was free from all this turmoil
   When I took up the cross in the Master's name.   10
   It was right for my heart to go along with me,
   But it told me its own steadiness forbade that.
   Right now I could be a rightful-acting man
   If only it would give up its silly will.
   Now I see, though, it doesn't give a damn,   15
   No matter what the end that comes my way.

3. All right, my heart, since I can never stop you
   From wanting to abandon me in distress,
   Then I beg God to guide you to some haven
   Where you will find a welcome without duress.   20
   Alas, poor little thing, what will be your fate?
   How could you dare to enter alone into peril?
   Who will help bring your sorrows to an end
   With all the steady loyalty I have shown?

---

[5] Friedrich von Hausen (*ca.* 1155–1190). Rhinelander prominent in the court of
Frederick Barbarossa. Served on imperial missions to Italy in 1175 and 1186. Died
in 1190, in Syria on the Third Crusade.

REINMAR VON HAGENAU, THE OLD[6]

[184]

Ich wil allez gâhen

1. I will go on the run
   Off to the love I possess.
   Even if a good outcome
   Lies beyond my fondest guess.
   But still I try it every day;   5
   I serve her without her bidding—
       She must soon change the sorrowful to the gay.

2. A twinge went sweeping over me
   When I heard something said:
   They told me she was a lady   10
   And a splendid life she led.
   I tested it—and yes, it's fair.
   No other woman could pull her down.
       There's no compare—even by the width of a hair.

3. If from any other land   15
   Some loving should ever come to me,
   That all lies within her hands;
   For other women I make no plea.
   She is my shining Easter day
   And fills my heart deep with love: 20
       He knows it's true, the One to whom men pray.

---

[6] Reinmar von Hagenau, The Old (d. *ca.* 1210). Major poet of Austria in the late 1100s, whose death was sung by his successor, Walther von der Vogelweide. Born in Alsace.

HEINRICH VON VELDEKE[7]

[185]

Tristrant muose sunder danc

Tristan stood, without giving thanks,
Among Isolde's loyal ranks,
For the magic philter could impel
Stronger even than love's spell.
My Lady then should give me thanks   5
Because that brew I never drank;
And yet my love fares valiantly,
Better than his, if that can be.

    O Lady fair,
    Of falseness bare,   10
    I'll belong to you
    If you will love me true.

HEINRICH VON MORUNGEN[8]

[186]

Ich hôrt ûf der heide

1. Voices loud and music sweet
   I heard once upon the moor;
   With those sounds I was replete

---

[7] Heinrich von Veldeke (*fl.* 1170–before 1210). Low German knight from Maastricht region; author of *Eneit*, German version of Vergil's *Aeneid*, based on French sources. Worked for Frederick Barbarossa in 1184.

[8] Heinrich von Morungen (*ca.* 1150–1222). Native of Thuringia who died in Leipzig. Very familiar with Provençal forms, as he shows in his Dawn Song (No. 187).

With joying and in sorrow poor.
Her who gave my mind a twang   5
I found dancing; and she sang.
Farewell sorrow! I too sprang.

2. There I found her all alone
With her cheeks bathed in sorrow.
For my death she made a moan   10
(She had heard it just that morrow.)
This new upset I could better bear
Than glib-given love, for as I knelt there
I watched the ending of her care.

3. I found her walking by the wall-edge   15
(All alone); I came at her call.
She would have gladly made the pledge,
Offering me true love and all.
I would have burned the land behind,
Except that she bound up my mind   20
And left my sense bereft and blind.

[187]

Owê, sol aber mir iemer mê

MAN:
Will it never again—o woe!—
Gleam for me in the night,
Shining whiter than the snow,
Her body cut just right?
It deceived these eyes of mine: 5
I thought it was the same
As the moon's soft glowing shine—
    And then day came.

WOMAN:

Will he never again—o woe!—
Spend the morning by my side?   10
Then as night from us will go
We will need no longer cry
"Alas! it's come—the day"—
A lament I heard him shout
When last by me he lay   15
    —Then day broke out.

MAN:

O woe! no one could ever count
The kisses offered me in sleep;
But later on, the tears fell down,
Steeping downward from her cheeks;   20
But as I held her lovingly,
Those tears she put away,
And wholly did she comfort me—
    But then came day.

WOMAN:

O woe! how he repeatedly   25
Devours me with those eyes!
That time when he uncovered me,
He'd let no cover lie
Over this poor naked frame—
Miraculously on and on   30
He never tired of that game—
    But then came dawn.

WOLFRAM VON ESCHENBACH[9]

[188*]

Sîne klâwen durh die wolken sint geslagen

WATCHMAN:
1. It has raked its talons downward through the clouds,
It has risen upward with an awesome might.
I see the gray of the dawning breaking out;
I see the end of the night,
And also that sweet companionship 5
I fostered when I let him in.
Now he must make a hurried trip.
A virtuous man I serve: no prey to sin.

LADY:
2. Watchman, my pleasure's fading as you sing.
You only bring addition to my lament. 10
Grief is the only thing you ever bring,
Every morning as the night is spent.
Please, your total silence keep.
I order: hold your pledging dear.
If my true love can share my sleep 15
I'll slip you something to bring you cheer.

WATCHMAN:
3. He must get out—quick! no delay!
Give him his leave there, my pretty wife.
Let him love you later the secret way,
To keep his name and save his life. 20
He put himself into my trust

[9] Wolfram von Eschenbach (*ca.* 1170–1217). Author of *Parzival* epic. From northern Bavaria of impoverished noble stock. Served the great patron of Minnesinger, Hermann of Thuringia. Only about eight lyrics survive. Here, a brilliant Dawn Song.

* Original text appears in Section X, p. 399.

That I should get him a safe egress.
Well now, it's day. It's long since dusk
When kisses lured him from me to your breast.

LADY:

4. Go on singing, Watchman, but leave him here.   25
   He brought me and he got some tender love.
   Your voice is always filling us with fear;
   Even when the dawn-star doesn't twinkle above,
   The man who's come to share my charms
   Is snatched before the night parts: 30
   You grab him quickly from my arms,
   From my white arms—but never from my heart!

POET:

5. As a gleam of daylight struck against the glass
   And as the Watchman warning sang,
   The Lady felt a baleful grasp   35
   And pressed her breast against her man.
   The Rider's courage did not surrender
   (The Watchman's song had failed on that score).
   They took their leave with rewardings tender:
   With kisses and with much, much more.   40

[189¹⁰]

Der helden minne ir klage

1. A lament for a love that can't be shown
   You always sang before the dawn shone,
   Of the sour following the sweet;
   He who love and womanly greetings
   In secret adores   5

---

¹⁰ Extraordinary love song that defies the courtly-love tradition by exalting the
joy of love from marriage.

Must part from both in the end;
This was the warning you did send,
As upward soared
The morning star; O Watcher, be mum!
Of these affairs be ever dumb!   10

2. Whoever swore or ever will say
   That he most fondly with his lover lay
   Unhidden from all suborning
   Should not from the fear of morning
   Slink away.   15
   No, he may the daylight abide.
   No man can ever take him aside
   His life to try
   If a trusted, tender, open wife
   Will give him love for aye and aye.   20

WALTHER VON DER VOGELWEIDE[11]

[190*]

Under der linden

1. Under the linden
   On the heath
   Where a bed for two was massed,
   There you could see
   Piled up neat   5
   Pluckings of flowers and of grass.
   At the edge of the copse within a vale—
                    Tandaradei—
   Sweetly sang the nightingale.

---

[11] Walther von der Vogelweide (*ca.* 1170–*ca.* 1230). Greatest German medieval lyric poet in vast range of genres. Born in Tyrolese section of Austria, but wandered from court to court. Frederick II rewarded him with a small fief near Würzburg.

* Original text appears in Section X, p. 401.

2. I went secretly   10
   To a meadow shady
   Where my sweetheart had gone before.
   He did greet me:
   "Pretty lady!"—
   Then made me happy forevermore.   15
   Did he kiss? Ach, a thousandfold!—
          Tandaradei—
   See, my mouth still holds the mold!

3. Heaped up there
   With royal pride   20
   Was a bedstead he formed of flowers.
   A laugh you'd hear
   From deep inside
   If a stranger ventured into our bower.
   From the roses he could tell—   25
          Tandaradei—
   Exactly where my head fell.

4. God forbid
   That our rendezvous
   Be known, for it would bring us shame.   30
   What we did,
   Just we two,
   We've sworn to hide in each other's name.
   O yes—and that little bird—
          Tandaradei—   35
   He said he would keep his word.

[191¹²]

Owê war sint verswunden alliu mîniu jâr?

1. Alas, where have they vanished, all of my years?
   Was my life a dream, or was it truly real?
   And all I thought truly was, was this not so?
   It seems I've been asleep and never knew it.
   But now I've wakened, and I no longer recognize   5
   Things as common to me before as one of my hands.
   These people, this land where I grew up from a child
   Have become as foreign as if I were never here.
   All of my former playmates are now run-down and old.
   The fields are all dry, the forest has been hacked.   10
   If it wasn't for rivers flowing as they've always flowed,
   I'd really think my misfortune was something great.
   Many now greet me aloofly who knew me once quite well.
   The world in its entirety is devoid of grace.
   And as I review those wonderful days gone by   15
   That have now disappeared like a pebble into the sea,
        Again and again: Alas!

2. Alas, how completely depraved the young people now behave!
   The ones who were once lighthearted have stifled their charm
   And now can only worry; why do they act this way?   20
   Wherever in the world I journey I find no one in joy.
   Dancing, laughing, and singing have all been forced to yield.
   No Christian fellow ever saw such a mournful state!
   Just look at the hats the women now put on their heads!
   And once-proud gentlemen go around dressed like hicks.   25
   Troubling messages are reaching us now from Rome:
   We are only allowed to be glum, never seize our joy.
   This troubles me greatly (after all, we once lived well),
   But now instead of chuckling, I can only choose to whine.
   This lament of mine has quieted even the wild birds.   30

---

¹² Lament that promotes a crusade that Frederick was trying to undertake; often titled "The Elegy."

L

Is it any wonder that I should feel depressed?
Yet what am I saying, a fool moved by bitter bile?
He who seeks worldly pleasures will lose whatever's to come:
    Again and again: Alas!

3. Alas, how all of our sweet things turn into poison!   35
    I see the bitter gall lurking deep in the honey.
    The world is outwardly pretty—white, green, and red;
    But inside the color is dark, as black as is death.
    And yet I'll show a comfort for those who have gone astray—
    With just a little effort they can still absolve their sins.   40
    Just think of it, knights! for this is your kind of thing!
    You're wearing the gleaming helmets, the hardened mail;
    You're carrying the thick shields, the bishop-blessed swords.
    Would to God I were worthy of this victorious crusade!
    For thus I, a needy man, could pile up a handsome hoard.   45
    O no, I don't mean some fiefs or some lordly gold.
    I just want to wear the crown of pure bliss forever;
    This any mercenary can win with just his spear.
    If I could make that yearned-for journey over the sea,
    O God, I'd sing, "Bravo!" and never again, "Alas!"   50
        No, never again, "Alas!"

[192¹³]

Ich saz ûf eime steine

I sat me down upon a stone
With kneebone crossed on kneebone,
And bent my elbow and my head
And in a palm that I outspread
I rested cheek and chin.   5
And then I pondered deep within
How man should guide his earthly stay,

---

¹³ Meditative poem composed during a period of civil strife in 1198.

And could not find a single way
That a man could win three things
And keep them all from spoiling: 10
Two are Rich Goods and Good Repute,
Which usually each other refute;
The third is Grace, which comes of God,
To which the others offer laud.
I'd like them all inside a chest.   15
Unfortunately, it's a vain request,
For worldly honor and the goods of men
And the blessing that from God descends
Seldom in a single heart are locked.
The paths and roadways lie all blocked.   20
Deception in ambush is always plotting;
Violence is in the streets marauding;
Peace and Right are sorely beset,
And if these two don't soon get better,
      The other three   25
      Will have no franchise to be free.

[193]

Sô die bluomen ûz dem grase dringent

1. As flowers out of the green grass spring
   As if they're laughing at the dazzling Sun,
   On a day in May when the morning is still new,
   And the little birds with skill begin to sing
   In the finest manner known to anyone,   5
   What delight can these ever be compared to?
   It is about one-half of a heaven's *Reich*.
   And if I try to say what it's really like,
   I'll have to speak about that great delight
   That often comes to please my eyes,   10
   And would do so now, if I just had the sight.

2. A noble lady, beautiful and pure,
    In fancy clothes wrapped well about,
    Walks among the people for delectation,
    High-spirited and courteous, not demure,   15
    Glancing on all the faces thereabout,
    Shining like the Sun against constellations:
    Let May bring us all of his many wonders,
    For which of them is something that can plunder,
    Compared to the royal splendor of this lady?   20
    Yes, we should let all of May's blossoms stand
    And stare on every hand at this worthy maid.

3. All right, you say, you prefer the outside world?
    Let us go then to a Maytime festival.
    Let us watch May come with his powers aflame.   25
    Look at him! Then cast your eyes on the girls.
    Tell me which merits the higher pedestal.
    See if I have selected the better game.
    O God! If somebody would just let me choose
    To treasure one, the other one to lose,   30
    My choice would be anything but random!
    My dear Herr May, I'd turn you into March
    Before my own sweet lady would be abandoned!

[194¹⁴]

Mir hat Her Gerhart Atze ein pfert

Herr Gerhart Atze shot my stallion dead
    Down by Eisenache way;
I lay my claim upon his head,
    To the lord whom we both obey.
The stud was worth three marks, no worse,   5
    But hear that man's lament,

¹⁴ *Spruch* or satiric *sirventes*.

Now that he knows he must reimburse
  Me for the deed he'd forget.
  He says he's become a lowly bum
  And my horse helped do the deed,   10
  For it was sibling to a steed
  That bit him recently on the thumb.
    Ah, what a laugh!
  I'll raise my hands in oath,
  Swearing it's not the truth   15
  If someone here will hold my staff!

NEIDHART VON REUENTAL[15]

[195]

Der walt

1. The wood
  With many sweet little sounds is filled;
  The songs of birds are never stilled;
  They've cast their grief away—
  With hearts now gay   5
  They greet the May!
  You maidens fair—break into pairs.

2. Now joy
  Swells in the streets in girls and boys;
  The linden will tell us summer's come;   10
  Its rich new leaves shine in the Sun
  And wonderful
  Its crown appears.
  You have the Maytime dear!

[15] Neidhart von Reuental or "From Ruing Dale" (*fl.* 1200–before 1246). Lower Bavarian knight who was master of realistic village poetry. Often penniless, though protected by Ludwig I of Bavaria and Frederick II of Austria.

3. The dew 15
   Falls in the fields in the flowers' eyes;
   Proud maids, boys should be there by your sides;
   Go slip your bodies into brocades,
   My tender maids,
   And dance away 20
   A welcome to the sweet, sweet May!

4. "How dear
   From other men I'd hold him apart,"
   Said Wodelhilt, a maid of changeless heart,
   "That man who undoes my bands. 25
   Hand in hand
   I'll tingle:
   I'll set his sword-hilt all ajingle.

5. "My hair
   With silken ribbons I shall bind 30
   For the sake of the man who pines
   To have me long in Reuen-Dale.
   Old winter's gale
   Is at an end.
   I love him. He's my one true friend." 35

[196^{16}]

Kint, bereitet iuch der sliten ûf daz îs!

1. Children, get the sleigh ready for the ice!
   This wearisome winter's cold,
   It's taken all our wondrous blooms away.
   Many a green linden stands there shivering gray,
   On its branches is no song. 5
   This has happened because of old Frost's anger.

---

16 Winter Song. A fourth stanza on women's fashions omitted.

Can't you see how he has done up our meadows?
It's his fault that all things fall.
Even the nightingale
Tells her tale far yonder.   10

2. Truly I need the words of some wise friend
   About a thing that's troubling me:
   That is: where can our children play?
   Megenward has a great big wide room
   And if you all consent,   15
   We'll spend our holiday there with roundelays.
   That is what his daughter wants when we are there.
   Go and tell your friends.
   Engelmar will dance quite ably
   All around the tables.   20

3. Go tell Kunegunde; that brings us all together!
   She has always loved the dance
   And bitches that we keep leaving her out!
   Gisel, go over to Jiuten and tell them too
   That Ella must join them balling.   25
   There's a promise between us, and it's fast.
   And, child, don't forget our Hedwig there!
   Demand that she come too! . . .

   (*The party begins.*)

5. Eppe's hitting Geppe Gumpen on the hand,
   And hard with his threshing flail.   30
   All is quieted then by the rod of Master Albert.
   This mess was caused when old Ruprecht found an egg
   (Found, hell! the Devil gave him it).
   He kept threatening to toss it over here.
   Eppe got just as burned up as he is bald: 35
   Gruffly he grumbled: "Hold it, man!"
   Ruprecht splattered him on the pate,
   And the yolk streamed down.

6. Friedlieb had to come here with Godelinde—
Just as Engelmar had dreaded.   40
I'm not going to tease. I'll tell it to the end.
Eberhardt the Bailiff had to step in between them,
And make the two make up.
If he hadn't, they'd have had each other's heads.
Like two dumb gawking ganders the whole day long   45
They eye each other intently.
And the man who leads our singing
Is our trusty Frederick.

7. Once upon a time my hair hung splendidly,
Twirling in locks around my band.   50
But that's forgotten now I've got a house.
Salt and grain I'm buying all the year.
Hell, what did I do to him
Who shoved stupid me into all these woes?
My debts to him were small,   55
But my curses now aren't little
When I'm there in Reuental
Without my victuals.

[197]

Der meie der ist rîche

GIRL:
1. "The May is rich about
And leads, without a doubt,
The wood to green again.
The trees are full of leaves:
The winter's at an end.   5

2. "Ah, the pleasure from the heath
As I watch the brightening sweep,

Yes, it's coming on to meet me,"
Proclaimed the well-shaped maid.
"Joyously I'll run to greet it!   10

3. "Mother, no lectures; let me be!
I'm going to the fields directly.
I want to leap and dance and spring.
Ah, it's been a long, long time
Since I've heard my playmates sing."   15

MOTHER:
4. "No, no, my dearest daughter, no!
All alone I've watched you grow,
Suckled you here at this breast.
O please, please do what I say:
Relax and let the menfolk rest."   20

GIRL:
5. "I want my lover's name to shine.
If you just knew him, you'd think him fine!
I'll rush away to see his face,
That gentle man from Reuental,
The man I'm yearning to embrace.   25

6. "Green across the branches is blent,
And all the trees will soon be bent
With blossoms down to the earth.
Ah, listen now, mother of mine,
I'm going away with that man of worth.   30

7. "Ah, my sweet honored mother—
He's calling me, my lover.
Shall I say never to romance?
He tells me I'm the most beautiful
Girl from Bavaria into France."   35

STEINMAR[17]

[198]

Ein kneht der lac verborgen

1. A farmhand lay all hidden,
   A farm girl by his side.
   The morning rays had smitten:
   A herdsman then outcried—
   "Get up! Let out the herd . . ."   5
   It startled them as they both heard.

2. He had to push the straw away
   And from the farm girl fly.
   He dared to brook no great delay,
   But clasped her closely by.   10
   The hay that around the maiden lay
   Flew away in the sun's bright ray.

3. Ah! how she had to laugh aloud
   As she saw him standing nude.
   Tomorrow morning he'll be allowed   15
   To take his place with her anew
   And play those games again with joy.
   Who ever saw such bliss with so few ploys?

[17] Steinmar, probably Berthold Steinmar (*fl.* 1250–1288). Gifted Swiss parodist who worked for Rudolf von Habsburg. Dawn Song Parody.

DER WILDE ALEXANDER[18]

[199]

Hievor dô wir kinder wâren

1. When we were little kids a while ago
And time was passing so very slow
That we could run across the meadow
Frisking endlessly to and fro—
Then we spent hours   5
With violet flowers
That cattle now cud as round they go.

2. We used to sit, I remember well,
Among the flowers trying to tell
Which the prettiest might be.   10
And our childishness anyone could see
As around we'd traipse
Garland-draped.
And so the time passed merrily.

3. Look! there we go from beech to pine   15
Trying to pluck a strawberry vine,
Rushing over the sticks and stones,
While all the while the Sun shone.
Then some gamekeeper pops
Out of the copse   20
Yelling: "Home, my laddies, home!"

4. How well I remember the spots and scratches
That we got from those patches—
Ah, it was such a kiddish skit!

---

[18] Der Wilde Alexander, "The Wild or Wandering Alexander" (*fl.* 1260–1300).
Swabian whose ceaseless travels earned him his name. Fond of riddles, hazy allusions,
and religious pronouncements. This poem is explicit in its allegorical implications,
although it seems for a time to be a simple song about childhood. Translated very
colloquially.

And yet, how clearly I recall it: 25
The game preserver's shout
Ringing out—
"Kids, up ahead's a snake pit!"

5. One went walking in the deep brush;
He yelled and screamed and out he rushed: 30
"Boys, hey boys! it just went in—
It's bit our pony on the shin,
And now he won't get well—
O hell!
God damn that wiggling thing!"   35

6. The gamesman cries: "Hey, hey! away!
And if you don't run and obey
I'll tell you what's in store:
You'll lose the light, for even more
Darkness is lurking in those woods;   40
Maybe for good
You'll lose the way; the tears will pour.

7. "Don't you kids know the Five Foolish Maids
Who over the meadows so long strayed
That the King had the door bolts slipped?   45
Ah, how they wailed! Their breasts they gripped
While wardens tore
The garments they wore,
And they stood for the world to see: stripped."

DER GUOTÆRE[19]

[200]

Hievor ein werder ritter lac

1. Once upon a time a worthy knight was lying
   Upon his bed, and they thought he was dying.
   In came a woman of such wondrous sheen
   She was a beauty no man had ever seen;
   Before all the others she did shine: 5
   She seemed a thing that must be divine.
   She stood before him, saying, "Tell
   Me, good rider, do I please you well?
   You've served me freely all of your days;
   I've come at your death your service to pay."   10

2. Her crown was all gold, and around her furled
   A girdle and belt and robe with pearls.
   He answered, "My lady, who might you be?"
   "I am Lady World," then answered she,
   "And now my back demands your eye;   15
   See! this is the great reward I ply."
   Her back was hollow, it lacked its skin;
   And there were worms and toads within;
   It stank like a foul and long-dead hound.
   "Christ! that I served you," was his weeping sound. . . .   20

[19] Der Guotære or "Good-Honor" (*fl.* 1265–1300). South German writer of
didactic verse. The Lady-World Poem tradition is common in German poetry. Three
more stanzas omitted.

[IX]
SONGS OF
GREAT BRITAIN

The lyric tradition of the British Isles falls into two linguistic classes: the Germanic, which is represented here in varying time phases of the English language; and the Celtic (Erse, Gaelic, Welsh, Cornish), which I have not translated. The Celts, particularly the Welsh, had a vital bardic tradition, and doubtlessly they made a contribution to the general development of British composition, especially in music. Another of their achievements lay in their narratives, which were the predominant vehicles for the early spread of Arthurian material. Although I have omitted work written in the Celtic tongues because of the linguistic difficulties, the Scottish-Irish ballads, though written in dialects of English, may perhaps capture some of the flavor of their composition.

Looking at the Germanic tradition, we find two major time periods: the Old English or Anglo-Saxon period, which began with the North Germanic invasion of Britain in the fifth century; and the Middle English period, which followed the Norman invasion in 1066. The Old English poetry has been translated into Modern English, but the Middle English work has merely been edited.

The Old English period supplies most of the oldest documents for Germanic languages. Cædmon's Hymn, for example, may be dated as early as 670. This literature is extremely valuable, for it gives us a glimpse of pre-Christian existence among the Teutons that we could not get as thoroughly from any other source. In a poem like *The Wanderer* (No. 201), one is struck by the hard, cheerless conditions of life, where tragedy is always vying with Christian assumption. The mind is drawn back to Norse mythology with its *Götterdämmerung* sensibility or forward to the melancholy films of Ingmar Bergman. The Christian coloring in the poem cannot entirely drive out the shadows.

Two of the most distinctive features of Old English poetry are its alliteration and its use of the rhetorical device called a kenning. The kennings are formulaic, imagistic ways of presenting more common objects: the sea is "swan's road," the sky is "dove's lane," buildings are "the halls of the Tall Folk (or the Giants)" (*Wanderer*, line 86). These devices, along with the interesting compound nouns, provide the poetry with great freshness. Since rhyme is seldom practiced, alliteration becomes the tool that binds the verse together, with a strong caesura in every line. One sound is repeated in each verse, usually three times. In my translations I vary this practice, sometimes using separate alliterations on both sides of the break. The alliteration tends to toughen the sound system, at least for the modern ear, which is accustomed to the more soothing effect of rhyme.

The Old English delighted in paradoxes. The Riddle Poem presented here (No. 202) is just one of a sizable body showing a continuing interest in the puzzles of life. By contrast, Cædmon's Hymn strikes the firm chord of Christian belief, and it is this new-found optimism that provides the joy that underlies much of the lyric tradition that follows.

The poetry of the Middle English period shows an undeniable lilt that suggests its closeness to the pulse of the people. If the Normans conquered and imposed their language, they still did not transform the "folk" in any immediately significant way. The pre-Chaucerian work is remarkably free of the conventions established in Provençal verse. Here only Number 222 and Charles d'Orléans' Number 223 indicate a following of the Continental traditions. Both of these are late, and the latter is by a North French writer.

One continuing feature of English composition is a love of ambiguity, which expresses itself in the use of puns. In Number 206, for example, there is a play upon "son" (Sone) and "sun" (Sonne). The supernatural descent of the Son on the Cross is imposed over the natural portrayal of the Sun sinking in the branches of a tree; the effect is striking. In the terse little Number 210 the sinister overtones of the opening lines come to a climax in the word "beste," which can mean either "beast" or "best one." The ambiguity of love is thus presented in as trenchant a way as Sappho's famous coinage "bittersweet." A poem like Number 214 is so elusive and haunting that it escapes any definite classification: is the maiden like Mary or Elvira Madigan or The Lady of the Lake? One cannot be sure.

The spirit of puzzlement is brought to the fore in the ballads, which are much concerned with the mysteries of life and death. We never really know why Lord Randal was poisoned by his sweetheart or who killed the lord lying in the green field (No. 228) or if the Wife of Usher's Well actually did see her sons. These works manage to capture the tragic spirit without destroying a sense of the fragile beauty of life. No one after reading *Barbara Allen* (No. 230) will forget the twining of the rose and the briar; here is symbolism in its most dramatic form.

The ballads, in fact, form the best link between the Middle Ages and the modern world. They cannot be accurately dated, and even if many were written down in the eighteenth and nineteenth centuries, they still were in the hearts and on the tongues of the people at a much earlier date. With them questions of time are unimportant, for the dilemmas they present are common to all time.

To assist the general reader, I have italicized those *e*'s and *i*'s that are voiced in Middle English in places where they might not be in Modern English. The selection of some words for voicing over others must necessarily be arbitrary in some cases. The reader is advised to pronounce all final *e*'s at the ends of lines, where I have not italicized them. The spelling has been normalized wherever possible.

A. OLD ENGLISH LYRICS

ANONYMOUS

[201]

The Wanderer: Oft him an-haga[1]

"Oft does the lone-liver   endure for some dowry,
Some mercy from the Maker,   although he be angst-filled
And long must he labor   yonder on wave-ways
Stirring with oar-stakes   the ice-speckled sea
On the road of the outtrod.   Fate so unflinching!"   5
So spoke the earth-roamer   mindful of miseries,
Victims of violence,   deaths of the dear-loved.
Sometimes I sounded   in dusk of the dawning
Words of my woefulness;   now there's no man,
None among quick ones   to whom in clear confidence   10
I dare declare me.   In truth I have thought
That a man is most masterly   in all of his manners
Who fixes down fastly   the broils in his breast
And hoards up the heartstrings   (let him think what he will!).
One who is spirit-sore   can't foist off fatings;   15
Nor can the mixed mind   hand over help;
And so great glory-seekers   stash down securely
Dreary-doomed gloom   bound in their breasts.
Thus have I shackled   thoughts in the mind that
Came to me, wretch-racked,   hewn from my homeland,   20
Far from kind kinsmen,   fixed thoughts with fetters
When in years yonder   my belovéd gold-giver
I buried in deep dirt   and thence I went forth
In woe, winter-weary,   over bindings of breakers,
Sore-seeking the grand halls   with outheavers of hoards,   25

---

[1] Lament of an exile who has lost his lord to death. Some critics consider the religious elements in the poem, especially at the end, additions by another hand. "Wyrd" in line 107 is Fate.

Where near or where far   I might perchance happen
On some man in mead-hall   who spoke of my folk
Or could bring me some comfort,   me lorn of my loved ones,
Could enjoin me with joy.   He who has felt it
Knows that sorrow as soul-mate   is so terribly tough   30
To a man who is banished   from friends who defend.
The exile-path gapes there;   no baubles are brandished;
Care is his cargo;   no fruit of the field.
He harks back to buddies,   the troving of treasures,
How him in his youngtime   some dispenser of doles   35
Feted with feastings.   O fun now how fallen!
He knows, when the need is,   to forgo for a long time
The talk of his teacher,   his sweet master of men,
When sleep and when sorrow   gathered together
To the unlucky loner   bind up the mind.   40
Then he will think that   he is kissing and clipping
His much-loved man-master   as he kneels on his knees,
Hand, head in that lap,   as in days long ago
He yarely yearned for   his due from the dole-stool.
Ah, he awakens,   that friend-bereft fellow,   45
And before him he sees   the black, spume-capped sea
Where brine-birds are bathing,   fanning their feathers,
Where freeze-frost and snow   come slashing with sleet.
How balefully laden   his breast then with bane,
Sorrow for some sweetheart,   sorriness renewed   50
As the images of kinsmen   swim into his mind.
Ah, with glee how he greets them,   eying them eagerly,
Those old fellow-fighters.   But off they go, floating.
These forms that are flitting   can proffer no comfort,
Rouse no lays long sung.   Care is the comer   55
To him who must fetch forth,   his spirit all weary,
Again and again,   out on breakings of brine.
And thus as I'm thinking   thoughts of the world's ways,
The mind's meditation   grows swart in the gloom.
When only the mere line   of men's lives is measured,   60
How suddenly they surrender   their space in the hall,
Those young, trusty thanes.   Mind how this midworld
In day after day   cracks and then crumbles.

Thus no man is master   of wisdom till winning
His winter's deal in world's domain.   Sage is foresuffering,   65
Is never hot-hearted,   not slick in his speaking,
Not weak in his warring,   nor yet vain in valor,
Neither fearless nor 'fraid,   and ne'er money-hungry
Nor brash into boasting   till true wisdom's his.
A warrior knows waiting   once his vow is out,   70
Till brimful of boldness   he clearly can call
Whither his heart-thought   will twist and will turn.
The smart man will gather   how ghastly the passing
When all of the world's wealth   lies there as a waste
As now hither-thither   throughout all the earth's realm   75
Stand walls that were racked   by the wind and the rain,
With hangings of hoarfrost,   dwellings dashed by the storm.
The wine-hall is weakening,   the lordlings are lying
Lorn of their lustihood;   the man-bands lie hacked,
Fallen proud by a wall.   War wore down many,   80
Jolted into last journeys.   Some did the birds bear
Over steepings of sea.   Grim came the gray wolf,
Dealing out death-shares.   Some by one glum-faced
Were dumped into trenches,   heroes left there to hide.
Thus did the Great Shaper   swipe down his setting,   85
Till the halls of the Tall Folk   stood idle and still,
And the bruiting of the burghers   was a noise voiced on wind.
He pondered profoundly ·   the pillage of the place;
He reflected then deeply   on the darkness of days;
Wise in the heart's ways,   he summons to mind   90
The crops of the corpses,   and these words he says:
"Where's the hero? the horse?   Where's the gift-giver gone?
Where the seats of the feast-hall?   Where joy and the noise?
O alas, those bright beakers!   Alas, armored man!
Alas, pomp of princes!   How time ticks away,   95
Hid under night's hood   as if it ne'er were.
All that's outlasted   is the wall wondrous high,
Cut with snake-carvings;   banished our bands.
The splinter of ash-spear   has hewn down our heroes,
With arms anxious for slaughter,   Fate famous as ere;   100
And storms now are striking   the slopings of stone;

A blinding blizzard is fast binding the earth;
Winter is howling and blasts black and blear;
Swartens the night-shadow; sent out of northland
Hailstones are hitting, a hell now for men.   105
The domain of menfolk is most dour and drear.
Wyrd works the ways of the world under heaven.
Riches soon run, and friends fade away;
Man cannot long stand; the kin spin away;
All earth's establishment soon will be empty!"   110
So spoke the sage one, sitting in sole pondering.
Good hap to the faith-holder, not brandishing breast-care,
Keeping grief deep inside, unless he kens curing
That can comfort with courage. Good hap to the grace-seeker
Humble to Heaven-Father, Who is our earthly fastness.   115

[202²]

Hwelc is hæletha thæs horsc

Who is so seerlike or crafty and clever
That he can answer what forces me forth?
For I rise up raging, wrathful and rueless,
Violent of voice and cruel in pursuit,
Faring o'er earthfolds, burning the folks' barns   5
Wreaking much ravage. The smoke rises high,
Black over thatchings. Ah, the din among dwellings,
The massacre of man as I fell the forest,
I break the bowers, I blast out the beams,
Welling with water, with the high, mighty powers   10
Impelling my pillage over land and o'er sea. . . .
Who am I?

² Riddle Poem. Answer: a storm. Some terminal lines omitted.

[203³]

The Wife's Lament: Ic this 5iedd wrece

I pour forth this poem   of my life pathetic,
Tracing the self's trip.   This I can say:
How I suffered miseries   once I had grown up,
Some new, some old,   but none more than now.
Fore'er I've experienced   expeditions in exile.   5
First fared my liegelord   hence from his land
Over waves' winnows.   I suffered wan-care,
Wondering where my lord   wandered abroad.
I took then to traveling,   seeking out service,
A winsomeless wanderer   out of woeful need.   10
The kin of my kind one   began to conspire
In soft, secret whispering   to split us apart,
So that sundered completely   I would be cast forth
To a most loathsome life—   ah, indeed how I longed!
Here did my dear lord   command me take dwelling.   15
I had little to love   here in this land,
Very few loyal friends.   And so is my soul sad,
For I found that companion   most fit for my side
Suddenly sad-spirited,   strangely ill-starred,
Mulling over murders,   hiding his mind.   20
Before we were both   blithe in our bearing,
Promising ever   that nothing would part us
Unless it were death.   All went helter-skelter:
And now it's as nothing   . . . . . .
Our loyal love.   Whether far, whether near   25
I must bide the bad cheer   of my cherished one.
A man has commanded: go live in that grove!
Under an oak tree,   deep in a den.
Old is my cave-lodge;   I languish with longing;
Dark are the dales round;   high are the hills;   30
Sharp are the hamlet-hedges   brittle with briars,

³ Lament of a woman parted from her husband. Line 24 incomplete. Lines 42–50
slightly emended.

A home full of groans.   The going of my good lord
Fills me with grief.   Other lovers are living
Lively on earth,   with leisure in the bedstead;
But I walk at daybreak   alone in the dawning   35
Under the oak tree   or deep in my den.
There I may sit   the whole summer day;
There I may weep   the wreck of my roaming,
Hardships so heavy,   never knowing any rest
From the dark depression   that dogs all my days   40
And seizes my soul now   for the length of my life.
A young man may ever be   melancholy and mourning,
Heavy in his heart,   yet he should e'er show
Blitheness of bearing   despite all his breast-cares,
His sufferings endless,   whether all the world's weal   45
He holds in his hands   or even if exiled
Among some far folk—   where my friend is sitting
Under some stone heap,   stung by the storm,
Ever mournful in mind,   wet by the water
In some ruined gloom.   Ah, my lord labors   50
With glumness that's great: too oft he remembers
Our hilarious halls.   Woe is the winning
Of one who's awaiting   a lover with longing.

CÆDMON[4]

[204]

Nu we sculon herian

Now let's give laudings   to the Lord of the Heaven-realm,
The main of the Master   with his firmness of mind,
The Miracle-Maker,   mighty Father everlasting

[4] Cædmon (*fl.* 670). First-known English poet. The Venerable Bede tells how this rude shepherd, hearing the voice of God, broke forth with this praise. Lived at Whitby; composed other poems.

Who worked in his wise   every wonder that was.
First did he form   for the offspring of humans   5
Heaven for roofing,   great Creator of all.
Then the Warder of mankind   worked out the world.
The Lord ever-living,   the Master all-mighty,
Fashioned the earth-folds   for the mansion of man.

B. MIDDLE ENGLISH LYRICS

ANONYMOUS

[205]

Summer is i-comen in

Summer is i-comen in,
Loude sing cucku!
Groweth seed and *bloweth meed*   *meadow blooms*
And springth the woode *nu.*   *now*
Sing cucku!   5

Ewe bleteth after lamb,
Loweth after calve *cu;*   *cow*
Bullock *sterteth;* bucke *ferteth*—   *starts (jumps)/ farts*
Murry sing cucku!
Cucku, cucku!   10
Well singest thu, cucku.
Ne swik thu never nu.   *Nor be quiet*
(Repeated in two parts:)

   Sing cucku nu, sing cucku!
   Sing cucku nu, sing cucku!   15

[206]

Nu goth Sonne under wode

Nu goth Sonne under *wode*.   *wood (Cross)*
Me rueth, Mary, thy faire *rode*.   *I pity/ face*
Nu goth Sonne under tree.
Me rueth, Mary, thy Sone and thee.

[207]

Say me, wight in the broom

Say me, *wight in the broom*:   *creature/ brush*
Teche me how I shall don
That min housebonde
Me lovien wolde.

"Hold thine tunge stille   5
And have all thine wille."

[208]

When the turf is thy tour

When the turf is thy *tour*   *tower*
And the *pit* is thy *bour*,   *grave/ bower*
Thy *fel* and thy white throte   *flesh*
Shallen wormes *to note*.   *feed*
What helpeth thee thenne   5
All the worlde winne?

[209]

Of oon that is so fayr and bright

1. Of *oon* that is so fayr and bright,   *one*
   Velut maris stella,   *Like a star of the sea (Latin)*
   Brighter than the day*e*s light,
   Parens et puella;   *Mother and maiden*
   I crye to thee: thou see to me.   5
   Lady, pray thy Sone for me,
   Tam pia,   *Thou so devout one*
   That I moot*e* come to thee,
   Maria.

2. Of car*e* counsel thou art best,   10
   Felix fecundata.   *Blessed by womb-fruit*
   Of all*e* weery thou art rest,
   Mater honorata.   *Honored mother*
   Biseech thou him with mild*e* mood
   That for us all*e* shed his blood   15
   In cruce   *On Cross*
   That we moot*e* come to him
   In luce.   *In light*

3. All this world*e* was forlore
   Eva peccatrice,   *By Eve the sinner* 20
   Till our Lord was i-bore
   De te genetrice.   *With you his bearer*
   With Ave it went away,
   Thester night, and cam the day   *the dark*
   Salutis.   *Of health* 25
   The well*e* springeth out of thee
   Virtutis.   *Of virtue*

4. Lady, flour of all*e* thing,
   Rosa sine spina,   *Thornless rose*
   Thou bar Jesu, heven*e*s King,   30

Gratia divina.	*By divine grace*
Of alle thou berst the *pris,*	*prize*
Lady, Quene of Paradis	
Electa.	*Chosen*
Mayde and milde Moder *es*	*Thou art (Latin)* 35
Effecta.	*Created*

5. Well he *wot* he is thy Sone	*knows*
Ventre quem portasti;	*Whom thou borest in womb*
He will not *werne* thee thy *boone*	*refuse/ prayer*
Parvum quem lactasti,	*The small one you suckled* 40
So *hende* and so good he is,	*gentle*
He hath brought us alle to bliss	
Superni,	*Of Heaven*
That hath *i-dut* the foule *put*	*shut/ pit*
Inferni.	*Of Hell* 45

[210]

Fowles in the frith

Fowles in the *frith,*	*forest*
The fishes in the flood,	
And I *mon waxe wood*—	*must go mad*
Much sorwe I walke with	
For *beste* of bone and blood. .	*best, beast* 5

[211]

Bitweene Merch and Aperil

1. Bitweene Merch and Aperil
   When spray biginneth to springe,

The littel fowle hath *hire* will   *their*
On hir*e lud* to singe.   *tongue*
I live in love-longinge   5
For *semlokest* of all*e* thing;   *the prettiest*
She may me bliss*e* bringe:
I am in hir *baundoun.*   *power*
    An *hende hap* I have *i-hent,*   *happy fate/ gotten*
    I *wot* from heven it is me sent;   *know* 10
    From all*e* women my love is *lent*   *taken*
    And light on Alisoun.

2. *On hew* hir heer is fayr enough;   *Of color*
   Hir brow*e* brown, hir eyen black;
   With *lossum cheere* she on me *lough,*   *lovely look/ laughed* 15
   With middel small and well *i-mak.*   *made*
   *But s*he me *woll*e to hire take   *Unless/ will*
   For to been her owen *make,*   *mate*
   Longe to live I shulle forsake
   And *fey*e fallen adoun.   *death-fated* 20
    An hend*e* hap I have i-hent . . .

3. Night*es* when I *wende* and wake,   *turn*
   Forthy min *wonges* waxen wan,   *Because/ cheeks*
   Levedy, all for thin*e* sake   *Lady*
   Longinge *is i-lent* me on.   *has come* 25
   In world is non so *witer* man   *wise a*
   That all hir bountee tellen can:
   Her *swire* is whiter than the swan,   *neck*
   The fayrest mayd in toun.
    An hend*e* hap I have i-hent . . .   30

4. I am for *wowing* all *forwake,*   *wooing/ worn out*
   Weery as water *in wore,*   *in a pond (?)*
   Lest any *reve* me my make   *rob from*
   I have i-yern*ed* yore.
   Bettere is *tholien* while sore   *to endure* 35
   Than mournen evermore.

Gainest under gore,   *Prettiest in gown*
Herkne to my *roun:*   *speech*
   An hende hap I have i-hent,
   I wot from heven it is me sent: 40
   From alle women my love is lent
   And light on Alisoun.

[212]

Lenten is come with love to toune

1. *Lenten* is come with love to toune,   *Spring*
   With *blosmes* and with briddes *roune,*   *blossoms/ song*
   That all this blisse bringeth;
   Daisyes in these dales,
   Notes sweet of nightengales—   5
   Eech fowel song singeth.
   The throstelcock him *threteth oo;*   *chides ever*
   Away is hire winter wo
   When *woderove* springeth.   *woodruff*
   Thise fowles singen *ferly fele*   *wondrous many*   10
   And *wlyten* on hire *wynne wele*   *pipe/ joyous wealth*
   That all the woode ringeth.

2. The rose *raileth* hir *rode.*   *puts on/ hue*
   The leaves on the lighte wode
   Waxen all with wille.   15
   The Moone *mandeth* hir *blee,*   *sends/ ray*
   The lily is *lossum* to see,   *lovely*
   The fennel and the *fille.*   *chervil-flower (?)*
   Wooen thise wilde drakes;
   Males merryen hire makes   20
   As streem that *striketh* stille.   *flows*
   Moody meneth, as doth mo;   *The brave laments, as do others*
   I wot I am oon of tho,
   For love that *liketh ill.*   *pleases poorly*

3. The Moone mandeth hir light;   25
   So doth the seemly Sonne bright
   When briddes singen *breme*;   *loud*
   Dewes *dunken* thise *dounes*;   *dampen/ hills*
   Deeres with hire *derne* rounes,   *animals/ secret*
   Domes for to deme.   *by which they talk*   30
   Wormes wooen under cloude,
   Women waxen wonder proude,
   So well it will hem seeme.
   If me shall wante wille of oon,
   This *wynne wele* I will forgon   *joyous state*   35
   And *wyght* in woode be *fleeme*.   *soon/ fleer (exile)*

[213]

All night by the rose, rose

All night by the rose, rose,
All night by the rose I lay;
Durste I nought the rose *steele*   *steal*
And yet I *bar* the flour away.   *bore*

[214]

Maiden in the moor lay

1. Maiden in the moor lay—
   In the moor lay—
   Seven-night fulle,
   Seven-night fulle.
   Maiden in the moor lay—   5
   In the moor lay—
   Seven-nights full and a day.

M

2. *Well* was her *mete*.   *Good/ food*
   What was her mete?
   The *primerole* and the—   *primrose*   10
   The primerole and the—
   Well was her mete.
   What was her mete?
   The primerole and the violette.

3. Well was her drinke.   15
   What was her drinke?
   The cold*e* water of the—
   The cold*e* water of the—
   Well was her drinke.
   What was her drinke?   20
   The cold*e* water of the well*e*-spring.

4. Well was her bour.
   What was her bour?
   The red*e* rose and the—
   The red*e* rose and the—
   Well was her bour.
   What was her bour?
   The red*e* rose and the lily-flour.

GEOFFREY CHAUCER[5]

[215]

Madame, ye been of alle beautee shrine

1. Madame, ye been of all*e* beautee shrine
   As fer as cercl*e*d is the *mapemounde,*   *map of the world*
   For as the crystal glorious ye shine,

---

[5] Geoffrey Chaucer (*ca.* 1343–1400). Greatest medieval English author. Composer of *The Canterbury Tales.* His Ballade to Rosemounde mixes formal North French conceits with realistic English detail (pikes, tubs).

And like ruby been your cheekes rounde.
Therwith ye been so merry and so jocounde   5
That at a revel whan that I see you daunce,
It is an oinement unto my wounde,
Though ye to me ne *do* no *dalliaunce.*   *offer comfort*

2. For though I weepe of teres full a *tine,*   *tub*
   Yet may that wo myn herte nat confounde;   10
   Your *semy* vois, that ye so small *out-twine,*   *delicate/ spin out*
   Maketh my thought in joy and bliss abounde.
   So curteisly I go, with love bounde
   That to myself I say, in my penaunce,
   "Suffiseth me to love you, Rosemounde,   15
   Though ye to me ne do no dalliaunce."

3. Was never *pik walwed in galauntine*   *pike wallowing in sauce*
   As I in love am walwed and ywounde,
   For which full ofte I of myself divine
   That I am true Tristram the secounde.   20
   My love may not *refreide* nor *affounde;*   *cool down/ go numb*
   I *brenne* ay in an amorous plesaunce.   *burn*
   Do what you list, I will your thrall be founde,
   Though ye to me ne do no dalliaunce.

[216[6]]

Adam scrivain, if ever it thee bifalle

Adam scrivain, if ever it thee bifalle
Boece or *Troilus* to writen newe,
Under thy long lockes thou moste have the *scalle*   *scab-disease*
But after my making thou write more true;   *Unless*

[6] Words to His Scribe Adam, who transcribed Chaucer's translation of Boethius'
Consolation of Philosophy (see No. 21) and his *Troilus and Criseyde,* apparently
rather sloppily.

So ofte a-day I moot thy werk renewe,   5
It to correcte and eek to rub and scrape;
And all is *thourgh* thy negligence and *rape*.   *through/ haste*

[217⁷]

Somtime the world was so stedfast and stable

1. *Somtime* the world was so stedfast and stable   *Once*
   That man*e*s word was obligacioun;
   And now it is so fals and deceivable
   That word and deed, as in conclusioun,
   Been nothing *lyk*, for turned up-so-doun   *alike*   5
   Is all this world for *mede* and willfulnesse,   *reward*
   That all is lost for lack of stedfastnesse.

2. What maketh this world to be so variable
   But *lust* that folk have in dissensioun?   *pleasure*
   For among us now a man is *holde* unable   *considered*   10
   But if he can by som collusioun
   Do his neighbour wrong or oppressioun.
   What causeth this but willful wretchednesse,
   That all is lost for lack of stedfastnesse?

3. Trouthe is put doun, resoun is holden fable;   15
   Vertù hath now no dominacioun;
   Pitee exil*e*d; no man is merciable;
   Through coveteise is *blent* discrecioun.   *blinded*
   The world hath maad a permutacioun
   Fro right to wrong, fro trouthe to fickelnesse,   20
   That all is lost for lack of stedfastnesse.

⁷ *The Lack of Stedfastnesse.*

Envoi to King Richard II

4. O Prince, desire to been honourable;
   Cherish thy folk and hate extorcioun!
   Suffer no thing that may be *reprevable*   *reproof-worthy*
   To thyn estaat don in thy regioun.   25
   Shew forth thy swerd of castigacioun.
   Dred God; do law; love trouthe and worthinesse,
   And wed thy folk again to stedfastnesse.

[218⁸]

To you, my purs, and to non other wight

1. To you, my purs, and to non other wight
   Complaine I, for ye be my lady deere!
   I am so sorry now that ye been light;
   For certes, *but* ye maak me hevy cheere,   *unless*
   Me were as lief be laid upon my *beere;*   *I'd as soon/ bier*   5
   For which unto your mercy thus I crye:
   Beeth hevy again, or ell*es moot* I dye!   *must*

2. Now *voucheth-sauf* this day, er it be night,   *please grant*
   That I of you the blissful sound may heere
   Or see your colour lyk the Sonne bright,   10
   That of yellownesse hadd*e* never peere.
   Ye be my lif, ye be myn hert*es steere,*   *steerer*
   Queene of comfort and of good companye:
   Beeth hevy again, or ell*es moot* I dye!

3. Now purs that been to me my lives light   15
   And sav*i*our, as doun in this world here,
   Out of this toun help*e* me thourgh your might,
   Sin that ye wol not been my tresourere;

---

⁸ *Complaint to His Purse.* In the Envoi, Brutus, a Roman, is taken as the legendary
founder of England (Albion).

For I am shaven as *nie* as any *frere*.   *close/ friar*
But yet I pray unto your curteisye: 20
Beeth hevy again, or elles moot I dye!

Envoi to King Henry IV
4. O conquerour of Brutus' Albioun,
   Which that by line and free eleccioun
   Been *verray* king, this song to you I sende;   *true*
   And ye, that mowen alle our harmes amende,   25
   Have minde upon my supplicacioun!

ANONYMOUS

[219]

I have a gentil cock

1. I have a gentil cock,
   Croweth me the day;
   He doth me risen erly,
   My matins for to say.

2. I have a gentil cock;   5
   Comen he is of *gret;*   *great lineage*
   His comb is of red coral,
   His *tayil* is of jet.   *tail*

3. I have a gentil cock;
   Comen he is *of kynde;*   *of good kin*   10
   His comb is of red coral,
   His tayil is of *Inde.*   *India*

4. His legges been of *asor,*   *azure*
   So gentil and so smale;

His *spures* arn of silver-whyt   *back-claws* 15
Into the *wortewale*.   *root of spur*

5. His ey*e*n arn of crystal,
   Looking all in aumber;
   And every nyght he percheth him
   In myn lady's chaumber.   20

[220]

I have a yong syster

1. I have a yong syster
   Fer beyonde the see;
   Many be the *drueries*   *love-tokens*
   That she sent*e* me.

2. She sent*e* me the cherry   5
   Withouten any ston;
   And so she did the dove
   Withouten any bon.

3. She sent*e* me the *brere*   *rose-briar*
   Withouten any *rinde;*   *bark*   10
   She bad me love my *lemman*   *lover*
   Withouten longinge.

4. How should any cherry
   Be withouten ston?
   And how should any dove   15
   Be withouten bon?

5. How should any brere
   Be withouten rinde?

How should I love my lemman
Withouten longinge?   20

6. Whan the cherry was a flour,
Than hadde it no ston.
Whan the do*v*e was an *ey,*   *egg*
Than hadde it no bon.

7. Whan the brere was *unbred*   *unborn* 25
Than hadde it no rinde.
Whan the maid hath that she loveth
She is without longinge.

[221]

I singe of a Maiden

1. I singe of a Maiden
That is *makeless;*   *matchless*
King of all kinges
To hir Sone she *ches.*   *chose*

2. He cam all so stille   5
Ther his Moder was,
As dew in Aperille
That falleth on the grass.

3. He cam all so stille
To his Modres bour,   10
As dew in Aperille
That falleth on the flour.

4. He cam all so stille
Ther his Moder lay,
As dew in Aperille   15
That falleth on the spray.

5. Moder and maiden
   Was nevere non but she.
   Well may swich a lady
   Goddes Moder be.   20

[222]

Have all my hert and be in peese

1. Have all my hert and be in *peese,*   *peace*
   And think I love you fervently;
   For in good faith, it is no *leese;*   *lie*
   I would ye *wist* as well as I.   *knew*
   For now I see, both night and day,   5
   That my love will not ceese.
   Have mercy on me as ye best may—
   Have all my hert and be in peese.

2. Have all my hert wherever I go:
   Hert, body, and all my might.   10
   Me for-thought we parted in two   *It grieved me*
   When I to you had most right.
   Have mercy on me, *mickel* of might,   *muchness*
   For of my love I cannot ceese,
   Tho I be selden in your sight—   15
   Have all my hert and be in peese.

3. It is a thing that me can *nye*   *bother*
   But if ye hold *that* ye have *hight;*   *Unless/ what/ promised*
   For traitors' tonges: "Evil *moot* they *thee!*"   *may/ thrive*
   I say to you, myn sweete wight.   20
   Therfore I sweere, as moot I dye,
   If I said aught whan ye *bad* peese,   *asked for*
   I will full meekly aske mercye—
   Have all my hert and be in peese.

4. Ye have my hert as I you highte;   25
   I pray God ell*e*s that I be dede.
   But I love you with all my mighte
   As he that weers furred hood on hede!
   This song was maad, *withouten drede,*   *doubtlessly*
   For you*r*e love that I first *cheese*;   *chose*   30
   Wher-so-ever I be, *in stall or stede,*   *in any place*
   Have all my hert and be in peese.

CHARLES D'ORLÉANS[9]

[223]

So faire, so freshe, so goodly on to see

So faire, so freshe, so goodly on to see,
So welle *demeined* in all your governaunce,   *conducted*
That to my hert it is a greete plesaunce
Of your goodness when I remember me;
And trusteth fully, where-that-ever I be,   5
I will abide under your obeissaunce—
So faire, so freshe, so goodly on to see,
So welle demeined in all your governaunce.

For in my thought ther is no *mo* but ye,   *other*
Whom I have serv*e*d without repentaunce;   10
Wherfore I pray you, see to my *grevaunce*   *grief*
And put aside all myn adversitee—
So faire, so freshe, so goodly on to see,
So welle demeined in all your governaunce.

---

[9] See Numbers 161–170. Composed in his English captivity.

ANONYMOUS

[224]

In what estaat soevere I be

1. In what estaat soevere I be,
   Timor mortis conturbat me.   *Fear of death disturbs me*

2. As I went in a myrie morweninge,
   I herde a brid both weepe and singe;
   This was the tenour of hir talkinge: 5
   Timor mortis conturbat me.

3. I axed that brid what she ment.
   "I am a *musket* both faire and gent;   *sparrowhawk*
   For drede of deeth I am all *shent.*   *mortified*
   Timor mortis conturbat me.   10

4. "Whan I shall *deye* I knowe no daye,   *die*
   What contree or place I cannot saye;
   Wherfore this songe sing I may:
   Timor mortis conturbat me.

5. "Jesu Crist, whan he sholde deye,   15
   To his Fader he gan saye,
   'Fader,' saide he, 'in Trinitee,
   Timor mortis conturbat me.'

6. "Alle Cristen peple biholde and see
   This world is but a vanitee   20
   And repleet with necessitee.
   Timor mortis conturbat me.

7. "Wake I or sleepe, ete or drinke,
   Whan I on my laste ende thinke,

For greete feere my soule doth shrinke—   25
Timor mortis conturbat me.

8. "God graunt us grace him to serve,
   And be at oure ende whan we *sterve,*   *die*
   And from the Feend he us preserve!
   Timor mortis conturbat me."   30

[225]

O Western Wind, when wilt thou blow

O Western Wind, when wilt thou blow:
The small rain down can rain?
Christ! that my love were in my arms—
And I in my bed again!

C. SCOTTISH-ENGLISH BALLADS

[226]

The Wife of Usher's Well: There lived a wife at Usher's Well

1. There lived a wife at Usher's Well,
      And a wealthy wife was she;
   She had three stout and stalwart sons,
      And sent them o'er the sea.

2. They hadna been a week from her,   5
      A week but barely *ane,*   *one*
   Whan word came to the *carlin* wife   *peasant*
      That her three sons were gone.

3. They hadna been a week from her,
 A week but barely three, 10
 Whan word came to the carlin wife
 That her sons she'd never see.

4. "I wish the wind may never cease
 Nor *fashes* in the flood, *troubles*
 Till my three sons come hame to me, 15
 In earthly flesh and blood."

5. It fell about the Martinmass
 When nights are lang and mirk,
 The carlin wife's three sons came hame,
 And their hats were o' the *birk*. *birch* 20

6. It neither grew in *syke* nor ditch, *gully*
 Nor yet in any *sheugh;* *furrow*
 But at the gates of Paradise,
 That birk grew fair eneugh.

7. "Blow up the fire, my maidens, 25
 Bring water from the well;
 For a' my house shall feast this night
 Since my three sons are well."

8. And she has made to them a bed,
 She's made it large and wide, 30
 And she's ta'en her mantle her about,
 Sat down at the bedside.

9. Up then crew the red, red cock,
 And up and crew the gray;
 The eldest to the youngest said, 35
 " 'Tis time we were away."

10. The cock he hadna crawd but once,
 And clappd his wings at a',

When the youngest to the eldest said,
"Brother, we must awa'." 40

11. "The cock doth craw, the day doth daw,
The *channerin* worm doth chide; *devouring*
Gin we be missed out o' our place, *If*
A *sair* pain we *maun* bide. *sore/ must*

12. "Fare ye well, my mother dear! 45
Farewell to barn and *byre!* *shed*
And fare ye well, ye bonny lass
That kindles my mother's fire!"

[227¹⁰]

Lord Randal: O where ha' you been, Lord Randal, my son

1. "O where ha' you been, Lord Randal, my son?
And where ha' you been, my handsome young man?"
"I ha' been to the greenwood; mother, mak my bed soon,
For I'm wearied wi' huntin', and fain wald lie down."

2. "And *wha* met ye there, Lord Randal, my son? *who* 5
And wha met ye there, my handsome young man?"
"O I met wi' my true love; mother, mak my bed soon,
For I'm wearied wi' huntin', and fain wald lie down."

3. "And what did she give you, Lord Randal, my son?
And what did she give you, my handsome young man?" 10
"Eels fried in a pan; mother, mak my bed soon,
For I'm wearied wi' huntin', and fain wald lie down."

4. "And wha gat your *leavins*, Lord Randal, my son? *leftovers*
And wha gat your leavins, my handsome young man?"

¹⁰ English version probably post-medieval, but the motif can be traced through
Italian to the Middle Ages.

"My hawks and my hounds; mother, mak my bed soon,   15
For I'm wearied wi' huntin', and fain wald lie down."

5. "And what becam of them, Lord Randal, my son?
   And what becam of them, my handsome young man?"
   "They stretched their legs out and died; mother, mak my bed soon,
   For I'm wearied wi' huntin', and fain wald lie down."   20

6. "O I fear ye are poisoned, Lord Randal, my son!
   I fear ye are poisoned, my handsome young man!"
   "O yes, I am poisoned; mother, mak my bed soon,
   For I'm sick at the heart, and I fain wald lie down."

7. "What d' ye leave your mother, Lord Randal, my son?   25
   What d' ye leave your mother, my handsome young man?"
   "Four and twenty milk *kye;* mother, mak my bed soon,   *cows*
   For I'm sick at the heart, and I fain wald lie down."

8. "What d' ye leave your sister, Lord Randal, my son?
   What d' ye leave your sister, my handsome young man?"   30
   "My gold and my silver; mother, mak my bed soon,
   For I'm sick at the heart, and I fain wald lie down."

9. "What d' ye leave your brother, Lord Randal, my son?
   What d' ye leave your brother, my handsome young man?"
   "My houses and my lands; mother, mak my bed soon,   35
   For I'm sick at the heart, and I fain wald lie down."

10. "What d' ye leave your true love, Lord Randal, my son?
    What d' ye leave your true love, my handsome young man?"
    "I leave her Hell and fire; mother, mak my bed soon,
    For I'm sick at the heart, and I fain wald lie down."   40

[228¹¹]

The Three Ravens: There were three ravens sat on a tree

1. There were three ravens sat on a tree,
     Down a down, hay down, hay down.
   There were three ravens sat on a tree,
     With a down.
   There were three ravens sat on a tree,   5
   They were as black as they might be:
     With a down derrie, derrie, derrie, down, down.

2. The one of them said to his mate,
   "Where shall we our breakfast take?"

3. "Down in yonder greene field   10
   There lies a knight slain under his shield.

4. "His hounds they lie down at his feet,
   So well they can their master keep.

5. "His hawks they fly so eagerly,
   There's no fowl dare come him nie."   15

6. Down there comes a fallow doe,
   As great with young as she might go.

7. She lift up his bloody hed,
   And kist his wounds that were so red.

8. She got him up upon her backe,   20
   And carried him to earthen *lake*.   *pit*

9. She buried him before the prime;
   She was dead herself at evensong time.

¹¹ Many alternate versions, such as the Scottish *Twa Corbies*. For recording, consult
Argo ZDA 72.

10. God send every gentleman
    Such hawks, such hounds, and such a *lemman.*   beloved one 25

[229¹²]

Sir Patrick Spens: The King sits in Dumferling Toun

1. The King sits in Dumferling Toun,
   Drinking the blood-red wine:
   "O whar will I get good sailor
   To sail this ship of mine?"

2. Then up and spak an eldern knight,   5
   Sat at the King's right knee:
   "Sir Patrick Spens is the best sailor
   That ever saild the see."

3. The King has written a *braid* letter   broad
   And seald it wi' his hand;   10
   He sent it to Sir Patrick Spens
   Was walking on the sand.

4. The first line that Sir Patrick red,
   A loud *lauch* lauched he;   laugh
   The next line that Sir Patrick red   15
   The teir blinded his *ee.*   eye

5. "O *wha* is this has don this deid,   who
   This ill deid don to me,
   To send me out this time o' the yeir
   To sail upon the see!   20

6. "Mak hast, mak hast, my merry men all;
   Our good ship sails the morn."

¹² Perhaps based on events in 1281 or 1290. For music, consult Argo ZDA 72.

"O say na so, my master deir,
For I feir a dedly storm.

7. "Late, late *yestreen* I saw the new moon   *yester evening* 25
Wi' the auld moon in her arm;
And I feir, I feir, my deir master,
That we will com to harm."

8. O our Scots nobles wer right *laith*   *loath, unwilling*
To wet their cork-heeld *shoone;*   *shoes* 30
But lang ere a' the play wer playd,
Their hats they swam *aboone.*   *above*

9. O lang, lang may their ladies sit
Wi' their fans into their hand
Befor they see Sir Patrick Spens   35
Com sailing to the land.

10. O lang, lang may the ladies stand
Wi' their gold *kems* i' their hair,   *combs*
Waiting for their *ain* deir lords,   *own*
For they'll see them na mair.   40

11. Half *oure*, half oure to Aberdour   *over*
It's fifty fadom deip.
It's ther lies good Sir Patrick Spens
Wi' the Scots lords at his feit.

[230¹³]

Barbara Allen: All in the merry month of May

1. All in the merry month of May
When green leaves they were swellin'

¹³ Composite version of a ballad that is largely post-medieval.

Sweet William on his deathbed lay
For the love of Barbara Allen.

2. He sent his servant to her then,   5
   To the place where she was dwellin':
   "You must come to my master dear
   If your name be Barbara Allen.

3. "For death is printed in his face,
   And sorrow's in him dwellin';   10
   Ah, you must come to my master dear
   If your name be Barbara Allen."

4. So slowly, slowly she got up
   And slowly she drew nigh him;
   The only words that she did say: 15
   "Young man, I think you're dyin'."

5. He turned his face unto the wall,
   And death was in him wellin':
   "Good-bye, good-bye to my friends all;
   Be good to Barbara Allen."   20

6. When he was dead and laid in grave,
   She heard the death bell knellin'
   And every stroke to her did say:
   "Hardhearted Barbara Allen."

7. "O Mother, Mother, go dig my grave.   25
   Make it both long and narrow.
   Sweet William died of love for me,
   And I shall die for sorrow."

8. Barbara Allen was buried in the old churchyard;
   Sweet William was buried beside her.   30
   Out of Sweet William's heart grew a rose;
   Out of Barbara Allen's a briar.

9. They grew and they grew in the old churchyard
   Till they could grow no higher.
   At the end they formed a true-lover's knot,   35
   And the rose grew round the briar.

[X]
SELECTED ORIGINAL TEXTS

Original Text for Number 6

1. Aeterne rerum conditor,
   Noctem diemque qui regis
   Et temporum das tempora,
   Ut alleves fastidium,

2. Praeco diei iam sonat,   5
   Noctis profundae pervigil,
   Nocturna lux viantibus,
   A nocte noctem segregans.

3. Hoc excitatus lucifer
   Solvit polum caligine;   10
   Hoc omnis erronum chorus
   Vias nocendi deserit.

4. Hoc nauta vires colligit,
   Pontique mitescunt freta;
   Hoc ipse Petra ecclesiae   15
   Canente culpam diluit.

5. Surgamus ergo strenue;
   Gallus iacentes excitat
   Et somnolentos increpat;
   Gallus negantes arguit.   20

6. Gallo canente spes redit;
   Aegris salus refunditur;
   Mucro latronis conditur;
   Lapsis fides revertitur.

7. Iesu, labentes respice   25
   Et nos videndo corrige;
   Si respicis, lapsus cadunt,
   Fletuque culpa solvitur.

8. Tu lux, refulge sensibus
   Mentisque somnum discute;   30
   Te nostra vox primum sonet,
   Et ora solvamus tibi.

Original Text for Number 10

1. Vexilla regis prodeunt,
   Fulget crucis mysterium,
   Quo carne carnis conditor
   Suspensus est patibulo.

2. Confixa clavis viscera   5
   Tendens manus, vestigia,
   Redemptionis gratia
   Hic immolata est hostia.

3. Quo vulneratus insuper
   Mucrone diro lanceae,   10
   Ut nos lavaret crimine,
   Manavit unda et sanguine.

4. Impleta sunt quae concinit
   David fideli carmine
   Dicendo nationibus: 15
   Regnavit a ligno Deus.

5. Arbor decora et fulgida,
   Ornata regis purpura,
   Electa digno stipite
   Tam sancta membra tangere!   20

6. Beata cuius brachiis
   Pretium pependit saeculi!
   Statera facta est corporis
   Praedam tulitque Tartari.

7. Fundis aroma cortice,   25
   Vincis sapore nectare,
   Iucunda fructu fertili
   Plaudis triumpho nobili.

8. Salve, ara! salve, victima!
   De passionis gloria,   30
   Qua vita mortem pertulit
   Et morte vitam reddidit.

Original Text for Number 12

1. Ave, maris stella,
   Dei mater alma
   Atque semper virgo,
   Felix caeli porta.

2. Sumens illud "Ave"   5
   Gabrielis ore,
   Funda nos in pace,
   Mutans Evae nomen.

3. Solve vincla reis,
   Profer lumen caecis,   10
   Mala nostra pelle,
   Bona cuncta posce!

4. Monstra esse matrem,
   Sumat per te preces
   Qui pro nobis natus   15
   Tulit esse tuus.

5. Virgo singularis,
   Inter omnes mitis,
   Nos culpis solutos
   Mites fac et castos.   20

6. Vitam praesta puram,
   Iter para tutum,
   Ut videntes Iesum
   Semper collaetemur!

7. Sit laus Deo patri,   25
   Summum Christo decus,
   Spiritui Sancto
   Honor, Tribus unus!

Original Text for Number 18

1. Dies irae, dies illa,
   Solvet saeclum in favilla,
   Teste David cum Sibylla.

2. Quantus tremor est futurus,
   Quando Iudex est venturus,   5
   Cuncta stricte discussurus!

3. Tuba mirum sparget sonum
   Per sepulchra regionum,
   Coget omnes ante thronum.

4. Mors stupebit et Natura,   10
   Cum resurget creatura
   Iudicanti responsura.

5. Liber scriptus proferetur,
   In quo totum continetur,
   Unde mundus iudicetur.   15

6. Iudex ergo cum censebit,
   Quidquid latet, apparebit;
   Nil inultum remanebit.

7. Quid sum miser tunc dicturus,
   Quem patronum rogaturus,   20
   Cum vix iustus sit securus?

8. Rex tremendae maiestatis,
   Qui salvandos salvas gratis,
   Salva me, fons pietatis!

9. Recordare, Iesu pie,   25
   Quod sum causa tuae viae:
   Ne me perdas illa die.

10. Quaerens me sedisti lassus;
    Redemisti crucem passus;
    Tantus labor non sit cassus.   30

11. Iuste Iudex ultionis,
    Donum fac remissionis
    Ante diem rationis.

12. Ingemisco tamquam reus;
    Culpa rubet vultus meus;   35
    Supplicanti parce, Deus.

13. Qui Mariam absolvisti
    Et latronem exaudisti,
    Mihi quoque spem dedisti.

14. Preces meae non sunt dignae,   40
    Sed tu, bonus, fac benigne,
    Ne perenni cremer igne.

15. Inter oves locum praesta
    Et ab haedis me sequestra
    Statuens in parte dextra.   45

16. Confutatis maledictis,
    Flammis acribus addictis,
        Voca me cum benedictis!

17. Oro supplex et acclinis,
    Cor contritum quasi cinis;   50
        Gere curam mei finis!

Original Text for Number 19

1. Stabat mater dolorosa
   Iuxta crucem lacrimosa
       Dum pendebat filius;
   Cuius animam gementem
   Contristantem et dolentem   5
       Pertransivit gladius.

2. O quam tristis et afflicta
   Fuit illa benedicta
       Mater unigeniti
   Quae maerebat, et dolebat,   10
   Et tremebat cum videbat
       Nati poenas incliti.

3. Quis est homo qui non fleret
   Matrem Christi si videret
       In tanto supplicio?   15
   Quis non posset contristari
   Piam matrem contemplari
       Dolentem cum filio?

4. Pro peccatis suae gentis
   Iesum vidit in tormentis   20
       Et flagellis subditum.
   Vidit suum dulcem natum

Morientem, desolatum,
   Dum emisit spiritum.

5. Eia, mater! fons amoris,   25
   Me sentire vim doloris
      Fac, ut tecum lugeam;
   Fac ut ardeat cor meum
   In amando Christum Deum,
      Ut sibi complaceam.   30

6. Sancta mater, istud agas,
   Crucifixi fige plagas
      Cordi meo valide;
   Tui nati vulnerati,
   Tam dignati pro me pati,   35
      Poenas mecum divide!

7. Fac me vere tecum flere,
   Crucifixo condolere,
      Donec ego vixero.
   Iuxta crucem tecum stare,   40
   Te libenter sociare
      In planctu desidero.

8. Virgo virginum praeclara
   Mihi iam non sis amara;
      Fac me tecum plangere,   45
   Fac, ut portem Christi mortem,
   Passionis eius sortem
      Et plagas recolere.

9. Fac me plagis vulnerari,
   Cruce hac inebriari   50
      Ob amorem filii;
   Inflammatus et accensus
   Per te, virgo, sim defensus
      In die iudicii.

10. Fac me cruce custodiri,   55
    Morte Christi praemuniri,
      Confoveri gratia;
    Quando corpus morietur
    Fac ut animae donetur
      Paradisi gloria.   60

Original Text for Number 44

1. Iamiam rident prata,
   Iamiam virgines
   Iocundantur, Terre
   Ridet facies.
   Estas nunc apparuit,   5
   Ornatusque florum
     Lete claruit.

2. Nemus revirescit,
   Frondent frutices;
   Hiems seva cessit;   10
   Leti iuvenes,
   Congaudete floribus!
   Amor allicit vos
     Iam virginibus.

3. Ergo militemus   15
   Simul Veneri;
   Tristia vitemus
   Nosque teneri!
   Visus et colloquia,
   Spes amorque trahant   20
     Nos ad gaudia!

Original Text for Number 48

1. Axe Phebus aureo
     Celsiora lustrat
   Et nitore roseo
     Radios illustrat.
   Venustata Cybele   5
     Facie florente
   Florem nato Semele
     Dat Phebo favente.

2. Aurarum suavium
     Gratia iuvante   10
   Sonat nemus avium
     Voce modulante.
   Philomena querule
     Terea retractat,
   Dum canendo merule   15
     Carmina coaptat.

3. Iam Dionea
   Leta chorea
   Sedulo resonat
   Cantibus horum,   20
   Iamque Dione
   Iocis, agone
   Relevat, cruciat
   Corda suorum.

4. Me quoque subtrahit   25
   Illa sopori
   Invigilareque
   Cogit amori.
   Tela Cupidinis
   Aurea gesto,   30
   Igne cremantia
   Corde molesto.

5. Quod michi datur,
      Expaveo,
   Quodque negatur,   35
      Hoc aveo
   Mente severa.
   Que michi cedit,
      Hanc caveo;
   Que non obedit,   40
      Huic faveo
   Sumque re vera:

6. Fidelis, seu peream
   Seu relever per eam.
   Que cupit, hanc fugio,   45
   Que fugit, hanc cupio;
   Plus renuo debitum,
   Plus feror in vetitum;
   Plus licet illibitum;
   Plus libet illicitum.   50

7. O metuenda
   Dione decreta!
   O fugienda
   Venena secreta,
   Fraude verenda   55
   Doloque repleta,
   Docta furoris
   In estu punire,
   Quos dat amoris
   Amara subire,   60
   Plena livoris
   Urentis et ire!

8. Hinc michi metus
      Abundat,
   Hinc ora fletus   65
      Inundat,

Hinc michi pallor
  In ore
Est, quia fallor
  Amore.   70

Original Text for Number 50

1. Dira vi amoris teror
  Et Venereo axe feror,
  Igni ferventi suffocatus;
  Deme, pia, cruciatus!

2. Ignis vivi tu scintilla,   5
  Discurrens cordis ad vexilla,
  Igni incumbens non pauxillo
  Conclusi mentis te sigillo.

3. Meret cor, quod gaudebat
  Die, quo te cognoscebat   10
  Singularem et pudicam,
  Te adoptabat in amicam.

4. Profero pectoris singultus
  Et mestitie tumultus,
  Nam amoris tui vigor   15
  Urget me, et illi ligor.

5. Virginale lilium,
  Tuum presta subsidium!
  Missus in exilium
  Querit a te consilium.   20

6. Nescit, quid agat; moritur,
  Amore tui vehitur,
  Telo necatur Veneris,
  Sibi ni subveneris.

N

7. Iure Veneris orbata,   25
   Castitas redintegrata,
   Vultu decenti perornata,
   Veste Sophie decorata:

8. Tibi soli psallo; noli
   despicere . . . .*   30
   per me, precor, velis coli,
   lucens ut stella poli!

Original Text for Number 55

1. Ab la dolchor del temps novel
   Foillo li bosc, e li aucel
   Chanton chascus en lor lati
   Segon lo vers del novel chan;
   Adonc esta ben c'om s'aisi   5
   D'acho don hom a plus talan.

2. De lai don plus m'es bon e bel
   Non vei mesager ni sagel,
   Per que mos cors non dorm ni ri,
   Ni no m'aus traire adenan,   10
   Tro qe sacha ben de la fi
   S'el' es aissi com eu deman.

3. La nostr' amor vai enaissi
   Com la branca de l'albespi
   Qu'esta sobre l'arbre tremblan,   15
   La nuoit, a la ploja ez al gel,
   Tro l'endeman, que·l sols s'espan
   Per las fueillas verz e·l ramel.

* Schmeller: "Psallo tibi soli;/ despicere me noli."

4. Enquer me membra d'un mati
   Que nos fezem de guerra fi,
   E que·m donet un don tan gran,   20
   Sa drudari' e son anel:
   Enquer me lais Dieus viure tan
   C'aja mas manz soz so mantel!

5. Qu'eu non ai soing d'estraing lati   25
   Que·m parta de mon Bon Vezi,
   Qu'eu sai de paraulas com van
   Ab un breu sermon que s'espel,
   Que tal se van d'amor gaban,
   Nos n'avem la pessa e·l coutel.   30

Original Text for Number 62

1. A la fontana del vergier,
   On l'erb' es vertz josta·l gravier,
   A l'ombra d'un fust domesgier,
   En aiziment de blancas flors
   E de novelh chant costumier,   5
   Trobey sola, ses companhier,
   Selha que no vol mon solatz.

2. So fon donzelh'ab son cors belh
   Filha d'un senhor de castelh;
   E quant ieu cugey que l'auzelh   10
   Li fesson joy e la verdors,
   E pel dous termini novelh,
   E quez entendes mon favelh,
   Tost li fon sos afars camjatz.

3. Dels huelhs ploret josta la fon   15
   E del cor sospiret preon.
   "Ihesus, dis elha, reys del mon,
   Per vos mi creys ma grans dolors,

Quar vostra anta mi cofon,
Quar li mellor de tot est mon　　　　　　　　20
Vos van servir, mas a vos platz.

4. "Ab vos s'en vai lo meus amicx,
　Lo belhs e·l gens e·l pros e·l ricx;
　Sai m'en reman lo grans destricx,
　Lo deziriers soven e·l plors.　　　　　　　25
　Ay! mala fos reys Lozoicx
　Que fay los mans e los prezicx
　Per que·l dols m'es en cor intratz!"

5. Quant ieu l'auzi desconortar,
　Ves lieys vengui josta·l riu clar:　　　　　30
　"Belha, fi·m ieu, per trop plorar
　Afolha cara e colors;
　E no vos cal dezesperar,
　Que selh qui fai lo bosc fulhar,
　Vos pot donar de joy assatz."　　　　　　35

6. "Senher, dis elha, ben o crey
　Que Deus aya de mi mercey
　En l'autre segle per jassey,
　Quon assatz d'autres peccadors;
　Mas say mi tolh aquelha rey　　　　　　40
　Don joys mi crec; mas pauc mi tey
　Que trop s'es de mi alonhatz."

Original Text for Number 63

1. Lanquan li jorn son lonc en may
　M'es belhs dous chans d'auzelhs de lonh,
　E quan mi suy partitz de lay
　Remembra·m d'un' amor de lonh:
　Vau de talan embroncx e clis　　　　　　5

Si que chans ni flors d'albespis
No·m platz plus que l'yverns gelatz.

2. Be tenc lo Senhor per veray
   Per qu'ieu veirai l'amor de lonh;
   Mas per un ben que m'en eschay   10
   N'ai dos mals, quar tan m'es de lonh.
   Ai! car me fos lai pelegris,
   Si que mos fustz e mos tapis
   Fos pels sieus belhs huelhs remiratz!

3. Be·m parra joys quan li querray,   15
   Per amor Dieu, l'alberc de lonh:
   E, s'a lieys platz, alberguarai
   Pres de lieys, si be·m suy de lonh:
   Adoncs parra·l parlamens fis
   Quan drutz lonhdas er tan vezis   20
   Qu'ab bels digz jauzira solatz.

4. Iratz e gauzens m'en partray,
   S'ieu ja la vey, l'amor de lonh:
   Mas non sai quoras la veyrai,
   Car trop son nostras terras lonh: 25
   Assatz hi a pas e camis,
   E per aisso no·n suy devis . . .
   Mas tot sia cum a Dieu platz!

5. Ja mais d'amor no·m jauziray
   Si no·m jau d'est'amor de lonh,   30
   Que gensor ni melhor no·n sai
   Ves nulha part, ni pres ni lonh;
   Tant es sos pretz verais e fis
   Que lay el reng dels Sarrazis
   Fos hieu per lieys chaitius clamatz!   35

6. Dieus que fetz tot quant ve ni vai
   E formet sest'amor de lonh
   Mi don poder, que cor ieu n'ai,

Qu'ieu veya sest'amor de lonh,
Verayamen, en tals aizis,   40
Si que la cambra e·l jardis
Mi resembles tos temps palatz!

7. Ver ditz qui m'apella lechay
 Ni deziron d'amor de lonh,
 Car nulhs autres joys tan no·m play   45
 Cum jauzimens d'amor de lonh.
 Mas so qu'ieu vuelh m'es atahis,
 Qu'enaissi·m fadet mos pairis
 Qu'ieu ames e no fos amatz.

8. Mas so q'ieu vuoill m'es atahis.   50
 Totz sia mauditz lo pairis
 Qe·m fadet q'ieu non fos amatz!

Original Text for Number 65

1. Can vei la lauzeta mover
 De joi sas alas contral rai,
 Que s'oblid'e·s laissa chazer
 Per la doussor c'al cor li vai,
 Ai! tan grans enveya m'en ve   5
 De cui qu'eu veya jauzion,
 Meravilhas ai, car desse
 Lo cor de dezirer no·m fon.

2. Ai, las! tan cuidava saber
 D'amor, e tan petit en sai!   10
 Car eu d'amar no·m posc tener
 Celeis don ja pro non aurai.
 Tout m'a mo cor, e tout m'a me,
 E se mezeis e tot lo mon;
 E can se·m tolc, no·m laisset re   15
 Mas dezirer e cor volon.

3. Anc non agui de me poder
   Ni no fui meus de l'or'en sai
   Que·m laisset en sos olhs vezer
   En un miralh que mout me plai.   20
   Miralhs, pus me mirei en te,
   M'an mort li sospir de preon,
   C'aissi·m perdei com perdet se
   Lo bels Narcisus en la fon.

4. De las domnas me dezesper;   25
   Ja mais en lor no·m fiarai;
   C'aissi com las solh chaptener,
   Enaissi las deschaptenrai.
   Pois vei c'una pro no m'en te
   Vas leis que·m destrui e·m cofon,   30
   Totas las dopt'e las mescre,
   Car be sai c'atretals se son.

5. D'aisso·s fa be femna parer
   Ma domna, per qu'e·lh o retrai,
   Car no vol so c'om deu voler,   35
   E so c'om li deveda, fai.
   Chazutz sui en mala merce,
   Et ai be faih co·l fols en pon;
   E no sai per que m'esdeve,
   Mas car trop puyei contra mon.   40

6. Merces es perduda, per ver,
   (Et eu non o saubi anc mai),
   Car cilh qui plus en degr'aver,
   No·n a ges, et on la querrai?
   A! can mal sembla, qui la ve,   45
   Qued aquest chaitiu deziron
   Que ja ses leis no aura be,
   Laisse morir, que no l'aon!

7. Pus ab midons no·m pot valer
   Precs ni merces ni·l dreihz qu'eu ai,   50

Ni a leis no ven a plazer
Qu'eu l'am, ja mais no·lh o dirai.
Aissi·m part de leis e·m recre;
Mort m'a, e per mort li respon,
E vau m'en, pus ilh no·m rete,   55
Chaitius, en issilh, no sai on.

8. Tristans, ges no·n auretz de me,
   Qu'eu m'en vau, chaitius, no sai on.
   De chantar me gic e·m recre,
   E de joi e d'amor m'escon.   60

Original Text for Number 95

Io m'agio posto in core a Dio servire,
Com'io potesse gire in Paradiso,
Al santo loco, c'agio audito dire
Si mantiene sollazo, gioco e riso;
Sanza mia donna non vi vorria gire,   5
Quella c'à blonda testa e claro viso,
Ché sanza lei non poteria gaudire,
Estando da la mia donna diviso.

Ma no lo dico a tale intendimento
Perch'io peccato ci volesse fare,   10
Se non veder lo suo bel portamento,
Lo bel viso e lo morbido sguardare,
Ché lo mi terria in gran consolamento,
Veggendo la mia donna in gloria stare.

Original Text for Number 105

1. Al cor gentil rempaira sempre amore
   Come l'ausello in selva a la verdura;
      Né fe' amor anti che gentil core,
   Né gentil core anti ch'amor, natura:
      Ch'adesso con' fu 'l sole,   5
   Sì tosto lo splendore fu lucente,
   Né fu davanti 'l sole;
   E prende amore in gentilezza loco
   Così propiamente
   Come calore in clarità di foco.   10

2. Foco d'amore in gentil cor s'aprende
   Come vertute in petra preziosa,
      Ché da la stella valor no i discende
   Anti che 'l sol la faccia gentil cosa;
      Poi che n'ha tratto fòre   15
   Per sua forza lo sol ciò che li è vile,
   Stella li dà valore:
   Così lo cor ch'è fatto da natura
   Asletto, pur, gentile,
   Donna a guisa di stella lo 'nnamora.   20

3. Amor per tal ragion sta 'n cor gentile
   Per qual lo foco in cima del doplero:
      Splendeli al su' diletto, clar, sottile;
   No li stari' altra guisa, tant' è fero.
      Così prava natura   25
   Recontra amor come fa l'aigua il foco
   Caldo, per la freddura.
   Amore in gentil cor prende rivera
   Per suo consimel loco
   Com' adamàs del ferro in la minera.   30

4. Fere lo sol lo fango tutto 'l giorno;
   Vile reman, né 'l sol perde calore;
      Dis' omo alter: "Gentil per sclatta torno";

Lui semblo al fango, al sol gentil valore:
Ché non dé dar om fé   35
Che gentilezza sia fòr di coraggio
In degnità d'ere'
Sed a vertute non ha gentil core,
Com' aigua porta raggio
E'l ciel riten le stelle e lo splendore.   40

5. Splende 'n la 'ntelligenzia del cielo
Deo criator più che 'n nostr'occhi 'l sole;
  Ella intende suo fattor oltra 'l cielo,
E'l ciel volgiando, a Lui obedir tole;
  E con' segue, al primero,   45
Del giusto Deo beato compimento,
Così dar dovria, al vero,
La bella donna, poi che 'n gli occhi splende
Del suo gentil talento
Che mai di lei obedir non si disprende.   50

6. Donna, Deo mi dirà: "Che presomisti?"
Stando l'alma mia a Lui davanti.
  "Lo ciel passasti e 'nfin a Me venisti
E desti in vano amor Me per semblanti,
  Ch'a Me conven le laude   55
E a la reina del regname degno,
Per cui cessa onne fraude."
Dir Li porò "Tenne d'angel sembianza
Che fosse del Tuo regno;
Non me fu fallo, s'in lei posi amanza."   60

Original Text for Number 108

Chi è questa che ven, ch'ogn'om la mira,
Che fa tremar di chiaritate l'are
E mena seco Amor, sì che parlare
Null' omo pote, ma ciascun sospira?

O Deo, che sembra quando li occhi gira,   5
Dical' Amor, ch'i' nol savria contare:
Cotanto d'umiltà donna mi pare,
Ch'ogn'altra ver' di lei i' chiam' ira.

Non si poria contar la sua piagenza,
Ch'a le' s'inchin' ogni gentil vertute,   10
E la Beltate per sua dea la mostra.
Non fu sì alta già la mente nostra
E non si pose 'n noi tanta salute,
Che propiamente n'aviàn canoscenza.

Original Text for Number 116

1. Donne ch'avete intelletto d'amore,
   I' vo' con voi de la mia donna dire,
   Non perch'io creda sua laude finire,
   Ma ragionar per isfogar la mente.
       Io dico che pensando il suo valore,   5
   Amor sì dolce mi si fa sentire,
   Che s'io allora non perdessi ardire,
   Farei parlando innamorar la gente.
       E io non vo' parlar sì altamente,
   Ch'io divenisse per temenza vile;   10
   Ma tratterò del suo stato gentile
   A respetto di lei leggeramente,
   Donne e donzelle amorose, con vui,
   Ché non è cosa da parlarne altrui.

2. Angelo clama in divino intelletto   15
   E dice: "Sire, nel mondo si vede
   Maraviglia ne l'atto che procede
   D'un'anima che 'nfin qua su risplende."
       Lo cielo, che non have altro difetto
   Che d'aver lei, al suo segnor la chiede,   20
   E ciascun santo ne grida merzede.

Sola Pietà nostra parte difende,
   Che parla Dio, che di madonna intende:
"Diletti miei, or sofferite in pace
Che vostra spene sia quanto me piace   25
Là 'v'è alcun che perder lei s'attende,
E che dirà ne lo inferno: 'O mal nati,
Io vidi la speranza de' beati.' "

3. Madonna è disïata in sommo cielo:
   Or vòi di sua virtù farvi savere.   30
Dico, qual vuol gentil donna parere
Vada con lei, che quando va per via,
   Gitta nei cor villani Amore un gelo,
Per che onne lor pensero agghiaccia e pere;
E qual soffrisse di starla a vedere   35
Diverria nobil cosa, o si morria.
   E quando trova alcun che degno sia
Di veder lei, quei prova sua vertute,
Ché li avvien, ciò che li dona, in salute,
E sì l'umilia, ch'ogni offesa oblia.   40
Ancor l'ha Dio per maggior grazia dato
Che non pò mal finir chi l'ha parlato.

4. Dice di lei Amor: "Cosa mortale
Come esser pò sì adorna e sì pura?"
Poi la reguarda, e fra se stesso giura   45
Che Dio ne 'ntenda di far cosa nova.
   Color di perle ha quasi, in forma quale
Convene a donna aver, non for misura:
Ella è quanto de ben pò far natura;
Per essemplo di lei bieltà si prova.   50
   De·li occhi suoi, come ch'ella li mova,
Escono spirti d'amore inflammati,
Che feron li occhi a qual che allor la guati,
E passan sì che 'l cor ciascun retrova:
Voi le vedete Amor pinto nel viso,   55
Là 've non pote alcun mirarla fiso.

5. Canzone, io so che tu girai parlando
   A donne assai, quand'io t'avrò avanzata.
   Or t'ammonisco, perch'io t'ho allevata
   Per figliuola d'Amor giovane e piana,   60
      Che là 've giugni tu diche pregando:
   "Insegnatemi gir, ch'io son mandata
   A quella di cui laude so' adornata."
   E se non vuoli andar sì come vana,
      Non restare ove sia gente villana: 65
   Ingegnati, se puoi, d'esser palese
   Solo con donne o con omo cortese,
   Che ti merranno là per via tostana.
   Tu troverai Amor, con esso lei;
   Raccomandami a lui come tu dei.   70

Original Text for Number 134

Or che 'l ciel e la terra e 'l vento tace,
E le fere e gli augelli il sonno affrena,
Notte il carro stellato in giro mena
E nel suo letto il mar senz'onda giace;
Vegghio, penso, ardo, piango; e chi mi sface   5
Sempre m'è inanzi per mia dolce pena;
Guerra è 'l mio stato, d'ira e di duol piena;
E sol di lei pensando ò qualche pace.

Così sol d'una chiara fonte viva
Move 'l dolce e l'amaro ond'io mi pasco;   10
Una man sola mi risana e punge;
E perché 'l mio martir non giunga a riva,
Mille volte il dì moro e mille nasco:
Tanto da la salute mia son lunge!

Original Text for Number 163

Le temps a laissié son manteau
De vent, de froidure et de pluie,
Et s'est vestu de brouderie,
De soleil luyant, cler et beau.

Il n'y a beste, ne oiseau,   5
Qu'en son jargon ne chante ou crie:
"Le temps a laissié son manteau."

Riviere, fontaine, et ruisseau
Portent, en livree jolie,
Gouttes d'argent d'orfaverie,   10
Chascun s'abille de nouveau—
Le temps a laissié son manteau.

Original Text for Number 171D

1. Se j'ayme et sers la belle de bon hait,
   M'en devez vous tenir ne vil ne sot?
   Elle a en soy des biens a fin souhait.
   Pour son amour sains bouclier et passot;
   Quant viennent gens, je cours et happe ung pot,   5
   Au vin m'en fuis, sans demener grant bruit;
   Je leur tens eaue, frommage, pain et fruit.
   S'ilz paient bien, je leur dis: "*Bene stat;*
   Retournez cy quant vous serez en ruit,
   En ce bordeau ou tenons nostre estat!"   10

2. Mais adoncques il y a grant deshait,
   Quant sans argent s'en vient couchier Margot;
   Veoir ne la puis, mon cuer a mort la hait.
   Sa robe prens, demy saint et surcot,
   Si luy jure qu'il tendra pour l'escot.   15
   Par les costés se prent, "C'est Antecrist!"

Crie et jure par la mort Jhesu Crist
Que non fera. Lors j'empoingne ung esclat;
Dessus son nez luy en fais ung escript,
En ce bordeau ou tenons nostre estat.   20

3. Puis paix se fait et me fait ung gros pet,
   Plus enflee qu'ung vlimeux escharbot.
   Riant, m'assiet son poing sur mon sommet:
   "Gogo," me dit, et me fiert le jambot.
   Tous deux yvres dormons comme ung sabot,   25
   Et au resveil quant le ventre luy bruit,
   Monte sur moy, que ne gaste son fruit.
   Soubz elle geins, plus qu'un aiz me fait plat;
   De paillarder tout elle me destruit
   En ce bordeau ou tenons nostre estat.   30

4. Vente, gresle, gelle, j'ay mon pain cuit.
   Ie suis paillart, la paillarde me suit.
   Lequel vault mieulx? Chascun bien s'entresuit:
   L'ung vault l'autre; c'est a mau rat mau chat.
   Ordure amons, ordure nous assuit;   35
   Nous deffuyons onneur; il nous deffuit
   En ce bordeau ou tenons nostre estat.

Original Text for Number 188

1. "Sîne klâwen   durh die wolken sint geslagen,
   Er stîget ûf mit grôzer kraft.
   Ich sihe in grâwen   tägelîch, als er wil tagen,
   Den tac, der im geselleschaft
   Erwenden wil, dem werden man,   5
   Den ich mit sorgen în verliez.
   Ich bringe in hinnen, ob ich kan.
   Sîn vil manegiu tugent michz leisten hiez."

2. "Wahter, du singest,   daz mir manege fröude nimt
Unde mêret mîne klage.   10
Mære du bringest,   der mich leider niht gezimt,
Immer morgens gegen dem tage.
Diu solt du mir verswîgen gar;
Daz gebiute ich den triuwen dîn.
Des lône ich dir, als ich getar: 15
Sô belîbet hie der geselle mîn."

3. "Er muoz et hinnen   balde und âne sûmen sich:
Nu gib im urloup, süezez wîp.
Lâz in minnen   her nâch sô verholne dich,
Daz er behalt êre und den lîp.   20
Er gab sich mîner triuwe alsô,
Daz ich in bræhte ouch wider dan.
Ez ist nû tac; naht was ez dô:
Mit drucke an brust dîn kus mirn an gewan."

4. "Swaz dir gevalle,   wahter, sinc, und lâ den hie, ·   25
Der minne brâhte und minne enphienc.
Von dînem schalle   ist er und ich erschrocken ie,
Sô ninder der morgensterne ûf gienc
Ûf in, der her nâch minne ist komen,
Noch ninder lûhte tages lieht.   30
Du hâst in dicke mir benomen
Von blanken armen, und ûz herzen nieht."

5. Von den blicken,   die der tac tet durh diu glas,
Und dô der wahter warnen sanc,
Si muose erschricken   durch den, der dâ bî ir was.   35
Ir brüstelîn an brust si dwanc.
Der rîter ellens niht vergaz;
Des wolde in wenden wahters dôn:
Urloup nâh und nâher baz
Mit kusse und anders gab in minne lôn.   40

Original Text for Number 190

1. Under der linden
   An der heide,
   Dâ unser zweier bette was,
   Dâ mugt ir vinden
   Schône beide   5
   Gebrochen bluomen unde gras.
   Vor dem walde in einem tal,
   　　　Tandaradei!
   Schône sanc diu nahtegal.

2. Ich kam gegangen   10
   Zuo der ouwe:
   Dô was mîn friedel komen ê.
   Dâ wart ich enpfangen,
   Hêre frouwe,
   Daz ich bin sælic iemer mê.   15
   Kust er mich? wol tûsentstunt:
   　　　Tandaradei!
   Seht, wie rôt mir ist der munt.

3. Dô het er gemachet
   Alsô rîche   20
   Von bluomen eine bettestat.
   Des wirt noch gelachet
   Inneclîche,
   Kumt iemen an daz selbe pfat.
   Bî den rôsen er wol mac,   25
   　　　Tandaradei!
   Merken, wâ mirz houbet lac.

4. Daz er bî mir læge,
   Wessez iemen
   —Nu enwelle got!—sô schamt ich mich.   30
   Wes er mit mir pflæge,
   Niemer niemen

Bevinde daz wan er unt ich
Und ein kleinez vogellîn:
　　　Tandaradei!
Daz mac wol getriuwe sîn.

35

[XI]
INDICES

A. AUTHORS

All references are to poem numbers.

B. TITLES AND FIRST LINES OF ORIGINALS

All references are to poem numbers.

C. SELECTED GENRES

(All references are to poem numbers.)

Alba, Aubade: see Dawn song

Ballads: 226–230

Begging poem: 26, 218

Chanson de toile: see Spinning song